INTO THE ENCHANTED FOREST WITH CALLUM

A HORSEMAN'S COUNTRY DIARY -

BOOK TWO

INTO THE ENCHANTED FOREST WITH CALLUM

A HORSEMAN'S COUNTRY DIARY –

BOOK TWO

Julian Roup

Copyright © 2025 Julian Roup.

This edition published in 2025 by BLKDOG Publishing.

Paperback ISBN: 978-1-915490-39-1

A catalogue record for this book is available from the British Library.

No part of this publication may be reproduced, stored in a retrieval system, or transmitted in any form or by any means, electronic, mechanical, photocopying, recording, or otherwise, without written permission of the publisher.

NO AI TRAINING: Without in any way limiting the author's and publisher's exclusive rights under copyright, any use of this publication to "train" generative artificial intelligence (AI) technologies to generate text is expressly prohibited. The author reserves all rights to license uses of this work for generative AI training and development of machine learning language models.

All rights reserved including the right of reproduction in whole or in part in any form. The moral right of the author has been asserted.

www.blkdogpublishing.com

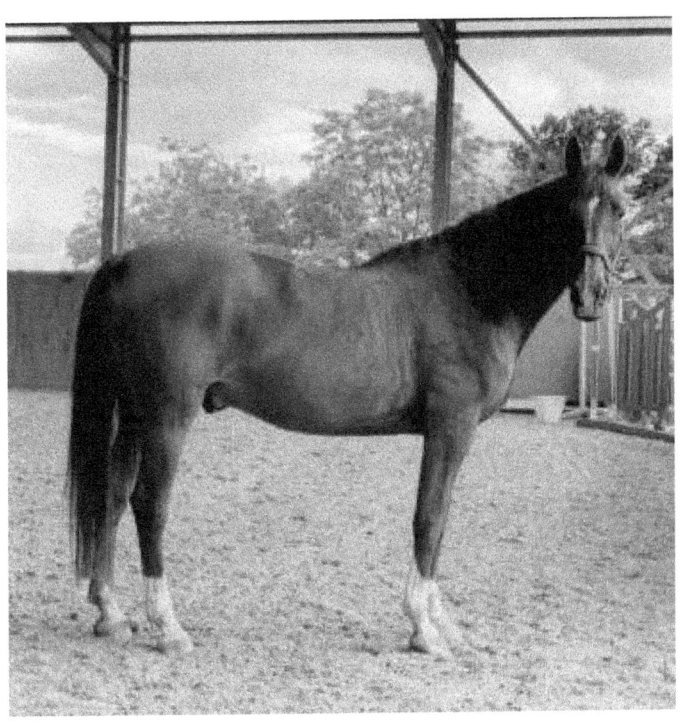

Other titles by Julian Roup for your consideration:

Life in a Time of Plague:
A Coronavirus Lockdown Diary

Into the Secret Heart of Ashdown Forest:
A Horseman's Country Diary

A Fisherman in the Saddle

First Catch Your Calamari: Travels with an Appetite

This Country I Call My Own

Boerejood

Acknowledgements

To Jan, who once again, aside from her current books-in-progress – including her debut poetry collection, *These Are the Things We Have Lost,* out in January from Fly on the Wall Press – has taken time to advise, encourage and edit this seventh book of mine with such style and finesse. Who after 48 years together, still rides with me and shares our lifelong, mutual passion for horses.

To Callum, who despite all his many faults, is one of the greatest characters I've known in the horse world. He stopped me dead in my tracks the first time we saw him and he is as special as he looks. And now he has become my co-author and my wingman when we take off for the woods.

My great thanks to the gifted artist and horsewoman, Abbie Hart, who illustrated the covers of this book with such charming images, as she did for my previous book – *Into the Secret Heart of Ashdown Forest.* I could not have found a better way of framing both books.

Julian Roup
East Sussex
August 2025

INTRODUCTION

This is a sequel to *Into the Secret Heart of Ashdown Forest: A Horseman's Country Diary*. Many readers who had enjoyed this book asked for more tales of the Forest and of Callum, so here it is: *Into the Enchanted Forest with Callum - A Horseman's Country Diary - Book 2*.

A long time ago, I read and enjoyed *Travels with Charley* by one of my literary heroes, John Steinbeck: the story of his drive around America with his wife's ten-year-old standard poodle, Charley. Though Callum, my 18-hand Irish Sports horse, is no poodle and while Ashdown Forest is not exactly a continent, it has been my world for 45 years, a place I have come to love and know intimately. So this book is a salute to John Steinbeck's travel book.

Just fifty miles southeast of London, it is in parts a secret world, this remnant of the great ancient forest of Anderida that the Romans found when they invaded Britain 2,000 years ago. My wife Jan and I bought Callum six years ago when I was 69. He was to be my 'old man's horse' - a less likely candidate for this job cannot be imagined.

But for all his failings, he has become a marvellous riding horse, whose sometimes hysterical nature adds interest to his personality and, on occasion, to our rides. I would not be without him.

I hope you will enjoy riding with us once more into the wild heart of Ashdown Forest.

Julian Roup

THE BOY WHO LISTENED TO TREES

When I was about 8 years old one of my favourite things to do was to slip out of our garden gate to go and play in the woods and streams on the back of Table Mountain, the iconic flat-topped colossus that broods over the city of Cape Town at the tip of Africa.

For a dreamy boy, always lost in reverie and books, it was a small slice of heaven among the oak, pine and blue gum woods where one rushing or trickling stream near our home, just 50 yards away, pooled and gushed over smooth grey stones.

The place was alive with bird life, and the occasional cough of a baboon, or the fluttering of an African Monarch butterfly. There was something gentle and intimate about the glade I always made for, with the stream running down from springs on the mountain slopes above. It was a welcoming place just above our 1950s neighbourhood called Newlands.

It was an ancient grove on the back of a mountain revered by its earliest inhabitants as a holy place. The Khoi and San peoples held Table Mountain in high regard, viewing it as a sacred place and a home to their supreme god, Tsui//Goab. They called the mountain 'Hoerikwagga', meaning 'Mountain in the Sea'. The mountain was believed to be a powerful and spiritual entity. This had been the mountain's character and history for the past tens of thousands of years. It was not Newlands at all. We whites were the new people. The land itself was ancient.

Is it any wonder then that an impressionable boy would hear whispers in the trees, feel eyes upon him, sense that he was being observed? In fact, he may well have been observed by the few early people who still lived on the mountain slopes in tiny groups of one or two. They were known to the whites as 'Bergies' – people of the mountain. But it was not members of this ancient tribe that I heard in my ramblings up the mountain, it was a presence far more ancient. It was the trees, plants and the grey sandstone rock of the mountain itself which truly held the spirit of this place. I felt that there was an inchoate reaching out, an attempt to communicate that I did not have words for.

Now, some 70 years later, I read academic papers by biologists who argue that plants and trees are themselves sentient beings who communicate with each other by chemical and fungal means and are fully aware of your human presence among them. So that slightly bewitched boy was indeed feeling and hearing and sensing something 'other' that he could not fathom. Now it appears that he was playing amid a community of trees and plants and that the place was more fully alive than he had sensed.

And then I discovered horses. My first ponies and horses took me galloping along the magnificent sweeping beaches of the Cape. This is where I developed my seat and my passion for horses. Here in the ice-cold South Atlantic Ocean, I swam my equine friends, and it was from here before long that I headed into the forested slopes of that storied mountain. And now I was more certain of the whispers, for I observed that my horse heard them too.

Life exiled me to England where I discovered woods as mysterious as those of the Cape, and here I rode Irish horses.

People always wonder why I ride alone, but the fact is when I swing onto a horse it is to be borne from one community to another – from human to vegetable society. Amid the greatest of their species, the oaks, beech and birch trees, I found that I was home once more, and once more besides hidden streams – the rising and falling streams within each tree – and once again among the whispers, the semi-silent conversations of the woods. And my horse hears them too, for he listens as keenly as I do.

Horses have been and remain my portal into this world of otherness, for they are far more attuned to this unseen thing. They sense the moving spirit of nature, much more than any human is capable of. So, when you are in tune with your horse, you find yourself communing with nature in ways that may surprise you.

As prey animals, horses are much as they were 10,000 years ago. Riding them, we are in partnership with something that understands, in an ancient way, the primordial character of nature, the eat or be eaten contract. That is why they quiver like tuning forks out there in the wild. And we are privileged to be part of that when we climb on their backs. A horse and rider among the trees of a dense wood are at some level time-travelling. No wonder we hear whispers.

So You Want a Warmblood?

It took me a year and five failed vettings to find Callum, my warmblood. I will spare you the full Gothic horror of the search story – all the miles and sad, mad, bad, damaged and broken horses we saw, and the owners who echoed those ills. Sufficient to say I had gone out seeking another pure-bred Irish Draught, a breed that has served Jan and me well over the years after first meeting them at the Dublin Horse Show back in the 1980s. There is so much to admire and respect about them, temperament, confirmation, honesty, and a capacity to stay fat on the meanest of diets. And despite their size they jump like stags. But my best efforts to find one had failed, there were simply none to be had in my modest price range. Their reputation has sent their prices into the stratosphere.

So, despite swearing at the outset of the search that we would not buy another warmblood – having had a Hanoverian who was happier on two feet than four – we set out on one last trek up country.

We'd been worn down by the desperately sad, fruitless year long search. But that day we drove up, rather despairingly, to see a dealer called Charley Young Equestrian Services in Bourne, Lincolnshire. She had advertised a 'Gentleman' for sale. I liked the look of him online and the advert sounded promising. And he was in our price range. We set off with not much hope.

The advert read:

> Callum
> *Super Genuine Gentleman*
> 'Cally is a classy full up 17 hand 11-year-old gelding by Aldatus Z! [later we measured him at 18hh]. He is schooling at novice level dressage and has competed successfully unaffiliated at prelim with a competent novice. He is a super hack, unfazed by traffic and has spent the majority of his life on a busy working farm.
>
> Cally loves to jump just needs more miles on the clock he has seen fillers including walls, water trays, gates as well as a variety of bright show jump fillers taking it all in his stride confidently.
>
> He has also been schooled round workers fences and showed real promise and talent in this area, I'm sure in the right hands he would excel in working hunter classes. He is comfortably off the leg and responds sensibly to aids, quick to learn and very much enjoys his work. He is only for sale due to owners' work commitments on the farm and they have owned him since he was 4.5 years old.
>
> Genuinely unspoilt and very sad sale! He is a loveable giant who is super easy to handle, happily comes in on his own without making a fuss, stands for hours to be groomed, plaited and pulled. Great to clip, bath, shoe, load etc. No vices and open to vet! He does have a small skin scar on the back of his hind leg that can be seen in photos but has never caused any problems!
>
> Genuine enquires and 5* homes only need apply!

We drove into Charley's rural yard in Lincolnshire, walked into the barn and there was Callum tied up outside his stable, gleaming gold, with all the curves in the right places. It was love at first sight.

Jan and I looked at each other and nodded. Each of

us rode him after Charley and though he was pretty much on his toes when I hacked him out with her, he took me up a hill at a fair hand gallop and pulled up smoothly. We'd found our horse. All thoughts of him being a warmblood had fled. That thought never crossed our minds.

Some years later, talking to a judge at the Dublin Horse Show, he described warmbloods as 'Dead Sharp'. And never a truer word has been spoken. When Callum arrived at our yard in Sussex in June 2019, I rode him out into the woods for the first time and wondered if I had not over-horsed myself entirely. He rode like a stallion, his neighs ringing through the woods as he pranced and danced down between the pines. At 69, I knew enough to know this was not an old man's horse. But we got home without any problem an hour later and so the love affair began. But it has been a love affair not without incident.

Callum is highly strung and riding him is like sitting on a very powerful 18-hand hysteric. Every now and then it feels as if someone has given him an electric shock and he will jump, jerk, shake, or whirl and run. One day this all got too much for me and I gave him a good whack with my stick. It was then that I was fully introduced to his incredible athleticism. His sire, an Oldenburg who jumped successfully for Germany and his dam, an Irish Draught x Thoroughbred, had given their son a capacity to leap that was second to none.

I found myself heading for a stream at a gallop, Callum having decided that the whip was not going to improve our relationship. I had a split second to decide to bail-out or go with him and I stayed put, fearing the self-induced damage a fall from such height at the gallop would do to my ancient limbs. He stood back from the bank and launched himself out over the water. There was a small stick-covered sandbank midstream, where by some miracle he touched down briefly, changed legs and then out over the rest of the stream we sailed into a dense pine forest. I felt branches whipping me and finally managed to pull him up. I started to laugh hysterically. Looking down I saw that one of the pine boughs had broken my left pinkie finger, but that was the only damage to me. Callum was without blemish, other than that to his character.

On the way home, we had a long and philosophical discussion about masters and servants, slavery, the human condition and the animal liberation movement. Callum more than held his own and by the time we reached his stable a sort of 'quid pro quo' had been established that has lasted to this day. The deal being that I would not mess with him if he did not mess with me. And, that if he could not help himself, now and then, I was not to even think of whipping him again, but to speak to him sternly. This has served us well. He now has the capacity to swear in three human languages.

The problem, you see, is that I do love him. And as we all know, love is a rocky road. I had started writing about him and in some strange way he'd become more than my ride, he'd become my muse. These days people stop us and ask if this is Callum from the books and when I confirm that it is indeed Callum from the books, all sorts of endearments are called on, much stroking and petting and very often the offering of an apple or a mint. Callum accepts these graciously, with the manners of the aristocrat that he is.

So you see, I'm stuck with a warmblood. But would I recommend one to you? Not on your life. Unless of course you want a life filled with alarms and excursions. And you can't really blame them, one has only to look at his breeding – warmblood!

If you've had the privilege of watching a performance of the Lipizzaners at the Spanish Riding School in Vienna, Austria, or the Andalucians in Jerez in Spain, you will be watching Callum's cousins do their incredible passades, caprioles and levades. These horses are as much at home in the air as they are on the ground. Their great-great-great-grandparents swam to the Irish shore from the sinking ships of the Spanish Armada in 1588 – off Kinnagoe Bay, in County Donegal. The Irish, not being slow at recognising a good thing, bred these horses to their cold-blooded draughts and so the Irish Draught came into being, an early form of warmblood, as the Andalusian carries the blood of the Arab and the Barb in their DNA. These are the horses that almost overran the whole of Europe as the Muslim armies swept out of the east and their brothers rode out of north Africa into Spain.

And of course it was the Andalusian horse that the Spanish Conquistadors took to America with them in search of gold and silver, the horse that became the root stem of the Mustang.

So Callum is indeed a 'gentleman' by blood, but let's not forget the good dollop of 'bastardry' in there too. It is what gives him and his warmblood cousins their power, size and scope. Callum is a lot of horse, as they say, and we more or less rub along together, as I too have a smidgeon of 'bastardry' in me. But would I go looking for another warmblood? Not on your nelly!

So, if having heard all of this, you still want a warmblood, then God help you! You will only have yourself to blame for the excitement and alarms and excursions that await you. But I should add that while you will be thrilled and terrified in equal measure, you will never be bored! And of course there is the risk of falling in love.

THE JOYS OF RIDING ALONE

For the most part, my riding life has been spent alone with my horses, in lonely landscapes far from the madding crowd.

It has been an active choice to ride alone and not in company. It began I suppose because I was extremely shy growing up, not that you'd know it now. I can talk for Africa and a sort of jokey persona has built up over the years which has acted a useful cover, to mask the shyness and the insecurities.

I also loathed and feared school and all the authoritarian nonsense and the macho bull that went along with it. Riding for me was all about escape from people, it was about being alone in a landscape with just my horse for company. My horses were the key to this hidden kingdom, the magic that took me through the looking glass into the secret garden of delight.

There is a pleasure to riding in company, but it is an altogether different experience. It is all about being social or sociable and just happens to take place on horseback. Frankly, I'd rather do that down at the pub or a restaurant, keeping the magic of horse riding pure and unadulterated. The profound experience that I have come to love and to depend on as the most life fulfilling activity I know is best done alone.

If this sounds impossibly precious and I come across as a weirdo, then so be it. I am never going to apologise for what has been the single greatest joy of my life – riding alone, free to dream, to imagine, to be still, to hear the voice of nature, to listen to the wind and the birdsong, the rustle and creak of the trees, to think, and to revel in the silence. To feel a thread of fear as my horse and I disappear ever deeper into our beloved woods, or deep into the dune country and the coasts of the Africa of my boyhood. If that makes me weird, I am happy to wear that as a badge of honour.

There are pleasures to be had with people. I am not unacquainted with love and friendship, but truly, mankind overall does not have a lot to recommend it. We have destroyed our planet, killed each other, and sent 80 per cent of animal life into extinction, a fate I fear we will all shortly follow. Why would one not wish to get away from the vast majority of mankind?

There is something that occurs when one is alone with a beloved horse and the two of you are distant figures in a landscape. There is no explaining it. To understand you will have to have experienced it for yourself. Something happens out there that changes you. When you return from that place of solitude you return a different person to the one who left two, three, four, six hours previously. You are at peace and also strangely buoyed up by the endorphins the riding has released into your bloodstream. You feel elated, energised. It is in short, my drug of choice, the only one I've been hooked on all my life.

And of course, besides the nature gazing and the peace there is another benefit to riding alone – your horse is completely focussed on you and your aids, as you are on him or her and out of this deep concentration on each other comes a relationship of trust and understanding, or indeed an acknowledgement that you'd best be damn careful on this particular horse. If it's the former, you can build on that burgeoning relationship to create the riding horse of your dreams and to improve your own riding skills. If it's the latter, time for a new horse maybe. But it's riding alone that will sharpen your focus either way on the strengths or weaknesses of this partnership on which your life depends, especially if you are riding solo.

Like so many activities that can be done alone, fishing, surfing, walking, running, climbing, sailing – riding alone adds a quality that can only be described as magic in part. Riding alone has been my passport to happiness, health and a heaven-sent dose of profound joy, and just maybe a little hard-won wisdom. And of course, the books.

One of the best things about riding alone is that you ride in unbroken silence – unless you talk or sing to your horse as I do myself from time to time. But generally, we are a silent pair that drifts around our woods, and this means you see more wildlife. Often the deer, foxes, badgers, rabbits stoats, squirrels, birds, only see you when you see them, especially if the wind is blowing towards you and your scent does not reach ahead to warn them. When you live just 50 miles from London, the privilege of seeing this much wildlife is a huge and valued bonus to riding alone.

Being immersed, engulfed, surrounded by so much beauty is the point of it all, the dangers are just the price one must be prepared to pay for this consciousness-expanding trip into another realm, far from the works of man. Your mind is cleared, your perceptions sharpened as you become one with the wood and your horse. It is a form of time travel into a pristine, almost primordial, past and the harsh croak of a crow raises the hairs on the back of your neck. This is the realest of real deals.

So, when Callum and I find ourselves once more enfolded in the leafy embrace of Ashdown Forest's beech, oak, birch, holly and chestnut woods, there is a sense of homecoming. A fixture of this place for four and a half decades I like to think the local wildlife see us and knows us. I imagine, as we brush our way past their homes underground or in the underbrush, in the tree trunks and branches and the forest canopy, that a badger might remark to a rabbit or a buzzard: 'There they go! Those two dreamy fools. The mad African and Callum. Lost again I imagine.'

I smile and pat Callum. 'We are OK fella.'

Riding Ashdown Forest

I like to tease my Scottish friends about living so close to the Arctic Circle and opting for just a month of summer with midges thrown in! But if the truth be told, I live in what the Scot Sir Arthur Conan Doyle, author of the Sherlock Holmes books, called 'Scotland in Sussex'. Walk here on any miserable day in winter, as he did for the 26 years he lived here, and you will get the full-blasted, haunted heath of *The Hound of the Baskervilles*. Ashdown Forest in East Sussex is a very strange place for a misdirected South African to have ended up in. It is the very opposite of the vast African landscapes I had grown up in, it is small, constrained by comparison and maybe a little bit twee to African eyes. But there are compensations.

Riding on Ashdown Forest provides many pleasures. These include the views your ten-foot-high eyes now see, scenery coming at you without effort, the magic carpet made flesh. Unlike a passenger in a car, you are in and part of the scene, and unlike a car or a motorbike you are not restricted to roads, and all is silent, but for the birdsong and the steady heartbeat of your horse's hooves. There is the pleasure of a horse walking actively beneath you. He swings along, alert and delighted with life, and it takes a hard heart not to be affected by that spirit. There is the feeling of power in a balanced, controlled trot, where the horse impulsion comes from behind and you float over the ground. Then there is the best gait of all, the slow, collected canter, which to the uninitiated can best be described as the feeling of riding a friendly dolphin as he rises and falls through the water; there is speed, comfort and that rocking, flowing motion. To be on a fit horse with a comfortable stride and a good canter, is to know bliss. I have such a horse.

There is, too, the pleasure of landscape, and if you are lucky, as I am, to live on Ashdown Forest, you have a varied and interesting riding country. Ashdown is high ground. It is nearly 1,000 feet above sea level, which provides you with far horizons to the South Downs, the North Downs, and views into Sussex, Surrey and Kent. The land is hilly, providing a series of bowls, amphitheatres, valleys, each with its own focus. On the hilltops stand circles of dark umbrella pines, the symbol of Ashdown, commanding the open heaths.

One such clump of hallmark pines marks the spot where Camelot came to Sussex. Near Birch Grove House they stand, Prime Minister Harold Macmillan's home, where President John F. Kennedy spent the weekend back in June 1963, just months before his death by an assassin's bullets. There are often secret hidden graves within these tree circles; some commemorated with a simple wooden board low in among the undergrowth, or simply with ash to enrich the soil. Perhaps my final resting place one day too?

Ashdown's 6,500 acres is the largest area with open public access in South East England and includes open moorland, deep deciduous woods, pine plantations on its edges and at least three golf courses that act as land bridges to nearby countryside at Forest Row, Crowborough and the East Sussex National Golf Club at Maresfield. Ashdown is the very heart of the Forest of Anderida, so named by the Romans. Today it still contains, in pockets, remnants of that ancient woodland that once divided London from the coast so effectively that a different Saxon dialect was spoken in each place. The Romans, in their brutal and effective way, punched a road through it, linking Londinium with the Sussex coast. Subsequently, kings hunted it, armies marched across it, and gypsies inhabited it, a landscape that Cobbett in his Rural Rides described as 'a poor, harsh, barren place'.

No wonder only gypsies called it home. Its acid soils are no good for agriculture. Its best crop is grass for livestock, for silage or for hay. Yet with the coming of the railways, many came here and found it charming.

Kipling's 'wooded, dim, blue goodness of the Weald' surrounds it. The views from its highpoints include Hilaire Belloc's 'hump-backed Downs'. Sir Arthur Conan Doyle lived here and walked Ashdown. Its brooding setting, and its microclimate of shrouding mist, rain and cloud, provided the inspiration for many of the landscapes in his Sherlock Holmes books. Holmes, of course, was the creature that England would not let die, the country going into black-armband mourning when Holmes was sent to his death over the Reichenbach Falls by Professor Moriarty, until he was somewhat reluctantly revived by the author. Finally, Sherlock was retired to beekeeping in Sussex. I, and many others, have our thoughts about this, and a retired army colonel (sadly passed on), who kept bees nearby was my chief suspect.

And of course, Christopher Robin of A.A. Milne's Winnie the Pooh books made it his, and so ours too; the perfect childhood playground. So one comes to it already biased in its favour, and the reality seldom disappoints. It is not grand country; it's not the Rockies, the Pyrenees or the Drakensberg. It is what my sister once called 'Mouse Country'. She got it right. Mrs Tittlemouse would feel right at home here. And so do I.

That huge, dim Forest of Anderida is now gone, the oaks providing ships for Nelson, the rest had by charcoal-burners burning fuel to smelt Sussex iron. It can be a lonely, eerie place in winter, so high above sea level and open to the worst storms off the Atlantic, brought in by howling South Westers that rattle the window of our cottage and lift the occasional tile.

The place names on the Forest show that many have loved this place, with many named after places in A.A. Milne's books. The Garden of Eden, the Enchanted Place, with its rock-centred picnic spot and the inscription in bronze: 'By and by they came to an Enchanted Place'; the Hollow on the Hill, Hundred Acre Wood. There are deep, still hammer ponds, those reminders that this was once England's iron country, and then there are the odd dips and craters made by V1 and V2 rockets, which crossed these skies and happily fell short of London.

Spring, announced by cuckoos and the hammering of woodpeckers in the hurricane-humbled woodland behind our cottage, brings forth bluebells and wood anemones. There is always yellow gorse, and in August and September, the purple swathes of heather lift the heart. Amid it all, the silver birch fights to reclaim its own, while the bracken rises and falls like a green tide.

Man has been here a long, long, time. His ancient presence is evident in the small fields bound by hedgerows and by the chestnut plantations regularly cropped for posts and staves. There are the old villages, Nutley, Fairwarp, Chelwood Gate, Crowborough, Chuck Hatch and Hartfield. However, there is also change, and new roads that bring walkers and day-trippers to picnic. Not all change is bad. There is a car park that holds our favourite ice cream van, a regular stop when the children were young, on the way home from school in summer.

There is also a large, and at times noisy, military presence, not as big as when the Forest was home to thousands of Canadian soldiers awaiting D-Day, but enough to make their presence felt. The rider regularly comes across lost soldiers learning navigational skills with their flapping maps.

'Can you tell us the way back to the Crowborough Army Camp?' they ask awkwardly.

It sits across the valley from our home and I always tell them, even when I know I should not. I recall my own national service in South Africa and the only creatures I might have asked directions from – ostriches, puff adders and one foolish tortoise, which ended up in the pot, my own lack of navigational skills and resulting hunger costing him his life.

There are the radio masts on Ashdown, which mark a vast underground warren, a remnant of the Second World War, now owned and occupied by the East Sussex Police Force. What, one wonders, are they doing down there in those mole-like spaces – certainly not catching burglars or muggers.

There are few pubs on the Forest. Our favourite is The Hatch, because of its food, the gardens, and for its snug space and warm fires. It's a regular place for lunch on New Year's Day, giving us a happy break from all the Christmas cooking at home. This place was old before Jan van Riebeeck set out from Holland in 1652 with his three small ships to create a vegetable garden at the Cape of Good Hope at the tip of the African continent, place of my birth back in 1950. Just over the hill from where I sit writing this, is the Horder Centre, an arthritis clinic, where hips and knees are replaced. It sits patiently under its green roof – waiting for me and my grinding, horse-worn joints – one day, perhaps, but not yet.

Ashdown appeals to man's spirit. It must do. The evidence is all around one here. It is of this world and it is not. Here be dragons, witches and Hollywood stars. There are more religions in this place than in Jerusalem. There is Wicca, the first and the oldest, whose time maybe has come once more. There are the Scientologists, who attract California believers and film stars to these parts, and the Rosicrucians up the hill. There are modest Church of England parish churches, where vicars hold tenuous sway over diminishing congregations, and there are the worshippers of the Open Air Church of our Lord or is it our Lady? No matter, this deity combines both masculine and feminine; its double nature fits well with the dual nature of this place.

It's a bog in winter and concrete in summer. Oh God, the mud, the mud! Not for nothing were Sussex girls called 'Sally Longshanks' for the long legs they needed to keep from sinking into the bottomless depth of it. Its ability to suck horseshoes off is legendary.

Into the Enchanted Forest with Callum

Ashdown is my adopted country. I am not English, nor ever will be, despite my British passport. I love the country, but I cannot claim to know it. I know Sussex and I love Ashdown Forest. So this is my place. It is enough. It is the endpoint for me in my family's second great trek - first out of Europe - Lithuania, Holland, France and Norway to South Africa - and then, after 400 years in Africa, back to Europe again. I share it with literary giants, wild animals, mystics, sheep and a few black Welsh cattle. It is home.

And I have a friend that I share it with and who shares my enthusiasm for it, not so much the hills, or the gallops, but the flat grassy bits and the shady woods in summer. Callum is always happy to go exploring, as long as he also gets a chance to eat, to browse, to absorb all edible stuff - grass, tender leaves and twigs, bracken, bark. No, he's not a fussy eater. Three wild geese fly regularly over my home at dawn each morning, heading for our neighbour's pond. They come in low with calls that thrill you to the marrow. They seem to say, 'Get up and see. Get up and live!'

And Ashdown is out there waiting to be discovered, and my horse is there, waiting to be fed.

A MODERN EIGHTEENTH CENTURY LIFE WITH HORSES

One of the least understood parts of the mystery of horse ownership is the way that they link you, embed you, into the kind of life that our great-great-grandparents would have known intimately – the simple daily rhythms of life that repeat themselves each and every day, the repetition needed to keep livestock alive. The work involved as regular and timed as that of a beating heart.

Even as cars, planes, trains, computers, satellites, radio, TV, laptops, phones and wristwatches inhabit our lives, controlling every waking moment it seems, the horses are there to keep us tethered to an earlier, ancient reality, that flows through our lives like an underground river, unseen though in plain sight.

There they stand in their intoxicating smells, amid the sharper scents of urine and manure, hay and straw, shavings and mash. These sights, sounds, smells, and physical touch are a descant to the sounds of our modern reality. There are stable brooms in my life, pitchforks, and manure lifters, water buckets, ropes, halters, saddles, and bridles. There is an array of horse blankets, scissors, and chests of liniments, ointments, bandages, things that are of another time, clinging on in this crass, demanding, modern world.

We who have horses are to some extent split personalities, ancient and modern in one skin. I have become inured to people gently picking pieces of hay off my coats and jerseys when I do the weekly food shop at the supermarket. I don't mind. I wonder what they would think of the pleasure I take in a well-kept muck heap! Truly at times I think I am living in the wrong century.

Few people meeting me in London during my years working in the art market would ever have guessed that my life included muck heaps, whips and spurs, leather chaps and a sprinkling of people who had almost never been to London, whose lives revolved around horses, woods and fields just 50 miles away. It was my secret world, my medicine, my life jacket. Nor could they have known that my closest friends were called Duke, Quest, Hombre, Xanthus, Max, Chancer and Callum. It was my secret hidden world. And the man who inhabited it was so much happier and more whole in it, than the man they met in a suit.

The horses are a daily reminder that the only real law of life is to LIVE, to inhabit one's senses as fully as possible to partake of the natural world as a means of living and a way to keep oneself healthy, both mentally and physically.

The demands of this twin life can be exhausting at times but even while I earn a living in the twenty-first century, it is the eighteenth century to which my soul pays homage and clings to, as if for dear life, horses and the love of horses runs in my blood.

I keep a close watch on the grass growing in the fields around us, yes, I watch the grass. For on the health of the grass depends the health of our horses, and what other feed they will need to supplement the grass. I watch Callum's digestion and worm him regularly. I know which local farmers can be relied on to grow the best hay, not selling you low quality or mouldy hay which the horse won't eat. I keep tab on the seasonal price of hay. And then there are those people whose very livelihoods are still eighteenth-century in most ways, the grooms, the farriers, although now they bring their furnaces with them in trucks, and they come to you rather than you going to them as in the past. There are vets, horse dentists, saddlers and tack shops all with their arcane knowledge. There are horse trainers who will back a young horse for you and sort out one that has got out of hand for a variety of reasons, many of these down to inadequate or insensitive owners. This is a world unto itself, existing in the modern world but with the same lexicon and skills as existed 200 years ago.

Living here in East Sussex, at 1,000 ft above sea-level, on the open miles of Ashdown Forest with its tucked away secret woods, it's not difficult at times to think one lives in the past. Our home, a 275-year-old stone cottage stands firm in the face of the Atlantic gales in winter, but the windows rattle and the front door makes a banshee wail when things get hectic and the wind takes a bone in its teeth. The lights flicker as the trees lash the power lines that bring us electricity through the woods. And then the lights go out and the central heating dies and the hot water cylinder cools.

Then it's time to light candles, stoke the wood-burning stove and thank God for the foresight of installing a gas hob. We get the matches out to light it when needed. Then, as we move about this old place that has been home to stockmen and their families for generations across three centuries, the flickering light on the stone walls takes us back in one swoop to 1760 when they built this cottage of local sandstone. Once the old place is made habitable using old technology, it's time to check on the horses. The fear of roofs flying off and corrugated iron wreaking havoc is in the forefront of our minds.

It is a privilege to be a slave to these beautiful beings for they give so much more than they take. Besides the joy of riding, there is this other thing they offer, keeping open a path to the past, the recent past, and the truly ancient past, when our lives were all rural and our hunting and gathering, our farming, was intimately linked to the lives of horses. They are not changed in any way, they are as they have always been, horses that inhabit their own natural world.

And thanks to them, that link to our past remains open to us, the path back is still there. If our forebears could join us for a brief day or two, they would be lost and bewildered by our lives today, until they came upon our horses in their stables and paddocks, and it is the horses that would connect us to them, giving us a shared, mutually understood subject that would provide a shared reality. They would stroke the horses and feel the heft of our pitchforks and would smile to see that something of their way of life lives on.

The horse is our time machine, that allows us to live across centuries, not just a few decades. And what a gift that is!

CONFESSIONS OF A HALF-ASSED HORSEMAN

You would think that seventy years of horse riding would have taught me something about horses and their management, but you would be wrong. I have some knowledge it is true, but the older I get, the more I realize just how limited my knowledge is. True, I've never killed a horse, and none of my horses have died as a result of my rather laissez-faire stable management. But much seems lacking.

Perhaps my biggest failure on the stable management front is my mucking out style. Or lack of it. Because of various age-related ailments I find it difficult to do the deep clean everyone else does every day, effortlessly. Instead, I remove manure on the top and dig out the worst wet patch and fill in with dry shavings. Over time this leads to a thinner bed which I will then add to with two more bales of shavings. My stable never looks like the pure thick immaculate beds I would not mind sleeping on myself, but Callum seems happy enough. Now and then, because my mucking out takes me half the time the others take, I jokingly offer to give them a tutorial, which leads to much mirthless laughter. I tell them they will be grateful to know my quick-style muck out when they hit 70, but it cuts no ice.

Anyone who has ever read anything of mine about horses and riding might be excused for thinking that I know what I am talking about, but they would be wrong. In fact, recently there have been one or two kindly emails seeking my advice on aspects of horse management, or deferring to my decades of knowledge. I feel a great need to come clean. I am no guru. And anyone who really knows me will be laughing at the thought of anyone asking for my advice about horses. A horse guru I am not.

What I do know a little about is the romance of riding, the beauties of nature and the horse, the mystery that happens when you and the horse become one and disappear into the woods for a few hours of dream time. But when it comes down to the practicalities, the sometimes back-breaking work involved in looking after a large animal, there is much lacking in my abilities and much improvement to be desired.

And now I find myself at a stable yard among women who know infinitely more than I will ever know about looking after horses, even though many of them are half or a quarter of my 75 years. And they give me no slack, no quarter, no excuses. I am picked on, pulled up, told off, bullied. And it is weary making, though they mean well. There is zero respect for age, for knees shot with arthritis, for a heart that has seen better days. I stand accused of being a half-assed horseman, directly, and sometimes indirectly but I hear what is being said. And at times it hurts. But they are right of course.

In the mornings when I turn Callum out to grass, I find myself looking round to see which rugs the other horses are going out in. A waterproof New Zealand rug is an easy choice through the winter, but as spring arrives and warm days alternate with freezing cold ones, it's sometimes tricky to know if a New Zealand is the right choice, or if the horse should go out in a fly rug with a fly mask as well, or if he should go out naked. If I get it wrong I am told, usually as a suggestion, it must be said.

The other day I was asked how often I clean my tack, Callum's saddle and bridle. Now I grew up reading horsey books and books about hunting and it was made clear that tack was to be cleaned daily. Yes – daily. So, though I know the answer, I can't resist winding my questioner up by saying: 'Oh, I do it regularly. At least once a month.' I won't repeat what my questioner then said, but it was rude. I can only imagine what she would say if she knew that sometimes months go by without a proper cleaning.

My riding style comes in for criticism too, though it has served me well for seven decades. I don't fall off much, which is just as well as I don't bounce these days as much as I did in my twenties. But nevertheless, my slack riding style comes in for criticism. An occasional riding partner, who in her teens rode for England, has strong views on my style. It does not help to say, 'I rode for South Africa,' (even though this is a lie), I get it in the neck anyway. 'If you kept your legs on Callum he'd be much more collected and wouldn't stumble nearly as much,' she says. I try for a few strides, gripping the horse's sides and Callum promptly obliges, getting off the forehand and it does feel nice having his rear end engaged and driving forward. But my legs tire quickly and we go back to just slopping along. Life's too short.

When it comes to feeding, I like to keep it simple. As much hay as he can eat and some non-heating mash and chopped alfalfa for breakfast and supper. Not good enough, I'm told, what about the supplements they need? Books have been written about supplements so I'm not getting into it here. He has a salt lick and is wormed as needed and his teeth rasped as needed. 'Keep it simple, stupid' is my motto and Callum it must be said looks good on it. His coat gleams.

Which brings me neatly to grooming. Now when I say Callum's coat gleams I mean it blazes with a sort of copper metallic sunshine all of its own. It's one of the first things I noticed about him on the buying trip that secured him as mine. But very little elbow grease goes into that gleaming coat. And he does love to be groomed. He will drop his head and almost fall asleep with the sheer pleasure of it. And I will give him a lick and a promise fairly often, but nothing like the proper strapping most horses in the yard get daily.

Some weeks ago, a stable friend saw me walking off home after putting Callum to bed. 'Do you sleep in your clothes?' she asked me. I'd put Callum to bed in his New Zealand rug as it was a cold night promised. 'Don't you have pyjamas?' Sheepishly I changed Callum into some more appropriate night rugs and sloped off guiltily.

When I get back from a ride these days, I hose off his legs and saddle patch. Cleaning a horse off after a ride is something relatively new for me. I was told in the past that wetting a horse's legs brought on mud fever. But fashions change and now everyone hoses their horse's legs off. Some even dry them off and add talcum powder.

My greatest moment of shame occurred recently. And I was indeed shamed. Callum is not the greatest water drinker, which has in the past led to a case of compacted colic which could have killed him. The vet gave him a sedative and poured a bucket or two of water down a pipe in his nose to his stomach. So I do worry about this water-drinking thing. I will often put the water hose into his mouth after a ride and he seems to enjoy drinking from that, as he does at the rivers we cross on our rides. But he's not a great one for emptying his water buckets like other horses in stables around him, who are the equivalent of 16-pints-a-night-men down at the pub; these horses empty two huge buckets nightly and pee for England.

I knew immediately that there was trouble brewing when one of the stable ladies asked me, all innocence, (which is a hard push for her), how often I washed out Callum's water buckets? 'Well,' I said, 'I give them a good swirl of water before filling them up in the morning.'

The look on her face was that of a cat that had a mouse trapped in its claws – a mix of devilment and delight. 'Ah,' she said, 'that would explain why he doesn't like to drink out of his buckets.' Maybe she was right, as I scrubbed both out with washing up liquid and he emptied one of his buckets in one long drink. He is a bit of a princess. Likes his bucket sparkling clean.

Then, giving me a long look, the kind a hangman gives a condemned man when measuring up the noose, the lady asked, 'If I come over to your place for a cup of tea what are my chances of getting a clean cup?' I admit I blushed. My moment of greatest shame had arrived. I assured her she would get a clean cup. But she was not satisfied. 'How often do you wash up your favourite coffee mug?' I hated telling her that it gets a quick rinse mostly until it finds itself in the dishwasher. So now each morning finds me scrubbing water buckets, though my back screams for me to stand up straight.

And then there are those who mean well and do take my age and my lack of fitness into account and somehow the kindness is in its way crueller, though not intended to be so at all. My young riding partner has been on at me for months to get a body protector which will keep me intact if I do come off when Callum decides to have one of his increasingly infrequent fits of horror at some strange object and does his version of the ice skating 'Triple Axel', spinning round and round like a dervish.

The body protector is rather like a solid exoskeleton which protects the vital organs and the spine when a rider hits the deck. And as Callum stands 18 hands and I am 6ft 2in there is a fair bit of ground to cover in a fall that ends in an impact. 'You need to look after yourself,' says my friend who wears a body protector herself. 'We want you around till you are 90 at least.' Oh, Lord help me, I think.

Some last bit of bloody-mindedness on my part wants nothing to do with this plan. After all, I've ridden most of my life unencumbered by crash helmets or body protectors. But like water dripping on stone, she does not give up. I used the pandemic as an excuse to keep out of the tack shops, I'm shielding I say, and indeed I am. But 17 May arrives, a day before my birthday, and I book a fitting session at the local tack shop. To my surprise and delight I find one that is a perfect fit and £120 less than the usual price of £260. Two days later I put this carapace of hard plastic and rubber on and look at myself in the mirror – Donatello from the

Teenage Mutant Ninja Turtles, that's me to a T!

But to my surprise when I ride out it feels snug and comfortable and reminds me of my teenage years when a girlfriend would ride pillion behind me, her arms holding me tight. It's a happy thought and I decide to stop being grumpy about it. Sometimes it seems being surrounded by bossy women has its upsides.

But they miss something, these people, these would be teachers, my critics. They ride round and round the indoor school, and up and down the road and briefly round the hill. They compete, they go to shows, they win prizes. But they and their beautifully kept horses do not disappear for whole mornings or afternoons, or evenings, into the woods, to dream awhile in the shade of beech trees, to listen to birdsong, to let the horse graze to his heart's content on whatever he fancies, as I scan the sky for buzzards or skylarks. They miss the snakes, badgers and foxes. They do not stop to watch the teeming ant mounds or listen to the woodpeckers. They don't enjoy the conversations of passers-by. The whispering of the trees and their windswept groaning are not sounds they know. They don't play hide and seek with country estate managers, or come across lovers in the bracken. They do not have children ask if they might pat the horse, or hear their squeals and laughter when the horse snuffles their hair.

If truth be told, I pity them, these experts, even as I own up to my latest shortfall. My horse and I own the Forest, we know its secret places, its hidden paths. We know where the ashes of friends lie scattered and where the best places are to pray. My horse I think is fitter than theirs, he eats up the miles, three hours or more of hacking is nothing to him, he comes home dancing. And even with my crocked heart I feel I am dancing too. Though I am required to appear humble in my failings. I am, by all accounts nothing but a half-assed horseman.

WOOD MAGIC

After 45 years of walking and riding Ashdown Forest, it is hardly surprising that I think the place is magic and a place of magic too. How else to explain the life force one finds out in the woods? How to share the sense of reinvigoration when crossing its miles on a walk or a ride?

For me, the very heart of the Forest's magic is its power to restore the spirit, never more so than now, in my seventh decade, following heart surgery and in this disease-blighted year of 2020. A potential death sentence provided me with a new lease of life. Facing the inevitable made me think hard about priorities and one of the first things I did post recovery from surgery was to buy a new horse, Callum - half German Oldenburger, half Irish Sports Horse. His sire jumped internationally on behalf of Germany and then for Holland.

So, not exactly an 'Old Man's Horse'. But when you fall in love with a horse, after a year of looking and four or five failed vettings, there is nothing rational in play. The heart wants what the heart wants, and I bought him despite some lightness up front and some sense of tightly coiled springs waiting to be unleashed.

Looking after him, feeding, grooming, mucking out and riding, has kept me fit and given me the chance to renew and deepen my love affair with the Forest, criss-crossing its every mile like an old wolf marking his territory. If this be magic, so be it.

Jan and I washed up in these parts back in 1980. Over the years, I've heard talk of magic hereabouts: ley lines on the Forest, white magic, witchcraft and the fact that this area seems to be a haven for alternative lifestyles and religions. Within a ten miles radius of my home, there are communities of Rosicrucians, Mormons, Catholic monasteries and retreats, Scientologists, Opus Dei and Druids.

I don't pay much heed to any of this, but it is very hard to spend some hours out in the deepest reaches of Ashdown Forest and not connect with something primordial as well as spiritual. It may just be the fact that here nature is still paramount, which is surprising, given that the Forest is smack bang in the middle of such a crowded place, East Sussex in the deep South East of England. But, like a whirlpool, it pulls you into its own reality and it's easy to feel something different here. There is magic, both light and dark.

It's not the teddy bears picnicking that you will find is the surprise, but the trees, the rare heathland, the gorse and the silver birches, the variety of mushrooms and the streams and their crossings. The Forest has much to teach us and to surprise us with.

I've come across some very strange things over the years while out riding. You cover a lot of ground on a horse in two or three hours – eight to twelve miles roll by easily. And now and again something has stopped me dead in my tracks. A crucified crow; a child's plastic doll with birds' feathers poking out of the eye sockets; strange constructions of wood lean-tos with circles before them; and once, near Pooh Sticks Bridge, a fully dressed male mannequin, seemingly a suicide, hanging in a tree. Maybe someone having strange fun, wishing to give passers-by the willies, or maybe something darker. I will never know.

The Forest of course is home to the redcap Fly Agaric mushroom, often associated with witches. Deadly nightshade, Belladonna, and foxgloves, source of digitalis, grow here too. It is a landscape of toxic plants and mind-altering mushrooms, amid the innocent vegetation.

Herds of deer move through these woods. If you are

on a horse, they will move off the path some yards and once in cover they stop and turn to observe your passing. Many eyes in the gloom.

There is an abiding silence in some areas. And in others the Forest is clothed in green moss. There are areas that are well-nigh impenetrable and then there are the majestic cathedral-like spaces amid giant beeches. Foxes and adders and badgers live here too. And pairs of buzzards quarter the fields and woods, looking for both the quick and the dead.

The magic I speak of and find in the Forest is not from man but from nature. When you ride among trees as I do, you ride among beings older, far older than you. And though they don't move from their position they feel and observe movement constantly, the movement of wind, of rain, of the sun, the moon and the stars and human and animal passers-by. They are rooted deep in the soil, yet they are beings of the air and the sky, and their music is that of the wind through their branches. To be among trees is to be aware of the slowing of your frenetic human mind to something calmer, more akin to a tree's state of quiet consciousness. That is magic enough.

And then there is the magic of light through the leaves and branches of a wood. The Forest cloud cover is ever changing and brings with it a movement of light that gilds the hills and valleys. Sunsets and sunrises provide their own drama and interest.

Because we don't suffer the light pollution you get in a city, the nights are themselves an opportunity to observe the display of starlight and moonlight across the Forest. About a week ago, just before heading for bed, I felt the need of some fresh air and went and stood in the garden for some minutes. I was met by the most fantastic light show provided by fast moving, low, broken cloud, racing below a full moon. This ever-changing vista seen from the darkness beneath the pines and beeches that fringe our garden was spectacular and the feeling it engendered was not dissimilar to the effect of the operatic aria, Nessun Dorma, (Let no one sleep), from the final act of Puccini's opera Turandot. I felt half whirled into an ecstasy beneath this light show. I felt my heart, spirit and soul lift as it never does in any place of worship other than the Forest. If this is not powerful magic, then I don't know what is.

I have crossed the Forest's rolling miles across four decades, on more than four horses, in states of grief, of sadness of heartbreak and of fear, and I've come to it too in states of joy, of gladness, of happiness and contentment. Always, always, without fail it holds itself out to you with comfort and companionship. Our human love for the Forest is returned in more than equal measure.

We are never entirely alone on the Forest. The dead lie thick about us here. In every beauty spot, human ashes are scattered. I have been at two funeral sites where the ashes of a very old woman and a young woman lie scattered.

There is the Airman's Grave too, with the fatal hill behind it and to the south the open skies to the South Downs and beyond them the Channel and France. The grave holds no bodies but commemorates the deaths of six young RAF airmen in the Second World War whose aircraft, Wellington Mk II W5364 QT-H, returning from a bombing raid on Cologne, ended its homeward journey here in fire and destruction on the last day of July 1941, impacting the Forest at this site. Passing by, I always stop to say thank you for their sacrifice.

Sadly, I know that Callum and my partnership on the Forest must end one day, this stitching of my life to the Forest cannot last, and I would not be human if that thought does not grieve me. But I would not have it any other way, horses and the Forest this last 45 years have been central to my life and my wellbeing. Saying farewell will be hard.

A Summer Evening Ride

Summer 2020

It was a summer's evening ride on Callum in which nothing much happened and yet, in a way, so much did.

Even after 70 years of riding, I still don't understand what happens when I get on to a horse, but it is deeply pleasurable and a kind of magic happens.

I brought Callum in from the field this morning at 7am as usual to get him out of the way of the flies which drive him and the other horses all bit crazy. He wears a fly mask and a light porous silky fly-rug which protects him, but he is always by the gate when I get there and happy to come in. Being chestnut, he is a bit like a redhead, thin skinned and sensitive to all sorts of things. So, he spent the day quietly in the cool of his box.

At 6pm, with the heat of the summer day dissipating I saddled him up, a lovely deep dressage saddle it is, and we slipped out of the yard with no one else around, and within 100 yards we were in the shade of the tree tunnel lane down to the lake. Having sprayed Callum top to bottom with fly repellent we wafted along, unbothered by stinging horse flies or midges, got to the bottom of the hill and turned onto the path that runs along the lake.

The hot weather really calms him down as it does with most horses and he slopped along, the sun gleaming gold on his coat.

I wear a pair of round blunt ball spurs – the gentlest

kind – to help keep his back end engaged with his front and a whip which is useful for flicking flies away. A sure sign that this horse has never been beaten – except for that one time when he hurdled the river with me – is evident in my slashing with the whip now and then at overhanging greenery as I ride past, and he takes no notice whatsoever. Other horses I've had would have been electrified by such behaviour. Not Callum. The whip and spurs gently used really do get him more collected under me and stops him being heavy on the forehand. One can feel the rear end engage in what is a fairly long-backed horse.

We crossed the lake along the top of its retaining dam wall and walked between two trucks belonging to carp fishermen and on along to the dogleg in the path which crosses the river that flows out of the lake.

There were midges dancing in the sunrays penetrating the woods and I heard the first owl of the evening; so did Callum, who lifted his head to look in the direction of the call.

Now and then he likes a bite of the greenery, his favourite is bracken, which is carcinogenic I'm told, so I try to stop him grabbing that. Then it was up the hill past all the warning signs against trespassing and alerts to the dangers of being shot or blown up by the outdoor adventure school that has taken root recently in this part of the woods.

And then we stopped short and despite his afternoon languor, Callum grew two hands taller as two deer leapt across the path 50 yards ahead of us. But we did not stop long.

And then on to the 'Hole in the Wall', the way through the hedgerow and trees and onto the road that runs down to the old Half Moon pub and the back entrance to Crowborough. Once across this road, you are on Ashdown Forest proper. We walked on into 100 Acre Wood – which is in fact 500 acres – and then down to the splash, where we stopped for Callum's obligatory drink and a bit of ferny stuff.

And then across the road that runs to Hartfield which

is home to the Pooh Bear Shop. A few hundred yards on and A.A. Milne's house is in view just below the hill that hosts the 'Enchanted Place' on its crest.

Sensing that we were now almost pointed homewards, Callum collected himself and had a jog up the hill, one of his most comfortable paces in a menu of comfortable paces. We entered the 'Enchanted Place' as usual to admire the view north and west, rolling green farmland and hills to the North Downs. One can see Sussex, Kent and Surrey from this vantage point. I held him on a fairly tight rein, as this is where he bolted out of the stone laid circle with Janice after hearing something in the undergrowth a week or two ago. But it was too warm to be bothered by much and a passing couple with a Labrador below waved a lazy hello.

We then meandered along the crest of the hill to the car park, passing a number of young crows fossicking for worms on the grass ride, none of whom were bothered by us, just hopping aside as we passed.

I greeted an old gent (older than me, anyway), reading on a bench who said, 'How is it up there on your horse?' and I said, 'Pretty good, thanks!' and he replied, but I missed it as we had moved past by then.

There was the slightest of breezes up on the open , so we did a slow rolling canter to the top. Then it was back down into the woods above our cottage. We stopped as usual to admire the three pigs that neighbours are raising on their smallholding along with three deep chestnut Sussex steers. Callum is happy to stand there endlessly, even though he knows we are now on the home run.

And then as we moved off, I saw a movement in the shadows of the path ahead, a small, rather ancient, flea-bitten fox stopped to look over his shoulder at us. Callum spotted the old fox too and lifted his head to peer at him, got his scent and walked briskly to catch up. We closed in on the fox who was totally unfazed, and he trotted up the earth bank into the woods on our left, stopping to peer at us from behind an oak, looking like something out of a children's book. I said, 'Good evening!' and he turned and walked another twenty feet into the wood and then, like an old dog, lay down and curled up at his ease on some leaf mould, a 'Prince of the Wood' at his leisure. It struck me that the three of us, fox, horse and man, are not that different, we all love these owl-haunted woods and know its paths and secret byways. It is home, after all.

The three of us admired each other for a minute more and then Callum and I went off down the hill until he caught sight of a horse in the huge grass field where a herd of twenty-five horses from the King's Standing Riding Stable graze when they are not taking riders out onto the Forest. A black mare in a fly mask came trotting up to inspect us and I let Callum say hello over the fence. She squealed as mares do and I thought, thank heavens I've stuck with geldings.

Just before we got to the river at the bottom of the hill that feeds the lake, we stopped to admire the two huge ant nests, which were a hive of activity, and then set off up the hill home at a brisk trot until Callum saw a friend in her paddock and stopped to watch her. Though these two are friends and stable companions, it was too warm for her to bother coming over so we rode up to the stables.

I dismounted by the shipping containers that serve as tack rooms for the yard. Callum grabbed mouthfuls of haylage as I unsaddled him and spray-washed his legs, which he enjoys. He likes to drink from the hosepipe, so he got a few long drags and then after I'd scraped the excess water off him, we strolled down to his paddock where he spends the summer nights.

I got back to the yard, mucked out his stable and filled the hay nets and water butt for the morning. And so home, sun setting and spurs tinkling.

And so, finally, a beer in the garden as the swallows feed on the wing. Peace, utter peace. I re-run the ride once more in my mind and wonder at how pleasurable it was to wander through the woods. So little happened and yet so much.

Riding Through a Plague

Winter 2021

As we enter the woods this last afternoon of the year 2021, it is foggy and slightly mizzling. The ranks of bare tree trunks look like longbow arrows shot into the bracken, now the colour of old dried blood, and it came to me that this was like a scene, writ large, from the Battle of Crecy against the French on 26 August 1346, won by the deadly English and Welsh longbowmen, who, from a distance, rained down arrowed death on the enemy.

Around me and my horse, the serried ranks of trees look thudded into the bracken making the earth bleed its bracken blood. The thought halts us, and just then a crow cries its haggard medieval challenge and the picture is complete. I shiver even though I am warmly dressed. I lift the reins and Callum strides on, ever deeper into the gloomy dripping wood.

The year is ending in days upon endless days of rain and the dire news of the Covid toll upon us. So I am more than usually grateful for Callum and the opportunity he provides to get out of the house and into the woods, no matter what the weather or the news.

There is much to be said for giving in to the weather, hunkering down at home with a good book, or to use the time to catch up with friends around the world. I am of a generation that still marvels at the fact that I can speak to my brother in California as he drives to work, or to my sister in

Cape Town on WhatsApp – and it's free. And you have the option of seeing them as well if you so wish.

But for all the attractions of staying indoors, it does pall after a while and I get a touch of cabin fever. Having a horse to look after requires you to leave the house at least twice a day to feed, water and muck out the stable, and a third time if you decide to ride in the middle of the day. So this keeps you up and at it and relatively fit. And it gets you out of the house.

It's strange how the simple act of getting outdoors lifts the spirits whether it's dull and foggy or raining and the wind howling. Wellies and a windcheater donned, you head out and immediately feel your spirit lift. Sometimes I think we were not meant to live in houses, and that they steal something of life by removing us from nature. A yurt or a tepee is probably the ideal shelter, keeping you warm and dry but leaving your senses open to the weather and the skies.

Now and then something unseen rustles in the bushes and Callum shoots forward for a stride or two, until he has established that it was a squirrel or a bird and not a sabre-toothed tiger. It keeps you on your toes, this habit of his. He is a warmblood after all with a highly strung nature. Even after a hard three-hour ride, he will still swing away so fast from perceived danger that I am at risk of sitting in the fresh air where he and my saddle had been a split second before.

What a year it has been, a roller-coaster through the Valley of Death and the rising tide of the Covid dead, national debt, failing businesses, lost jobs, and devastated families. God help us all.

Against this tidal wave of darkness, there is its opposite to celebrate, the doctors and nurses of the NHS and everyone who staffs it, the ambulance service, the army, and the service personnel, delivery drivers to shelf stackers, postmen and women, the people who've kept the country's infrastructure going, who fed and clothed us, emptied the bins and kept the country ticking over. And the scientists who rushed a vaccine to the rescue.

Into the Enchanted Forest with Callum

The final words of *When Death Comes* by poet Mary Oliver echo in my ears:

> When it's over, I want to say: all my life
> I was a bride married to amazement.
> I was the bridegroom, taking the world into my arms.
> When it's over, I don't want to wonder
> if I have made of my life something particular, and real.
> I don't want to find myself sighing and frightened,
> or full of argument.
> I don't want to end up simply having visited this world.

These thoughts rode with me today until I reached a favourite spot where the horse likes to take a breather and observe the life of the Forest, and where I like to stop to say my thanks. There was so much to be grateful for, my life for one, and not to be counted among the dead yet.

After a long moment, I clicked my tongue and Callum moved on home. And my wish for the year ahead? That on New Year's Eve next year, I will be sitting once more on Callum in the woods.

CHECK MATE

Summer 2022

Into every life a little rain will fall and yesterday it poured on Callum and me. Twenty minutes from home and heading up the hill past King Standing's huge field with the Southern part of the Forest our planned destination, Callum went dead lame. I dismounted, thinking stone in the hoof, for which I carry a hoof pick, but there was nothing in either front or back hooves. Callum was all for carrying on, up the hill, out on a ride, but I thought better of it and led him home, back down the hill to the two bridges and then up the hill, the two of us hobbling in sympathy, me on my broken knees and Callum with who knew what.

At the stables, Lee, one of the resident professional grooms, took one look and said, 'Check ligament. Probably the best of the four to get. Ice it.' Our vet, Duncan from Priors Farm, was with us in twenty minutes and confirmed Lee's judgement. Hosing and icing to bring the heat down got underway and Callum now faces anything from three to nine months recovering. After a week or two of box rest, he will start walking out on a lead as expert opinion says recovery must come under some stress. So the far reaches of the Forest will not be seeing us for some time.

After a few months, Callum's check ligament is healing slowly, not made any easier by his occasional shy or buck due to pent up energy. Actually he is being a good patient and puts up with my cack-handed ice bandaging with good humour. It's been almost five weeks now that he has been on box rest with just a break morning and evening when I muck out and a ten-minute walk each day.

I started off leading him in the indoor school but as he jumps around now and then that is not helping so I am now riding him instead with the vet's blessing. We alternate with a ride in the indoor one day and then a walk out to the edge of the woods and back the next day. I see the chestnuts are falling. On fine days I also get him out for some grass on the lead. We pass the window of a horse called Monty who is now a friend of his, and they have a natter and share whatever the other one has been munching on, grass in Callum's case, hay in Monty's. The horsey contact seems to be helping my boy.

I cannot know what Callum really feels about this drastic change to his routine, but like most horses, he seems accepting of it. I on the other hand miss our rides very much, both the exercise and the sheer lift to the spirit it provides. But another month and we may get into the woods for 15 minutes of forest bathing. It was a long hard worrying slog from then on in for months and though Callum proved to be a good patient, he found being cooped up difficult.

Three months passed, then Duncan arrived to scan Callum's ligament. I tried not to hope. I prepared myself for disappointment. Duncan had said this was going to take nine months and be a long haul. But a tiny part of me did hope and I did my best to damp it down.

I had been doing my best to manage Callum's frustration at the enforced box rest this past three months, with just 30 minutes of walking exercise allowed. The big lad was a model patient, patient to a fault, but walking him in the indoor by hand proved to be life threatening – my life – and so with Duncan's approval I started to ride him out. Over the weeks we pushed it to 40 minutes and quite recently I let him jog. He was sound throughout after the initial fortnight.

Only once did he lose his head, when he spotted his neighbour, the even bigger horse, Lennie, up the hill from him as we headed home in a hailstorm. He totally lost it and let rip, rearing and bucking and cantering sideways. I hung on for dear life and wondered if he'd buggered his tendon all over again. But he stayed sound in the days after.

And now I would shortly have the result of the scan. Duncan, sensing how tense I was, kept things light. It's a skill vets learn early. Some have better bedside manners than many doctors I've met. Callum's drugged head hung heavy against my chest as we waited the outcome of the scan.

The result showed that the ligament had healed perfectly in three months. I found it hard to say much. I managed a thank you, I think. And then the relief swept over me. Callum and I would be out on the Forest once more in the Spring. For now I was advised to stick to our regime of regular light work and not risk putting him out to grass for fear that an over excited gallop could take us right back to square one.

Ten days have passed since the scan and my horse and I are feeling our way back into the woods, greeting old friends, the candelabra tree, the hump-backed bridges, the lake and the weir, the streams and the secret places of 100 Acre Wood. The woods are winter-bare now but to us they have never looked more beautiful; filled with sun, or mist or rain, they are beautiful. And as is his way, Callum stands and stares and stares and I wonder what it is he sees.

It has been a hundred days since the nightmare started, my horse dead lame and hardly able to hobble back to his stable. It is a hundred days and I am happy.

There are moments when my horse makes me laugh, at something funny or odd he has done. He regularly gives me frights too, which keeps me on my toes. There are moments when compassion for him washes over me when I find him sleeping in his field like this morning, dead to the world, and on waking he lets me put his headcollar on without bothering to stand up. And gently I rub his ears, which are unusually level with my knees.

And then there are those moments, even after his

being with me for a few years, when I look at him rapt, amazed that anything in this world so beautiful could be part of my life. It may be him lifting into an electric trot in the paddock, snorting explosively, the curve of his neck and back accentuated by his excitement, or it may be the sunlight flashing off his golden coat, or a gentle nuzzle out of nowhere. Then I stand before him, humbled by this horse-god that allows me on his back and carries me willingly through my days.

He does not like to be fussed, he has his own dignity and he keeps his own counsel. How is it that I have the right to call him mine? More truly, I am his.

The Seven-Month Summer

This strange and bizarre year of 2022 has been filled with many challenges, politically, economically and health-wise, but it has provided a seven-month summer from April to October.

Callum and I came out of the winter in good order and from March we were back to our routine of two hour rides most days, covering about 10 miles of country. His ligament is cool and just has the slightest thickening. The vet says he has healed well. So doing the maths, I reckon we've done about 50 miles of hacking a week, criss-crossing the heathlands and the woods alternatively. By my reckoning, that is 200 miles a month, some 1,400 miles for the past seven months of good weather. Had we trekked south, we'd be at Gibraltar by now!

The year has seen more trees down than at any time since the hurricane of 1987. My 'church' in 100 Acre Wood is no more, just a wreck with three giant beeches lying in the clearing like so many pick-up-sticks. The beetles and fungi must be having a party in there. And the snakes have loved the warmth. The deer, too, seem more numerous than ever and the recent rut has been as noisy as the weekend parties at the B&B next door.

The treefalls have meant a certain amount of bushwhacking to find a way around them and I am constantly amazed by how this highly strung horse of mine will stand while I prune a passage around the obstacles. He will munch leaves quite happily as I cut and break branches, steady as a rock. I am pleased with him. He has also learned to curb his enthusiasm and his 18-hand stride to give me a ground covering hand canter that he will hold for miles. So it has been a good summer.

The autumn past has been spectacular with colour and the biggest display of mushrooms and fungi I've ever seen. I so regret not knowing which are safe to eat and wish we had the French service offered by local pharmacies willing and able to do the identifying for you.

The grass has verged from lush to parched in the heat of high summer and then it came back lush again after some early autumn rains. So Callum goes into the winter well covered and muscled.

FALLEN GIANTS

Winter 2022-3

Maybe it's this year's weird weather that has fooled the trees into keeping their leaves so long into autumn and beyond. Some have paid a price for it. For it is now November and 18 degrees outside – unheard of.

The poor trees carrying that huge freight of leaves could not cope with the torrents of rain and howling winds that we've suffered this past week and I've now counted twelve trees down on my favourite riding area on Ashdown Forest.

The fallen giants add a frisson of excitement to my rides, as finding a way round them is not aways easy. But Callum and I are both up for it and generally, after some bushwhacking, we find a way through. On Wednesday, we were almost home, just past our friends and neighbours the Rotberg's lovely house in the woods, when we found our way completely blocked by an enormous beech branch the size of a trunk lying right across the telephone cables and the track that carries you over the two Victorian stone bridges recently repointed by a talented local stone mason. Dead stop and a very confused Callum. He approached the leafy obstacle but could see no way round or through or over it, so swung away and then decided to look again but gave it up for a hopeless task.

What to do? There was no possible way round the

huge fallen branch and my first thought was that we would have to retrace our ride the two hours back home, the way we'd come.

But then I realised that I could cut through the woods and down to the lake and take the lake ride home, a 15-minute journey at the trot with a canter up the hill. Halfway into the wood we came to a rivulet still bubbling and splashing after the rains. I put Callum at it, urging him to cross it where it was narrowest, but he was having none of it. No matter that both his parents had jumped for Germany and Ireland. And I was not going to remind him of his river-hurdling capacity with a crack of the whip.

So, it was up the hill for us, about a hundred yards and round the spot where the rivulet emerges from the earth and then back down the hill to the lake path. Once there we headed east to see if I could get through the gate on the other side of the treefall. But side branches held the telephone lines to just six foot off the ground. I considered my options, while Callum ate leaves.

In the end, by lying prone along his neck and with his head held sensibly low we scraped below the cables and saved ourselves a longer ride. We were home in ten minutes, filled with a great sense of satisfaction. For a sometimes crazy horse, Callum has come a long way and these days, mostly, makes a fine riding horse.

Now the BT Openreach team must get their chainsaws to the tree and clear the path and the telephone lines. How long I wonder will it be till all telephone lines are removed from our streets and landscapes thanks to the arrival of mobile phones. And if we can then lose the electricity powerlines and pylons, we will be back to an eighteenth-century landscape, and so much the better for it.

Hell In the Hail

Winter 2022-3

In this week of rain, hail and snow, Callum and his mates had four days of enforced box rest, broken by walks in the indoor school or a brief lunge in the paddock. The only time I tried to lunge him during a break in the rain we were caught out by a hailstorm and Callum, like Queen Victoria, with whom he shares some typically high-handed qualities, was not amused. On exiting the lunge paddock he dragged me back to his box tossing and shaking his head at the stupidity of mankind in general and his own human in particular.

It has rained torrentially for the best part of five days, not the usual drizzle or mizzle, but stair-rods. This history-making summer of 2022 was finally broken after seven months, just six weeks from Christmas.

It's been so wet the mushrooms have taken to climbing the trees to stay out of the damp, keeping their feet dry, something that fascinates Callum.

For the student of English weather, and aren't we all, this summer would have had us scratching our heads twenty years ago, when weather such as this was forecast but not yet experienced. The temperatures this summer has reminded me of the summers of my youth in South Africa's Cape, when one lived in a swimming costume or shorts and flip flops. We never gave winter two thoughts; summer was all encompassing.

But today Callum finally got out – twice. Once for a pre-breakfast canter in the lunge ring and then a lunchtime walk in the woods. The paths were boggy and running with rivulets, making their way through the fallen leaves, twigs and branches.

Looking after horses is a very social business and, as such, is a life-enhancing activity. For someone who lives a fairly solitary life as a writer, the stables are my interface with the world. Today the chat was all about the weather and a huge hay delivery that is imminent from a local farmer.

I was asked about the treefalls in the woods and how passable the rides were and if I had remembered to wear a hard hat instead of my soft peaked cap, something I nearly managed last week but for an eagle-eyed friend. There were brief chats with other friends before and after my ride. Inconsequential chat but underlying it a checking in, a wish to connect, to know you are well. And as such, heart-warming.

I did a huge muck out too, as the forced box rest had built up a small muck heap in Callum's box. My horse care is not of the highest order. Now and again, when I've finally got Callum's box looking half decent I like to tell people to take a look and learn something about horse management as I know this will wind them up, given my usual slackness.

As usual, our hour-long meandering ride round the lake coloured the rest of my day with rainbow-like endorphins. It ended with me crossing paths with two riders from another nearby yard who made a fuss of Callum, which as ever he took as his by right.

As I dismount, my age of 20 in the saddle jumps 52 years and I am 72 once again, all too obviously, as I hobble up the yard, leading Callum to his stable where I strip him, rub his head, brush his back and wash down his legs. Then I strip myself – crash helmet, body protector and leather chaps. Long gone are the days when I rode out in jeans, a T-shirt and tennis shoes in the dunes of the Cape, going for a swim after a gallop on the beach and then a slow ride home.

But the deep-seated pleasure of this latest Sussex ride still suffuses me. The joy is the same, my sinews, tendons and muscles not so much.

The couch is calling me. I put my feet up and relive the ride, the sunshine through rain and snow, yellow autumn leaves, dappling onto a carpet of yellow, orange, russet and red with a sprinkling of storm-torn green. The light glimmers on the lake once more and the river sounds like a jet taking off. I sip my drink and count my blessings.

Julian Roup

Snow Dancing

Winter 2023

This winter is having a last snowy fling with some minus zero weather. It is tricky enough to manage this weather on your own two feet, but with a horse it requires an added dimension of care, getting his rugs right, his exercise safely done, managing turnout to pasture when possible, and all this with crocked hips and knees I have to factor in. Long gone are the days when a one-mile walk was the same as a five-mile walk and stairs presented no challenge.

So last thing each night before turning out the light I check the weather for the next day and in the morning once more I take a look at the forecast and plan my day accordingly. Working from home makes my job easier than in my commuting to London days and I am able to fit my horse's demands in around it.

We have amber weather warnings of possible snow and sure enough it was snowing lightly when I pulled the curtains back at 6.30 am, but happily there was no wind. As Callum spent the day out at grass yesterday, it was an easy decision to keep him in for the day and have a ride to stretch his legs. First, I popped over to the stableyard and fed and watered him and mucked out, then home for breakfast, a shower and two hours of work. At 11am I had him saddled and myself warmly dressed and we set off down the back hill heading out into the woods.

He walked out with a will, the cold setting him on his toes and we swung along at a good extended walk, cutting through a pinewood and down to the small stone bridge spanning the river. A trot along the valley floor and then a fast canter up the hill to the Church Hill Car Park, festooned these days as are all the car parks on the Forest, with signs demanding payment for what used to be free. But if it means saving the Forest, it is a small enough price, I suppose. The work on the Forest this spring has seen giant machines cutting gorse that is stacked into prickly hills.

We edge through the holly hedge into Five Hundred Acre Wood, trespassing once more, keeping an ear and an eye out for lurking Land Rovers, but all is peaceful and we slant down to the pond over windblown trees, Callum making light work of them. We push on into the heart of the Forest, observing the buds on trees and the start of new growth. There is an old collapsing wooden board bridge over a rivulet we cross and soon we are into Hundred Acre Wood, back in public access land.

The snow has held off thus far but now It begins to fall lightly, making Callum throw his head around as he does when bothered by midges in the summer. I'm not fooled, I've known him five years now and this head-tossing is an indication of his feeling the weather and wanting to run. I give him his head and he surges up through the trees . When we pull up, I can feel that he is still full of running, but we walk on the gravel path. When we are once more on grass the head shaking starts again and I know what is coming. It's his snow and hail dance, which is his way of saying to me, 'Sorry, but I just have to give in to this feeling of slight craziness, better hold on tight, who knows what I might do?' I know only too well what he might do and I speak to him soothingly and stroke his neck while keeping him on a tight rein.

He finally relaxes as we arrive at Wood Reeves car park on Black Hill, cross the road and head down the bridlepath. Now he walks as though the furies are behind him, ignoring his favourite stopping places where he likes to take in the view. The snow is at the forefront of his mind and we are on the way home. He feels very light beneath me; airs above the ground are still on the cards. I keep talking quietly and he relaxes but keeps walking strongly down the hill.

We pass Woodmans and then cross the two bridges, pass the candelabra tree and finally face the home hill. Without my asking, he takes off in giant strides but I hold him to a fast canter rather than the gallop he wants. I am saving him and his off fore from his temperament, though he does not thank me for it. We top the hill smartly enough, setting off the seven horses in the field on our left, having a run themselves, tails up. The snow eases off and clears just as we reach the stable. I strip him and hose off his legs, especially his right front leg, and rug him up.

It's been an hour and a half of living intensely in the present on the back of a horse doing his snow dance and I am buoyed up by that feeling for the rest of the day. My spirit is the lighter for the ride, despite the cold and the snow. I am at one with the weather and I find myself whistling.

The Ambling Horse – Britain's Lost Heritage

As a boy growing up in South Africa, I was lucky enough to own a gaited horse, that is a horse that has two additional gears to walk, trot, canter and gallop; it has a running walk or amble and a rack, a very fast flashy amble. For someone who spent days in the saddle and covered long distances, it was a great advantage to have that wonderful mile-eating amble where you simply sat back deep in the saddle as the rocking horse motion covered ground. It did away with the need to post at the trot (the rising trot) or try to sit a jarring jogging trot.

Four decades later, living in England, with dodgy hips and knees, my thoughts returned to those horses and that comfortable pace. Some research showed few such horses for sale in England which is strange, as this is where the ambling horse and mule originated. They were a much-loved means of getting around in the Middle Ages. The thousands of monks who moved between their network of churches and abbeys in Catholic England made them a firm favourite. They are just so comfortable. Some mules also offer this gear.

And the lady's palfrey was another horse that provided this gentle, comfortable pace. The palfrey was highly valued during the Middle Ages for its smooth gait, making it the preferred choice for women and nobility on long journeys.

Horses who have this gait are sometimes shown off in

the showring with the rider holding a glass of water in one hand, losing not a drop, even with the horse going at a good clip. American Saddle Horses, the Tennessee Walker, The Rocky Mountain Horse, the Paso Fino and others offer this balm for the butt, hips and knees.

Technically, ambling describes a four-beat intermediate lateral pace, in which fore and hind feet come down separately rather than together, although other movements come under the same name.

In Africa, the hardy Basuto pony offers this pace and the odd Boerperd too. In Iceland, there is the 'tolting' Icelandic horse, which has the same gait. And that provides the clue to the spread of the ambling horse.

The New York Times reports that a recent study has found through tracking horse DNA that the gene mutation which allows for this gait originated in England and these horses were taken by Viking raiders to Scandinavia and wherever they roamed the seas.

The article states:

> In a study published in Current Biology, scientists have proposed a hypothesis for how horses with this ability came to be found around the world. They suggest that ambling horses arose in Medieval England and then were brought to Iceland by Vikings, who subsequently spread the animals across Eurasia by trade. The study is a follow-up to the discovery in 2012 that the ability to amble can be traced to a single gene mutation. It's called DMRT3 or, colloquially, the 'gaitkeeper' mutation.
>
> In the new study, the researchers analysed DNA from the remains of 90 ancient horses. They found the gaitkeeper signature in horse samples from England dating back to the 9th century. They also found the mutation in early Icelandic horses from the 9th to 11th centuries. When they looked at horses from the same time period in mainland Europe, however, they failed

to find the gene.

The great thing about ambling, this mile-munching pace, is that it's easy on the horse as well as the rider. Not the fast-racking version which remains comfortable for the rider but takes a great deal of energy from the horse. But if you keep your Ambling Rosie to the amble, you can pretty much go all day.

And despite this huge recommendation for a pace that is ground covering, comfortable and easy on the horse, ambling horses are unheard of in England these days; they are lost to their birthplace. Why? Maybe it's because the major drivers of horse sport – racing, hunting, jumping, eventing, dressage – have no need for ambling. And for the millions of happy hackers, it's just not on offer in its place of origin.

This is such a pity as it's the ideal gait for the older rider who suffers from arthritic knees and hips. Maybe it's time to bring back the ambling horse to this green and pleasant land that was its birthplace? In Callum, I am blessed with four incredibly comfortable paces, walk, jog, trot and canter, but were he to have that amble and rack as well he would be incomparable!

ASHDOWN FOREST IS BURNING

Winter 2023

Ashdown Forest, home to Pooh Bear and his friends Christopher Robin, the donkey Eeyore, Piglet, Owl, Kanga, Roo and Rabbit, is not a happy place this week. There are drifts of choking smoke across the miles of open heathland. The Forest is aflame, and my horse Callum is not impressed.

But it is all in a good cause, the Foresters are cutting back and burning the prickly gorse that threatens to engulf this scientifically rare heathland, an area of outstanding natural beauty and scientific interest. They are saving the purple flowering heather and many other plant species, including orchids, that would otherwise be engulfed by the yellow flowering gorse that strangely enough always smells of coconut and petrol to me when in bloom.

The other invasive species that is getting the chop is the silver birch. Left to nature, these rolling hills so beloved by walkers and riders would revert in a few decades back to woodland, returning to what was the impenetrable Forest of Anderida for thousands of years, home of the wolf, fox, bear, boar, deer and badger.

Callum keeps a sharp eye on the leaping flames and the rolling plumes of smoke. But other than that, he continues on his way, even though the paths he knows so well are now no longer hemmed in by ten-foot-high walls of gorse, but lie open to the faraway views of the Forest, to the South

Downs, the North Downs and the country west towards Gatwick Airport.

This cutting back of the gorse gets my partial approval as its disappearance means that at least one reason for Callum to spook is gone. He suffers from an over-active imagination, not unlike his rider, and in his warmblood mind, the gorse hides every imaginable kind of predator, so that as we do a nice, collected canter I will suddenly find myself ten foot to the left or right of where I was just a split second ago. These violent actions are all part of Callum's menu of moves to stay clear of the lions, tigers, and other horrors that he is convinced lurk deep in the gorse, not to mention the heffalumps and Woozles, just waiting to pounce.

He and I have words about this tendency of his from time to time, but as yet I've not found the argument that convinces him that there is no need to deviate from a straight line. He has a very highly developed sense of humour and more than a little mischief, qualities not unknown to his rider either. Do we become more like our horses, or do they become reflections of ourselves? It's a worrying question. I don't really want to be riding something that suffers my foibles thanks very much, it's bad enough having to live with them myself.

My jinking, jumping, whirling dervish of a horse emerges from the smoke unscathed. But now and then he does unsettle dog walkers of a nervous disposition who grab hold of their Labradors, Cockapoos, mongrels and Jack Russells. Callum has a habit of stopping the herding instinct of the black and white collie dogs dead in their tracks, when they note this 18-hand chestnut hill doing airs above the ground. They are highly intelligent dogs and run back to their owners, tails between their legs. No bad thing either!

The Foresters have chosen their cutting season well. It was an immensely wet autumn which went on and on into an extended Indian Summer until the English skies could no longer hold back their load of rain and the is wet, wet, wet. So, there is no chance of the controlled burn getting out of

Into the Enchanted Forest with Callum

hand. For that you'd need napalm. This work now also avoids the nesting birds from March to August.

Two thirds of the Forest is heathland, which provides a wonderful habitat for birds such as the nightjar, which comes all the way from Africa to breed here (as Jan and I did), and the resident Dartford warbler. The Forest is also home to a wide variety of beautiful butterflies, including the silver-studded blue, rare insects and spiders. It also hosts ancient breeds of sheep, cattle and ponies, grazing, as they have done for centuries. Across the heathland there are foxes, rabbits, stoats, weasels, shrews, bats and badgers, many of them safely below ground no doubt during this burn.

Callum is happy as ever to take the tree tunnel home, leaving the smell of burning behind him on the high ground, his gleaming chestnut coat carried down into the woods pulsing and shining like a burning coal. He knows for a fact that he is hot stuff, so very unlike the elderly man who barely manages these days to stay with him. It's not only the Forest that is burning now – Callum is on fire to get home for a bite of grass and freedom from this burden on his back!

RIDING A DRAGON

Winter 2023

This winter has taken English weather to new levels of misery for the horse-riding community who have the daily responsibility of keeping large, boisterous animals exercised.

The first few months of the winter were unrelentingly wet, with trees down across the wooded parts of the Forest, then in January we had a record freeze with overnight temperatures dropping to minus 5 Celsius – not as cold as a Montana winter – but bad enough to make exercising a horse tricky. And then we had the tail end of Storm Isha, with high winds gusting to 60mph up here on the heights of Ashdown, 1,000ft above sea level.

My best and most reliable judge of wind speed is our front door which provides an organ note of protest when hit by high-speed gusts. Last night the noise from the door was so unrelenting that I stuck an ebony letter opener into the crack to jam the door closed and the noise finally stopped. During the night, the wind claimed a roof tile.

This 1760 stone cottage has seen some storms in its 264 years of existence. It stands in uneasy proximity to two giant trees, a yew and an oak some 30 and 50 feet to the west of us. With the prevailing winds from the west those trees will fall across our driveway and hit the cars and then the cottage if brought down by a storm. It adds additional stress, listening to the keening wind.

By Monday, I had not ridden Callum for ten days. This added to my stress, the pressure building in the horse evident with each passing day that I could not get him out for a run. Most days I managed to lead him over salted ice in the yard to lunge him for half an hour in the round sand paddock, but it was not enough exercise for this lad. Really, I have no right to be riding a horse like this at my age. He has some moves that would not shame John Travolta, or Nureyev come to it.

So it has been a tricky time. But this morning, the storm winds had blown themselves out and the sun was shining a pleasant 10 Celsius – time to ride the dragon. After feeding and mucking out, I popped back to the cottage to have some breakfast and as I munched marmalade toast, I scanned the news. The first thing I spotted was the rapturous and tearful reception given to the documentary film Super/Man at the Sundance Film Festival about the fall from a horse that paralysed Hollywood actor Christopher Reeve.

> **Christopher Reeve documentary brings tears to Sundance**
> 'A standing ovation met a powerful new film looking at life for the Superman star before and after his paralysing accident.'

Reading that gave me pause I can tell you. Was the Universe trying to tell me something? Magical thinking kicked in big time. I've never been too fussed about a fall killing me, but the thought of being wheelchair-bound for what remains of life does give me the willies.

I tacked up, debating whether to lunge Callum first before riding but decided against it as the weather window seemed to be closing again and I just wanted to get him out. He stood like a rock as I mounted at the block and then did his light-footed 'Oh the ground is hot' dance out to the yard, snorting like a good 'un. I kept him on a short rein, my legs telling him to stay collected and that I was watching him.

Living on a hill has distinct advantages, allowing for wind-blowing gallops that take the edge off a horse in no time, but with a horse this long out of work, I did not wish to take any chances with his previous ligament damage, so we danced, ducked and shimmied our way down to the bottom of the hill, the horse feeling at least another two hands taller than usual. By the first bridge across the stream, the path flattens out and I put him into a brisk trot. Each fallen branch was reason to jig and jump but I kept him at it. His eyes were as much on the path as they were in the woods where he searched for monsters. Finally as we reached towards the top of the hill I put him into a slow, controlled canter, sitting deep into my saddle, legs braced for hops, skips and jumps. At the top of the hill, I let him blow at the walk and then doubled back on myself going back down the hill. So far, so good.

We did a loop around the lake, keeping up a good fast trot with some head shakes indicating a wish for more speed, but trot I'd said and trot it remained. Checking my watch, I saw we'd been out for an hour and I could feel the steel tightness of the horse soften somewhat. I relaxed too a little and we walked along with no more drama. We reached the old ivy- and moss-covered Victorian bridge where he likes to grab some green and I gave him a minute or two at the ivy. And then it was uphill all the way home and I let him canter off the rest of his excitement at being out with a good ten-minute walk at the top back to his stable.

It had felt like being on a dragon at times, but he had not really put a foot wrong. Maybe like me, his age is catching up with him, but I would not put money on that bet, not just yet anyway.

IRRESPONSIBLE OLD CODGERS

Summer 2023

Last winter, Jan took a tumble off Cara, her beautiful 17.2hh grey Irish Draught mare, landed on a gravel road and broke her left wrist, two ribs and her right hand. Britain's beleaguered National Health Service rose to the challenge magnificently and repaired her after numerous scans, X-rays, a bunch of analgesics, some bone setting and a two-hour operation to put a titanium rod into her left wrist. Total cost: zero.

But despite the wonderful care, kindness and skill involved, there was a slight undercurrent of unspoken wonder, surprise, and maybe just the slightest unstated criticism that someone over sixty was still getting up to shenanigans like this. There was a sense that Jan was old enough to know better than to be horse riding at her age. The hospital would be better used looking after the truly sick and dying, not a bunch of old farts with self-inflicted wounds. The staff in A&E and the bone clinic mentioned that in the past 24 hours there had been three other horse-riding accidents.

I can understand this feeling all too well. What the hell do we think we are up to? Are we irresponsible, stupid, crazy? I would have to plead guilty to all those things as I am a decade older than Jan and should be even more aware of my 'irresponsible' behaviour.

I hate to think what this accident would have cost us without the NHS healthcare in the UK. Maybe, I thought, sitting by

Jan through that long night, the time has come to bid farewell to riding? But once home again, there is as yet no talk of giving up. A smaller horse, yes; but that is the sum of our forward planning.

Our adult children also think we are pushing our luck and making nuisances of ourselves with the medical fraternity. Our oft-stated concern with our son's motorbike riding elicits a ream of statistics which show conclusively that many more people are crippled or killed in horse riding accidents than in motorcycle crashes. We hang our heads a bit but carry on regardless, like junkies just out of rehab.

Are we mad? Is there something wrong with us? Yes, to both these charges. The problem is we've been mainlining this horse drug for six and seven decades respectively and in some ways it is one of our main reasons for living, our single greatest pleasure. We've fought off cancer and heart disease, so we are not unaware that this time on earth is a fragile thing and is drawing to a close. This makes us even more wedded to this so-called irresponsible behaviour called horse riding.

There seems to be an ever-greater unwillingness in the West to live a bit dangerously. But it is this very thing that adds salt and savour to what otherwise would be a very bland life. We are wedded to the adventure that awaits us in the woods, out in the landscapes beyond people, even beyond help in some cases. We are not unaware of the risks and use FindMy on our iPhones in case we fall when riding alone – our son's suggestion. But it would be hard to land an air ambulance where we disappear into the Forest.

It would appear that for better or worse we are indeed irresponsible old codgers. And all the better for being just that. The poem says, 'When I am old I shall wear purple.' Stuff that, I hate purple. But riding a long-striding horse into the sunset or sunrise for that matter, that is my drug of choice and I'm buggered if I'm giving it up to keep the medics happy. See you in A&E.

Courage and the Loss of Nerve

When you start riding in your childhood, you are totally without fear. And that is despite the odd tumble from your pony and later your horse. But somewhere around your sixties, little niggling worries start arriving. Age definitely brings with it a loss of bottle. I don't know why this happens, but it certainly does. Maybe it is due in part to the fact that one is more physically fragile, one doesn't bounce as well as when you were 10 years old. The late Christopher Reeve, the actor known for his Superman role, was left paralysed by a horse-riding accident. Reeve, who played Superman in four films, experienced his life-changing spinal injury in 1995. And if that can happen to Superman, why should it not happen to you?

If you've ridden all your life, chances are that many of your friends are horse riders too and you will have seen or heard of their falls and injuries. All of this stuff builds up in your mind and the risk-taking side of you begins to urge caution. You do all the right things, wearing a good crash helmet and a body protector, finding a horse that is sensible and reliable and riding in weather that is not likely to cause the horse to be worried.

But however reliable the horse, there will be incidents from time to time when this 1,000 to 1,700lb creature slips and falls with you, is hit by a car, bucks, rears or bolts. There is not a horse born, even the most 'bombproof', that will not on occasion, given the right inputs or circumstances, do something that could potentially injure you. Banging you into a gate, or standing on your foot, or spooking as you lead him or her to the paddock and sending you flying. This stuff happens; it is the stuff of life with horses.

So, a time comes, creeping in quietly which brings with it a new caution in one's riding style or distances covered. Some, like me, who have ridden mostly solo all their lives, will start looking for company. Having someone with you rules out the horror of lying injured miles from anywhere with nobody knowing where you are.

Nobody particularly wants to die, and certainly nobody wishes to be immobilised in a wheelchair, and as both these outcomes are potentially on the cards – just look up the stats – a wise counsel in our heads begins to whisper, 'Be careful'. But a love of riding is enough to see off these fears generally, and we do what we've been told to do, programmed to do, we get back on the horse!

Most people who have ridden for four, five, six or seven decades will have gone through the odd wobble, especially after a serious horse-riding injury. So how to cope with the arrival of this unwanted guest, fear?

In my family, we've had some experience of this business recently. In my case, having Callum, a high-mettled horse, stable-bound for three months while his damaged check ligament knitted together again. And when he finally emerged, he was more wildcat than horse. It certainly gave me pause at the age of 72, and it took some getting over, believe me. The joyous walk to the stable became more akin to the last walk of a condemned man, as I battled the butterflies.

There came a day when we hit rock bottom. We'd reached the half-hour exercise mark and all was going well, Callum was healing nicely and calming down too. And then the gods of circumstance came out to taunt me. It began to hail, pellets like bullets, and even at the best of times Callum is not a fan of water in his face, never mind hail. And just

Into the Enchanted Forest with Callum

then when he had started acting up, a rider on a grey horse crossed the bridge home just ahead of us, riding fast uphill to get to the stables and out of the hail. Something tripped in Callum's mind, and he reared and bucked, throwing himself inside out, not wishing to be held back by a tight rein to his mandatory walk. Not in the hail and not with another horse cantering fast up the hill ahead. I had a second to decide, keep fighting him and come off or give him his head and risk the check ligament snapping this time. I took a risk giving his head, knowing that if I came off, he would tear up that hill like a lunatic. I gave him his head in as controlled manner as possible in the circumstance and his great powers of acceleration sent us flying up the hill, all the while the hail whipping him to a frenzy.

And then we had a moment of luck. The other rider had pulled up under a huge beech tree to get himself and his horse out of the hail. We stopped there too, joining them. Soon the hail eased and ten minutes later we were home safe, with Callum rugged in his stable. Getting on him the next day pretty much scraped the 'bravery barrel', believe me. But I did, we never had a repeat of that madness and despite the excitement, his ligament healed completely. Everyone needs a little luck and a smidgen of courage now and then!

Jan has had her own problems with falls. Great credit to her for still riding four years after coming off Callum and breaking her shoulder. This after riding him very happily for two years. But, as horses do, one day he saw a deer on the Forest, caught her unawares, dropped a shoulder, spun round in a split second and galloped for home. This on the day after she'd bought a body protector! She called me and I found her chatting animatedly to the group of people who had come to her aid and caught Callum when he stopped to graze. I rode him home and Jan got a lift to the local cottage hospital, where they called an ambulance and sent her straight to A&E. It took a couple of months to heal but the real, long-lasting damage was to her nerve after six decades of riding and competing. Mind you, after a few weeks she was back on her own lively 16.3hh Irish Sports Horse Traveller, cantering him across the Forest single-handed – such was the trust she had in him.

Ben, a handsome 6-year-old 16.2hh chestnut Irish Draught we bought her after Traveller's death at 21, provided further excitements. We discovered that as a lockdown buy, he had never – and I mean never – been ridden out on a hack in his two years with his previous owner in Ireland. Naturally enough, he found our woods and the Forest, full of deer, cows, rabbits and badgers, terribly frightening! Even birdsong startled him. But after six months, Jan had gentled and taught him enough that he was an enjoyable ride. She had even persuaded him that his preferred method of napping – running backwards – was not to be tolerated. But one day, when I took off ahead without warning, he gave a giant buck and got her off. Then he did the same thing to her friend. Off he went to another loving but more suitable home! Then it happened again. After the fall off Cara, her injuries, and the long healing time, she thought her riding days might be over.

Instead, she downsized. She found a chunky 15.1hh piebald cob, her second Traveller, who helped to rebuild her lost confidence to such an extent that she is riding solo once more across the length and breadth of the Forest. But it's not been easy. She had to force herself to ride alone, and it took many months. But as she says, quoting Michael Rosen's picture book *We're Going on a Bear Hunt*: 'You've got to go through it to get over it.'

As I've said, I've been there myself, so I understand all too well what she has been through. But unlike Jan, I have not had broken bones as an added incentive to be fearful.

Courage is not the absence of fear; it is being beset by fears but getting on the horse anyway and soldiering on. It is just another of life's lessons that the horse gives us: 'You've got to go through it to get over it.'

CELEBRITY HORSE

When your horse is better known than you, life can become tricky. A few years ago I started writing about Callum, and now it has begun to impact on my riding. Every now and again a rider or walker on the Forest will ask in passing: 'Is that Callum from the books by any chance? Are you the writer chap?' Half embarrassed, half delighted, I pull up and we have a chat. Callum gets most of the attention, which seems only fair, as he did not actually give me permission to write about him quite so frankly; all his foibles and mannerisms are well covered. So I allow the walkers to pat him and give him a mint or two.

To say that he enjoys the attention would be to understate the case. He loves it! And why not? It gives him a chance to stop, grab some grass, enjoy a mint and be the centre of attention. There is something about this horse with his four white socks that indicates a mind of his own. He comes first, second and third in the galaxy of his important relationships, so no doubt feels he is rightly due the attention. And irritatingly, the walkers are often completely charmed by him. It's a bit like a parent collecting a child from a party where the hostess tells you how wonderful Jonny is, how beautifully behaved, when at home he is a little devil. It's much the same with Callum. One of his old tricks is to perform what the ice skaters call a 'Triple Salchow', when they suddenly pick up speed, jump into the air and spin around three times, landing on the ice if they are good, or on their butts if less so. Callum never lands on his butt, but I've come close on occasion. The admiring walkers, of course, see none of this.

And Callum is no fool. These days, he actively looks out for admirers on our rides. If he hears people talking in the woods he picks up speed till he can see them and as they approach he slows and then stops. If he is not recognised, it means I am sitting there trying to get the great lump moving again with the slightly bemused walkers wondering why I stopped and why I am now kicking my horse to urge him on. I can't imagine what they would say if I told them, 'He considers himself a literary celebrity and is wanting you to acknowledge that with pats, mints and admiration.' They would think both horse and rider are patently bonkers and would get away from us as fast as possible. And who could blame them? It's downright embarrassing. But as he is chestnut, you can't see Callum blush. I'm the pink one!

Thank goodness he can't read yet, there would be no living with him then. But with AI who knows, one day they could well be able to translate English into Horse, and then all hell will break loose in this quiet corner of the Forest. It won't be Pooh Bear, Piglet, Tigger or Eeyore who will surprise you when you go down to the woods today – it will be my horse Callum saying to walkers: 'Actually, I prefer Ferrero Rocher to Polos.'

It's all got a bit out of hand with Callum. He keeps his press cuttings file in a waterproof plastic binder in his grooming tack box – they are all there: Country Life, The Field, the Guardian, Sussex Life and a handful from Canada, the US and South Africa. Recently I found him and his new next-door neighbour, a 12-hand coloured pony, paging through them and I swear the pony was rolling its eyes. But like all vain creatures, human or not, Callum was oblivious as he pointed out particular elements of his conformation and how I had the bit too low in his mouth. He has little good to say about me. So I shrug and carry on. Having a celebrity horse is no easy thing and when you only have yourself to blame it's hard. Very hard.

Stay Alert, Stay Alive

Two of the many gifts that horses have bequeathed me – living in the moment and developing lightning-fast reflexes – have served me well. If you've ridden for most of your 70-plus years, you cannot help but learn a thing or two about horses. The cost of not learning is broken bones, hospitals and big costs. Horses make good teachers – they help you focus something wonderful.

Horses share the fly's ability to move 30 times their body length in a lightning-like leap. In the case of Callum, who is something of an hysteric, it's done in the blink of an eye. It's in his DNA. So, when you are riding a horse like this it's not a good time to ruminate on that idiot who stole your parking space, or what you'd like to do to that teacher who said to you, 'This is tennis, Julian, not ballet!' or the tax inspector who went through your books and found nothing amiss. You had better focus on the job in hand, horse riding, and staying alive.

I've attended a few meditation classes in my time and found that horses are much better meditation teachers than any human I've met, and I've met a few. Boy, do you live in the now up there in that saddle! It's a kind of moving meditation on steroids. You are so fully immersed in the now that you are part of it, much like a deep-sea diver is part of the underwater world the moment his head sinks beneath the waves.

There is a moment when this focus and being in the present wobbles a little bit as you get older. That is when magical thinking enters your life to some extent. You start looking for omens and signs from above as to whether this is a good time to ride. For me, the collywobbles set in if I drop my riding helmet or struggle more than usual to put my body protector on, or, like this week, when the strap buckle of my spurs caught for a moment on the inside of my left stirrup. I twiddled it free and as I did, the little devils of the future imperfect smiled cynically at me and muttered: 'Not a good way to go, dragged by the heels like Mussolini!' Where does this BS come from? Maybe the overwrought imagination of a writer?

But ignoring all noises off, I settle deep into my comfy dressage saddle and the warmth of Callum's flanks calms me down; I am soon back in the present. And focused, alert and ready to rock and roll, 20 years old once more, with 55 years evaporated like the steam from a kettle as that long raking stride carries us deep into the overarching chestnut, oak, beech and birch tunnels. I'm once again at home in my saddle.

The state of heightened awareness ushered in by the knowledge of your vulnerability is such a gift. You see with the detail that only artists usually notice. The stripes and stipples and splashes of sunlight on the pine trunks, turning them into wooden barber poles, but brown and gold, not red and white, though red and white are here too. The first fungi of the autumn dot the pine needled forest floor, the cleverest among them climb trees to escape the forest floor foragers, looking like a MENSA meeting of geniuses. And like geniuses, this move up the trees is not the brightest idea, as they stand out like beacons. Here and there, the red and white fly agaric awaits its own specialised feeders, those not put off by its toxins. The Fly Agaric (Amanita muscaria) is as enchanting as it is highly toxic. Home of fairies and magical creatures, it is most at home in birch woodland, where it helps trees by transferring nutrients into their roots. But do not be tempted by its beauty; if eaten it can cause hallucinations and psychotic reactions.

And to add to the green, brown, gold, white and red, there is the bluebell blue haze of Spring. We may ride in the woods, but the rainbow has followed us in.

And that brings me neatly to the lightning-like reflexes. When your horse starts the business of impersonating a fly, you'd best be a fly too, or you are going to be that squashed thing on the ground. I tend not to drop things. Even when an object slips out of my hands, I manage to catch it mid-fall, thanks to the lightning-like reflexes my horses taught me.

And best to stay alert once you put a foot in that stirrup. I like to let my horse graze on a ride now and then, it gives him a really good incentive to leave the stable yard knowing, like this morning, that there was a banquet awaiting him in the woods, blackberries, picked carefully amid the thorny briars, lush grass, beech leaves and bracken. This gives me a moment to check my phone or do whatever I please while his mouth is actively engaged in green pursuits.

But I watch him like a hawk. The moment he pauses in gobbling, stops chewing and cocks an ear at something he heard in the woods or lifts his head suddenly level with my own, I make full contact on the reins, being oh so aware that a flight may be imminent without any cabin crew to advise the fastening of seat belts.

At some level, I have begun to think like a horse, to react like a horse, to some extent anyway. I listen for sounds that will switch Callum on to flight mode, squirrels, deer, badgers in the woods, a fat woodpigeon ahead, about to flap noisily away. Helicopters, drones, buzzards, motorbikes, flying plastic or paper.

It sounds exhausting, doesn't it? And the strange thing is it is not at all tiring. It keeps you in the present and all that other stuff, money, status, people, dissipate like mist in the valley on a warm summer's morning.

I have long thought that one's mindset on horseback reels back time to when we were hunter-gatherers emerging from Africa as a species. We were as much hunted as hunter, easy meat on two legs, and that meant we needed to be super alert, just as the horse, a prey animal is alert. On horseback, you are more alive and in tune with nature than normal, and what a gift that is.

And once you are home, beer in hand, sprawled on the couch barefoot, the endorphins kick in and you ride the high until the beer hits the spot and adds its own feel-good factor. Horses have been my best teachers, my gurus, my pals, but they can also be a bit crazy. Best stay alert, stay alive, live in the moment.

A LOVE LETTER TO ASHDOWN FOREST

As a horseman, I try after a ride to produce words that encompass landscape, horses, friendship, and a search for belonging. Simply put they are love letters to Ashdown Forest after a forty-five-year affair. My riding is also about peace of mind, most evident to me during a time of the Covid 19 pandemic in which a return to the woods offered both solace and peace.

I've been privileged to spend the last four decades living and riding around the fabled Forest and found the place, and my horse, almost magical during the pandemic.

My passion for horses I hope shines through in these pages, as my horse offers a reduction in stress and an entry point into a totally different mindset. After the best part of a year in lockdown thanks to Covid-19, it became clear to me as never before how much I owed to the place ... and to my horses, Callum most recently, who have carried me across its green miles.

Both the Forest and the horses have brought me health, peace, and deep spiritual contentment when life offered just the opposite. The pandemic truly brought it home to me how important nature is to our well-being. So my writing is a kind of thank you to the Forest and to Callum, the big chestnut, who has been my companion during this plague year. On his back I have reconnected in a deeper way with the Forest and seen how and why we need to cherish what remains of the few wild places left here in the busy South East of England.

I have always loved horses, riding, and landscape and they provided an escape and a balm from the pressures of a fairly unhappy schooling experience. I started riding at the age of six in Cape Town, South Africa, where I was born and now in my mid-seventies, I am riding what will probably be my last horse.

What inspired me to write about all this? Well, it's been my passion, my salvation in a way, and certainly cheaper than seeing a psychiatrist. During the past 18 months of the Covid-19 pandemic the importance of horses and riding became doubly important to me, as did the beautiful heathland and woodland of Ashdown Forest – the walking ground of Sir Arthur Conan Doyle, who wrote the Sherlock Holmes books. And for three years, 1913 to 1916, it was the winter home of poets Ezra Pound and W.B. Yeats, who shared a cottage on the and drank cider in the Hatch Inn.

For me, Ashdown is a dreamscape and a literary landscape combined and I love it and wanted to share something of it with others. Having emigrated from South Africa in 1980 at the age of 30 I was very unsettled for some years and then slowly but surely, Ashdown began what I can only describe as a 'nature cure' and the place entered my heart. These days, after owning so many horses, my real home is in the saddle. When I am riding, I am home.

Some years ago, I had heart surgery and some stents were placed in my heart. I also have a blood condition which impacts my immune system, so for these reasons and even since being vaccinated, Jan and I have been in effective lockdown. Horses have always been a lifeline and now they became a lifeline with a capital H. So in effect I've spent the last year and a half writing and riding like fury on Callum who as I've recounted, I found when I went in search of an 'old man's horse' but fell in love with what is probably the single most inappropriate 'old man's horse' imaginable! But what the hell, you only live once.

What is the spiritual and meditative power of the horse? Where do I begin? This is such a vast subject. We are all aware now of the way horses are used with emotionally troubled people and the benefits this brings. The book The Horse Boy by Rupert Isaacson is one of the best on this subject and it moved me greatly.

I find that when I'm riding a very large animal that has the capacity to kill you, it forces you to live in the now; the past and the future have to take care of themselves for a while as you negotiate your way through the woods. This helps you focus on the present to an unusual degree and I believe this brings about an activation in our minds better known and understood by our hunter-gatherer forebears. You are truly alive and the natural world takes on an almost luminous and numinous presence. I, for one, feel I am riding through a sacred space.

This is the gift of the horse to humans, or those who have the sense to tune into what the horse offers. After some hours out in the woods, I am a different person to the one who left some hours before: more still, more centred, more at peace. And the activated endorphins released by the riding give you a natural high.

So my advice to any exhausted/stressed-out horseperson would be to say: Cherish your horse as a purveyor of horse medicine. They will, if you allow them, give you the single most powerful connection with nature and its power to fill you with joy. Forget any form of competing if that is your thing and let the horse give you a lead in slowing down, finding the time to simply stand and stare, as the poet tells us, and to remind yourself of all those things that bewitched you about horses to begin with.

All of this slightly woo-woo stuff is accentuated by my riding in this Forest.

Today the Forest is owned by the local authority, the East Sussex County Council and is the largest natural park and woodland southeast of London with some 6,500 acres to walk and ride on. It is special scientifically as one of the last remaining heathlands in Britain and is a beautiful place to explore on foot or on horseback. It is astonishing that such a place even exists so close to London beneath the flight paths into Heathrow and Gatwick airports.

The pandemic brought many thousands of new visitors to the Forest as they grasped the importance of what it provides in terms of good physical and mental health. So I was not alone in having a fresh respect and understanding of the value of nature to us as human beings. There was in these parts an ancient belief in the Green Man of the woods, a sort of nature spirit. I believe something of the spirit of the Green Man haunted me during this time.

I have come to realise that unless we see nature as sacred, as something worthy of veneration, we as a species are lost. After all, we can see with increasing clarity that this 'spaceship' we call the Earth has no lifeboats. If we destroy it, we destroy ourselves. What better reason do we need to worship the earth in ways earliest man did instinctively, believing as he did if one listened, the trees and the stones 'spoke'? Looking at the landscape in this way transforms everything, us, and the landscape. And horses, through their sensitive nature, are the perfect guides into this new reality; spirit guides if you will.

HORSES SLEEPING ON A HILL

I wake at 6am as usual and get up to bring Callum in from pasture for the day to avoid the heat and flies. Sleepily, I leave the house, climb over the back fence and walk through the little wood. Below me, the valley is hidden in mist, just the first two paddocks visible.

This high-summer morning is pregnant with smell: fecund, rich, growing, wet, earth and grass and a tang of sharpness from the dung heap. But no breath of air, no wind. Stillness heavy on the dew wet grass.

I walk slowly down the hill, still feeling the effects of my ride yesterday, in my muscles and spine and knees. I place my feet with care. Seventy summers have come and gone and the gift of horses is still with me for now, but not much longer. I treasure it all the more.

Descending the pasture hill I pass the show jumpers and dressage horses, sleeping in the grass in their light summer fly rugs. Some lie flat, some have their heads up, some snore softly.

I pass grey Storm and chestnut Conker, and the lovely grey Andalusian. Not all lie prone on the grass, some stand sleeping, as horses do. The black pony Jack looks dead to the world, half buried in grass, Donty the piebald gelding is dreaming at the far end of his paddock, the bay Finch and his pony friend Benny are grazing, as is golden Callum.

I call out to Callum who comes from mid-paddock, strolling to meet me at the gate, and I click on the lead rope. He is dry, and round with the night's grazing.

As I turn back up the hill the mist is lifting and the horses with it, some who were lying asleep now stand to watch us pass. It is going to be a warm day.
I return home to bed with a coffee, and repeat the walk, touching each part of it with care, like a jeweller arranging gems for a forget-me-not-ring.

DESPERATE TO GET OUT – AND BACK IN AGAIN

Maybe it's just Callum, gentle flower of a horse that he is, of high-strung nonsense, erring on the side of his warmblood sire rather than his dam, a grey Irish Draught cross – supposedly of a more laid-back temperament.

Like any horse that has been stuck inside for too long because of torrential English rain and mud, or ice and snow, or this winter's two Atlantic gales, Callum makes his feelings known. He gets jumpy in the box and starts to box-walk. I then get him out for some lunging which begins in a way that would not embarrass a well-hooked swordfish.

So when the day dawns warm and sunny – relatively speaking – I get him into his New Zealand rug, put on a headcollar and Chifney bit and walk him the quarter mile to his paddock. I note on the way down, out of the protection of the stable yard, that there is an icy wind blowing, but Callum is on the bit and champing to get to the grass.

After a quick release that I've perfected after many an excitement at the gate, Callum turns into an Arab stallion, tail bent right over his back, has a little gallop, then a roll and finally it's head down for some serious lawn mowing.

Three hours later it's coming up to lunch time and I look down the valley from our cottage windows and blow me down, His Imperial Highness is by his gate looking around, evidently wishing to come back in! I gear up for the weather and the walk and in we come, Callum snatching at the grass all the way back to the stables.

Is it him, or is it me? Or is this just nonsense? The strange thing is that he is not alone in this behaviour, some of his stable mates are just as fickle in their 'in or out' needs.

Many years ago we kept our horses out 24/7 in the summer in a field with a huge three-sided lean-to barn that allowed them to get out of the sun and away from flies when they wished to. It was an ideal arrangement. Sadly we no longer have access to it. The barn is no more.

When we lived briefly in Idaho, we came across American barn stables which provided individual runs for the horses, from their two-gated stables, which in minus 20C snow-bound winters worked well. But we do not have such luxury.

What is your view of this strange 'in-and-out' requirement of Callum and his mates? It seems to me that much as they are always gagging to get out for a run and some fresh grass, the novelty soon wears off and they wish to be in their nice warm stables. There is something innately human about this which I find endearing, even as it exasperates me at times.

BRITISH WATER TORTURE, WITH HORSES

Winter 2024

There comes a point in a movie about spies where the man or woman has been tortured to within an inch of their life and is about to confess everything just to get some sleep and an end to pain. That is how March in the UK feels to me. I don't know if I can hack another month of this misery, unsure if summer will bring relief, or if it's going to be a wet summer this year, adding insult to injury with just more rain.

I have the greatest respect for anyone who can survive a Scandinavian or Canadian winter, but truly to see a British winter through, with horses as part of the mix, also takes a certain bloody-mindedness and something of the spirit of the Blitz!

And it's one thing to be born into it – though even the Brits moan. I think they see griping about the weather as another pleasure, like tea and scones. But to come from sunny climes as I did, the British winter is a test of one's mettle.

The great walker and writer, Alfred Wainwright, famously said, 'There is no such thing as bad weather, only unsuitable clothing.' But however well dressed for the weather you may be, there is a part of you that you cannot cover in Gore-Tex – your mind. And it is your mind that takes the hardest hits when the weather is unrelentingly awful. It becomes depressing to say the least.

People use SAD lamps – Seasonal Affective Disorder lamps that is – but they have limited impact, in my experience. The answer is to fly out of this cold, dripping wet purgatory for some sun. The whole British package holiday business is based on a craving for sun in winter and it sends turnip-white Brits abroad into the midday sun like mad dogs, to roast as red as beetroot.

Even the horses don't want to go out in this misery. Their field is a mudscape of brown craters and slides, Passchendaele revisited. And despite New Zealand rugs, they patrol the fence with the exit gate like guards outside a royal palace – marching up and down, up and down, and now and then the moment comes when they curse – 'Bugger this! I'm done' – and they just come straight through the electric fencing. Done, done, done, and back they gallop to their cosy stables and the hay nets and deep beds of straw or shavings. Who can blame them?

Recently I was out hacking on my own, as is my way, and Callum and I found ourselves miraculously under a blue patch of sky. 'God smiles on the just,' I thought to myself – too soon. The sky grew dark, and the heavens opened, and Callum took off like a woman without an umbrella who has just spent three hours and £200 at the hairdresser and is now caught in a downpour. He put his head down and galloped like a good 'un for the shelter of a hilltop pine copse and stood there shaking. I was with him all the way. We waited till the storm passed and then slip-sliding, we skated home.

So, the horse version of Russian roulette has become part of my winter routine, as we've had very limited turnout. Callum gets a daily lunge or a ride, but misses the turn out. So, each day, as his springs get coiled tighter and tighter, I ask myself, like Hamlet,' To ride or not to ride, that is the question.' And riding means that it's a 50-50 chance as to whether I will continue to 'be or not to be' – it takes some thinking about I can tell you. At my age, one doesn't want to be bouncing off the ground from an 18-hand horse. But usually what remains of my bottle wins the day and out we go to play in the woods. So far, so good.

Every winter, we say this one we are going to escape from or have a break midwinter, but then there are the animals to consider, cats, dogs, horses. And once again, post-Christmas, we find ourselves looking out of the rain-lashed windows with the whites of our eyes showing like a spooked horse. Why do we do it? I'm not the person to ask. But do it we do. Forty-five winters and counting.

The only things that do well around here in winter are the potholes in the roads and paths. They just grow like Topsy, without planning or design. The only ones who like them are the area's garage owners who are all doing well on fixing smashed tyres, bent wheels and bust shock absorbers. And the hospital A&E is inundated with broken ankles, arms and wrists. Around here, the potholes rule and even people with 4x4s drive defensively.

The Met Office tells us that 'February 2024 has been the mildest and wettest on record'. No kidding? And they warn that thanks to global warming, England will increasingly have mild, frost-free winters that are wetter than what we are used to.

But there will come a day when the cuckoos, the woodpeckers and the skylarks are once more heard in the woods, when midges dance in shafts of warm sunshine and the scent of bluebells fills the air like an elixir. Then the New Zealand rugs are washed and stored away, the grass grows lush and the horses fat on it, content to spend days and nights in the paddocks, not giving the gate or fences a second glance. Then, then, 'Oh to be in England now that April's here!' And the time of testing torture is but a dim memory once more.

Dear Lord, send spring soon!

Ashdown Unchanged -- A Horseman's Prayer

Spring 2024

Each day, as my horse and I slip into the woods for a spot of forest bathing, I celebrate the changeless changing of the seasons. Each time of year brings its pleasures – the green shoots of spring with its violets, wild garlic and then the azure haze of bluebells beneath neon green new leaf on the beech trees. The bee-filled buzz of lazy summer days and the horse nodding away the midges round his nostrils. The splendour of autumn as seen in a deciduous wood, the mushrooms of every kind, messengers from the underworld. The barking of stags in rut and the busyness of squirrels. Then winter reveals the tree scaffolding, bare skeletons of wood, leafless. The wind and rain bring pruning shears to these groves and old friends groan one last time and fall down, a feast for the beetles and new light on the forest floor.

This home range of mine is a tiny remnant of an ancient forest that existed here before man arrived. As my horse and I make our way alongside streams and through hidden secret valleys, I mark the changes with care. A section of blue spruce culled to rid the woods of their endemic spruce beetles, the ever-busier car parks bringing walkers and dogs, the roar of Gatwick-bound jets overhead and the odd tent hidden among the pines of someone driven by my own passion to hold the earth close for what may well be its last few centuries. Let us pray for an end to change and a return to a world made whole by its changelessness.

Just imagine for a moment a world without change, a world so in balance that there is no change, other than the seasonal changes. This is how our distant ancestors lived. It seems impossible to imagine such a world; the culture of 'progress and development' is embedded so deeply within us that to turn away from it seems retrograde, crazy. And yet it has only been in the last few hundred years that dramatic radical change has become the norm. As a species, our brains are wired to cope with change, to be adaptable. This is surely a good thing, as it helped us cope with massive change imposed by nature, floods, fire, the pulses of the Ice Ages.

But between these natural changes, our species lived for millennia in a symbiotic balance with the earth as hunter gatherers. We were too few and too thinly spread to make any meaningful change. If a hunted species thinned out, we could move on to where they were more plentiful, giving our old range time to recover its animal inhabitants.

With this changelessness came many gifts. There was no loss of habitats, no loss of forests, no loss of landmarks, no loss of caves, or sacred places. Our world then was in balance and stasis was good. Whole generations would experience the earth in the same way and our culture would celebrate the omniscience of nature. We were like ants moving over the face of our god, our nature mother, and it must have filled us with a kind of quiet ecstasy, to know we were a part of this deep rhythm of life.

As Callum and I move through these beloved woods we cannot help but notice the changes. The tents and caravans of people who have bought small plots of Tilhill Forest, an outdoor adventure playground, the cars of fisherman at the lake. Where all was unchanged for years and decades, change is now nibbling away at the Forest and one can only wonder when and where and how it will end?

Horse Fly Season

Summer 2024

When I went down to get Callum in from the field for the night, he came running to the gate despite the heat, tossing his head and almost bowling me over. I looked to see where the horse flies were and sure enough there was one on each side of his neck, just about in the throat latch area. I killed both in quick succession and rubbed his neck hard. If a horse could speak, Callum would have said a heartfelt thank you.

I put on his headcollar and waited for the other horses to be collected so that we could do our evening march up the hill to the stable and supper. Trust those damn horse flies for finding the one spot on the horse that was not covered in a fly rug or fly mask. Horse fly IQ must be around genius level, or they just home in on unprotected skin.

Jan's new horse, who we've nicknamed Traveller Too (he is the second Traveller she's owned) is a piebald and the bastard horseflies are smart enough to avoid the white patches where they would show up and settle instead on the black for a spot of bloodletting.

Now that summer has, post-solstice, finally graced us with her presence, she seems to wish us to know that late or not, she is here! For two days now here in South East England the temperature has peaked at around 27C, which seems like a heatwave after the nine months of extended winter we've had this year. And with the heat have come the flies.

Jan bought two new Formula 1 style fly swatters for the house which I have been putting to such good use that our dog Gus now perks up when he sees me grab the thing, knowing there might be a dead fly coming his way if he is quick enough. Sadly, riding with a fly swatter would look a bit off, so instead the first thing I do after leaving the stable yard is to pick a good leafy beech branch and brush it up and down Callum's sides and all over his head. He is most appreciative, and the head tossing stops almost immediately.

The women of the yard cover their horses in fly repellent to such an extent that the horses leaving for rides smell like an A&E hospital ward. I'm not crazy about the stuff, which seems to me to have a limited success rate and rather spoils the wood and smells, which both Callum and I enjoy so much. So, for us, it's beech branch swishing and that does us fine.

After all these years you would think I'd know where the horse flies are thickest, out on the open sunny heathlands or in the gloom of the woods, but the damn things seem equally distributed to me.

And of course, the horse flies are not the only bugs to bug us at this time of the year, it's party time for midges too, dancing in the sunbeams and making an audible murmuration over the dung heap. It sounds like rush hour in the air just now. My pet hate besides the horse flies and the midges are the big blue lazy flies that sound like outboard motors who dive bomb your head and go round and round a room until they find you again and venture another dive bomb. Now and then a rage comes over me when I open the fridge and one of these fat horrors tumbles out barely able to fly so gorged is it on butter, cheese, ham or last night's leftovers.

Back in the day when I was a stripling lad living in Cape Town, each stable boasted a branch of a Port Jackson tree soaked in some fly killing toxin and that seemed to work pretty well. Fly sheets had not entered my ken back then.

Into the Enchanted Forest with Callum

These days, when Callum and I sally forth, he wears a violet-coloured fly fringe over his eyes, the faded blue over the bright gold of his skin makes for a nice contrast and seems to do the trick. I'm not too crazy about riding him in a fly mask as he is inclined to stumble a bit, anyway, preoccupied as ever with what devils the bushes might be hiding and so anything that impairs his vision doesn't get my vote. It also seems to have the effect of making him even more jumpy than usual – so the fly fringe and our leafy beech branch has to suffice.

As we ride out, I look like a baseball player coming onto the pitch testing the heft of the bat with full arm swings up and down the horse's flanks. And all this just to keep those damn flies at bay. Ah, summer.

Forest Bathing with Callum

Autumn 2024

It's an early September morning and Callum is making brisk work of the grassed hill that rises steeply from our river crossing to the small country road we have to cross to get into Five Hundred Acre Wood for a spot of forest bathing. This wood is adjacent to Hundred Acre Wood. Sometimes forest bathing can get the blood racing as both the horse and I know that these are huntsman-haunted woods.

Callum eats the hill, cantering in 20-foot strides. He wants to let rip but the grass is still carrying its freight of night dew and I don't want him to have another injury, nor me. I pull him up and look back at my home town, Crowborough, on its hill basking in sunshine and racing cloud. It has been home for 44 years and I feel real affection for it.

We cross the tarred road as quickly as we can, hearing the sound of approaching cars. Up an earthen bank bearing signs of my own previous passing and that of recent deer, and we fold ourselves silently into the chestnut and oak forest. Some 30 yards in, we are invisible to the odd car pelting down the hill.

Callum's ears are like two steel points as he takes in the forest sounds and its scents. He is making soft snorts to let off steam and also to let me know to sit tight, and I put my legs on him. As we make our way down the green tunnels, breaking off an overhanging beech branch here and there to keep the way clear, he seems more settled now.

Into the Enchanted Forest with Callum

I have breakfasted well, and the two mugs of coffee want to see the light of day again. I need to pee and pull up near a two-foot-tall chestnut stump to dismount, which I manage without too much bother. I am just done peeing when I feel Callum tense.

Suddenly about a 100 yards down the hill, I see two dogs on long leads and three men in forest green bearing shotguns broken open over their arms, coming my way. They have not seen me yet, but the wind is blowing their way, and the two brown and white English Pointers know I'm here on their patch.

A second later, I'm zipped up and in the saddle. A random thought flashes through my mind – do I really need knee surgery? I'm not entirely sure how I vaulted onto my 18-hand horse from that tree stump. Fear lends springs to our legs!

I am in the saddle, but not quite secure. Callum, good Christian that he is this morning for once, stands planted while I wriggle myself deeper into the saddle, sniff, wipe my nose, adjust my specs, eyes on the dog party all the while. Callum is well disguised in his flaming gold against the autumn foliage of the sweet chestnuts. Collecting the reins, I edge us back into the undergrowth before turning him uphill on a faint deer trail almost obliterated by the leaf-fall.

Phew! The pheasant hunters have not loosed the dogs. I make my escape, Callum's legs feeling as springy as mine were a moment ago. I check my zip. It's stuck halfway down, and a bit of T-shirt is sticking out down there. Never mind, we are safe.

I hear rustles around me. Callum and I find ourselves among a crowd of nervy escapees, pheasant yes, deer too, and squirrels zipping up trees. The work on their winter nut caches is left for now as they peep out at the hunting party.

The woods open up into cathedral like spaces and I lift Callum into a nice jog trot, still uphill, making sure we are well clear of the men and dogs and the fine birdshot-loaded guns.

Half an hour later, as I ride into the stable yard, three much younger friends ask where I rode this morning. I grin and say Five Hundred Acre Woods and as one they all raise fingers and wag them. But they are grinning too. 'You devil!' says one and just for a moment this old 'has-been' does feel a tad devilish!

Callum too, by the feel of his bounce. He enjoyed it as much as me, this illicit forest bathing, which in retrospect feels more like power-showering. Yes, there is definitely a lightness to Callum's step as I head for the dismounting block. He enjoys these games of hide and seek as much as I do – a bit of ducking and diving in enemy territory.

Going the Extra Mile for the Love of a Horse

Winter 2024

This morning, as I walked home after feeding and mucking Callum out, following a night of heavy rain that left his breakfast hay net nicely sky-soaked, I heard a clip-clopping coming down the lane and looked up to see who was abroad to so early on a Sunday. It was Kirsty, one of the young women who stable at the DIY yard next door to our cottage, where Callum is based. She was riding Bea, her 17-hand, 22-year-old dark bay Hanoverian mare, whose distinctive white stripe on her head and a grey patch in her black mane sets her apart.

I was surprised and delighted, as Kirsty and Bea have been like ghosts this winter, haunting the very early hours of each day and the late evening dusk. Kirsty, a professional groom, has been working quietly for six months with dogged determination to save her mare who had also damaged a check ligament like Callum did some time back, something which horses of this age and breeding are prone to. And she was doing this first thing in the morning just as the sky lightened before dawn and last thing at night after a full day of caring for many other horses at two other yards.

Bea is Callum's neighbour in their individual grass paddocks and had done herself an injury in the field back in the autumn. As Callum had a similar injury, I had a very good idea of the long hard road facing Kirsty and Bea. Many owners with a 22-year-old horse like Bea, who has the disconcerting habit of falling down now and then, even before the ligament injury, would have called time on the horse and had her put down. This thought never crossed Kirsty's mind. She has had Bea for many years and the pair have done well at cross country, show jumping and dressage and the bond between them is exceptionally strong.

When Christ said, 'Love thy neighbour', we assume he meant people, but maybe he meant our working animals too? Kirsty seemed to work on that assumption and needed no exhortation from on high to act with love. And so her 5am days began just as one of the wettest of English winters set in.

Bea is a highly strung warmblood, easily set off to high jinks, something that would not help her leg to heal. So Kirsty bandaged her at the crack of dawn each morning and walked her the five minutes a day allowed by the vets, the idea being to avoid all the normal activity of a busy yard, horses being taken to the horse walker, to the lunge ring, to the indoor school and others being hacked out. Tractors moving muck trailers and dragging sand ploughs. Cars coming and going. Anything that would set Bea off into airs above the ground.

It must have been a very lonely winter for the two. And having been there myself, I know something of the feelings they would have had. As a fisherman, I know how it feels to be surrounded by others hauling in fish when you don't even get a bite, or are busy unpicking over-winds. It's maddening. And it's the same when your passion, horse riding, is put on hold while all around you, others continue their busy horse schedules amid much cheerful chat and you plod alone in the dark to give your horse five minutes at grass, with worry your constant companion.

So this morning, when I hailed Kirsty in the lane and asked how she and Bea were doing, I was delighted to hear that they were doing twenty minutes of walking work a day now and the vet is coming next week to see if this might be extended. I complimented Kirsty on a job well done and she replied, 'She has done all I've asked of her over the years so I owe her my best in return.'

Bea is lucky in her owner, many others would not have had that commitment, though it must be said that many an old horse is treated just as well by their owners. There is a tribe of women, mostly women, who are nursing old horses through their last arthritic years, too fragile to ride, but loved just the same. Kirsty and Bea are just one such pair, who this winter have lived out this love across the human horse gap. Quietly, silently, uncomplaining, seeking no praise, in the midst of people riding, riding, riding. Kirsty represents the very best of what 'for love of horses' means. I wish her and Bea a summer of riding quietly through the woods and much joy; they have earned one more summer at the very least and hopefully more than that.

I wrote this almost two years ago and this evening I bumped into Kirsty and Bea coming home from their evening walk in the dusk. I asked her how things were going with Bea and she said she seemed well, though not well enough to ride. The mare has completely accustomed herself to her new, less active life and is now completely retired. It has been a long spell of not riding for Kirsty though she does exercise some horses at other stables where she works, but not her own horse. She remains to my mind the epitome of a horsewoman with the horse's wellbeing coming first, second and third.

In Search of Callum's Mother – Message in a Bottle

This story is a message in a bottle, launched into the sea of Facebook, in the hope that it will wash up on the Irish, German or Dutch shore and help me find my horse's dam.

It is one of the strangest leftovers of paternalistic thinking that makes it easy to find your horse's sire but not his dam, the mother that gave him life, carried him, gave birth to him, nurtured him. How weird that the horse world continues in this strange practice that relegates horse mothers to the darkness of unknown history!

When I bought Callum, he came with his passport and breeding papers that showed him to be half German, half Irish. He is the son of Aldatus Z, a distinguished and successful Oldenburg stallion who show-jumped internationally for Germany and Holland. There are images of this big white-faced chestnut stallion available on breeding sites, with photos and videos of his jumping career.

But as for his Irish Draught mother, there was not a single image to be found, or any mention of her beyond her name on the Irish Sports Horse breed papers – Coevers Line (Premium Broodmare). Her sire is listed as Coevers Diamond Boy and her dam as Minteck. Her grandsire is Diamond Lad. The legendary stallion, King of Diamonds, is one generation back. Her history includes Lochnaver Lady, Glacier Mint and Darrig. And there the trail goes cold. Search as I may, I have not been able to find an image of her.

And there are images of the stallions in Callum's dam line, Coevers Diamond Boy and Diamond Lad, but no image or history of his dam.

Coevers Diamond Boy. Born in 1989, Coevers Diamond Boy is an Irish Sport Horse that has been an important breeding stallion, sired by Diamond Lad (King Of Diamonds) out of the mare Lochnavar Lady, who is a daughter of Coevers.

Coevers Diamond Boy has produced a number of proven jumping horses including Richmont Park, who was competed by Rodrigo Pessoa.

Sire of international showjumpers including Richmont Park, Falsterbo Grand Prix winner. Coevers Diamond Boy (ISH) - Sire: Diamond Lad (RID) x Dam by Coevers (TB). So my lad Callum, with all his lazy sharp quirkiness, and jumping ability mentioned in his family history, is bred in the purple, but there is no sign of his dam. Can you help?

For heaven's sake, let's start celebrating our brood mares with images and video and history. Let's put them in the spotlight where they deserve to be!

Postscript: And then one day, my letter in a bottle landed on an Irish shore and my question was answered by the kind person who replied with images of Callum's mum - he is the spitting image of her but in chestnut, not grey. I was also provided with the name of her breeder and owner, and so the circle closed. I now know Callum's full history and have in effect 'met' his parents, and what a handsome pair they are!

My Talismanic Ride

When you do a ride that you love, that brings you peace, that fills you with beauty, that carries you some way closer to Enid Blyton's 'Faraway Tree', after some while its elements, its paths, its woods, its waters, its trees, its hollows and hills take on a talismanic quality, a magic that is greater than its parts, as you and your horse move through it with all the familiarity of the Shipping Forecast's place names. The ride becomes a mantra, a clicking of rosary beads; it becomes a semi-submerging of your soul in nature.

You are no longer a horseman passing by, a mere figure in a landscape, you are part of it and it is part of you, much like a swimmer is at any moment a potential part of the sea, so much at one with this watery element that it might claim him or her forever. That is how my talismanic ride is for me, it is a merging of my everyday reality with something that is eternal, and yet I am alive. If that is not magic, I don't know what is.

It begins with a 6am coffee in bed. I check the weather forecast and it looks reasonable. There has been rain overnight and I make a mental note to go easy in some spots that are likely to be slippy. Callum is a total klutz, he falls over his own feet all the time. He is so busy looking for spooks or new ways home or walkers and dogs or grabbing some leaves that he allows his feet to look after themselves. Once he actually fell right down and since then I work much harder at keeping him collected. That is how each day begins for me.

I shower and dress and head for the stables (breakfast will have to wait till I'm back).

I feed him a light breakfast, groom and tack up, get into my leather chaps and body protector and we are out of there in fifteen minutes tops. Long gone are my days of riding bareback in shorts or a swimming costume, as I did growing up in the Cape in South Africa. We slope down the hill to the little Victorian stone bridge that crosses the stream in Tilhill Forest. It is in full flood, the first of this autumn. On the way down, we pass a number of deer who are not too bothered by us and a stag who is; still high on the rut, he stands his ground, a wisp of greenery still in his antlers. The colours of the bracken are gold and bronze and auburn and the chestnuts lie thick on the forest floor. Here and there a tree stump shows that squirrels have used it as a dining table, with just the husks of the chestnuts left as evidence.

Before crossing the B2188 I stop the horse to look back at Crowborough on its hill. There is sunshine and cloud shadow and a mixed palette of green, yellow and auburn as the new season takes hold. Callum shifts beneath me, he wants to get on with it and we do. The road is clear and we cross it in good order and then I lift him into a jog to help him carry his 1,500 pounds over the 2ft high sand berm that is our marker into Five Hundred Acre Wood. Now we are trespassers, and my level of awareness begins to approach that of a wild animal. I do not want to have another confrontation with the game keeper or the estate manager. We've been using this wood for four decades and I am not about to stop now. I feel it is my small contribution to the fight for the 'Right to Roam' that has been taken from us and which I want to see returned to us before I die.

There are places in the wood where we regularly stop. These are usually places that Callum has decided he likes to stop at and do whatever it is he does, looking deep into the woods. Here I listen and absorb the woods, I say a word of thanks sometimes to the spirits of this place, I check my mobile - a mix of the sacred and profane. This particular stopping point is just below what I call the 'glass box on the roof house', an enormous mansion with a lovely meadow that in spring is a riot of bluebells. The scent is bewitching and that is why both Callum and I agreed that it is a good place to pause on our meanderings. Another such place is in the midst of huge beech trees where there is a depression in the ground that might have been made by a V1 rocket falling 50 miles short of London during the Second World War.

I listen to the wood music, groaning and squeaking trunks when there is any wind, the rustle and susurration of leaves and the birdsong. Now and again I hear the cry of the buzzards that patrol these woods.

The sameness of this ride through country I know as intimately as my hands soothes me. I know every pothole and boggy bit, every windfall branch, every angled camber to the path, anything that might cause my horse to take a misstep. Here and there I reach out to break a branch that obstructs our way, or to stroke a moss-covered trunk.

We work our way through the wood and emerge to a view that looks out across the valley to the Enchanted Place, with its memorial to A.A. Milne and E.H. Shepard, writer and illustrator of the Pooh Bear books. They are not the only bookish ghosts to haunt this place. Sir Arthur Conan Doyle of Sherlock Holmes fame passed this way as did William Butler Yeats, the Irish poet and writer of the poem The Lake Isle of Innisfree, with its bee loud glade and its dream of an escape to the wild, a poem that opened an inner eye in me and set me on my own writing path.

> 'I will arise and go now, and go to Innisfree,
> And a small cabin build there, of clay and wattles made;
> Nine bean-rows will I have there, a hive for the honey-bee,
> And live alone in the bee-loud glade'.

Into the Enchanted Forest with Callum

In this place during the First World War, from 1913 to 1916, Yeats and his American friend Ezra Pound wintered for three years at Stone Cottage near the fifteenth-century pub The Hatch and grew ever more reluctant to return to London after weeks down here, a feeling I understand and subscribe to myself.

As we emerge from the wood onto a heathland path, Callum lifts into his slow but ground-devouring canter. It feels, I imagine, like riding a dolphin at sea, there is a fluid movement so softly in contact with the earth there is no jarring. For once he is all collection and we flow up the hill like a glowing chestnut wave. He knows he is headed home now.

But this does not stop him from turning off the path to a Forest pond where he and I both like to soak his legs. Since the excitements of that check ligament issue on his front right leg two years ago, this water spa treatment can only help to keep him sound. He uses his time paddling and drinking and looking to the North Downs on the horizon that hides London and to the west, the glidepath to Gatwick Airport. I sit deep in my dressage saddle that came with Callum and count my blessings, not least that I am not cooped up in one of those passenger jets.

At Wood Reeves car park we once more cross the B2188 and enter the long, wooded tunnel down the hill to the lakes, two bridges and then the final home hill. It has been an hour and a half of dreamtime, of living utterly in the present, of forest bathing.

As a product of many cultures, Christian and Jewish, South African and English, French, Lithuanian and Norwegian, my vocabulary includes words that have different meanings and interpretations. One example is the word 'talismanic'. To me, a Talis is a silk prayer shawl in blue, white and silver, and manic is a kind of high. So this talismanic, prayerful ride has left me once more on a high. Not a bad cross-cultural definition at all, for my talismanic ride.

I rub Callum down, hose his feet and walk him down to his paddock for the rest of the day. Once more, we have marked out our territory. How many more such days I have I do not know, which makes each ride something to be treasured. This talismanic ride of ours.

No Time to Be Sick

What is it about horse people? If we were not already sure that our club of choice - the horse-riding world - was filled with nutters, the arrival of sickness just confirms it!

I've lost count of the numbers of sick women and the odd man, who religiously turn up to do their horse chores morning and night, even when sick to death with colds, flu and even with Covid. I know, I've got the T-shirt too.

When a horse person gets sick, their first thought is, 'Yikes! How am I going to do the horse?' Not 'Woe is me, I'm sick!' Oh no, being sick will just bloody have to fit round doing the horses. If this is not crazy behaviour I don't know what is, yet it is a commonplace.

At my yard I've now been beside those going through death, divorce and illness; they just soldier on. I think they get something from the horses that makes soldiering on a bit easier, even when life's a bitch. Isn't that the absolute truth? Horses are better in their way than any analgesic, even when you are down, depressed or just common-and-garden type sick.

We've seen the growing popularity of petting animals in hospital and horses used in therapy with trauma victims, so there really does seem to be some scientific proof that these creatures provide you with a shot in the arm even when you are hors de combat, excuse the pun.

And the weird thing is, the other folks at the stable don't get in a tizz, they just observe the two-metre rule and maybe help you stuff hay nets. They know that sooner or later they may in turn need your help.

Horses are not a hobby or a passion, they are a disease themselves, one for which there is no tablet or inoculation. And maybe one of the side effects is this loss of judgement we suffer when we get sick. Instead of taking to our beds with hot water bottles and whisky, we ensure that the horses are comfy, well fed and exercised.

And have you noticed the age of our fellow riders? Sure there are plenty of young women as ever, but the hard core is made of up of women and the odd man of a certain age. So maybe ignoring illness has life-giving properties not yet fully understood by the medical fraternity? In my next life, I do hope that I will be a chess player or a knitter. But truly what kind of life is that?

Achoooooo! Sorry, I've got the sniffles. Never mind, the horses are fine. And isn't that what really matters?

WHAT IS IT ABOUT HORSES THAT YOU LOVE?

When non-horsey people ask, 'So why do you love horses so much?', it's hard to explain it to them. It starts, if you are lucky, when you are a kid and you get on a pony and suddenly you have speed and power and four legs and you can outrun the bullies. And the pony, generally speaking, does whatever you ask it to do. It looks after you and brings you home safe from the most amazing adventures. When you are on its back you are not just a little boy, you are a prince.

When you are a tormented teen, the horse is always there for you, in ways that even your best friend can't be. It takes you away from your problems into another dimension. It lends you a distance and a perspective to examine your life. And it comforts you. It makes you feel good about yourself.

When the time comes that you start dating the horse is your wingman, the best in the world, because most girls respond to horses, love horses, the beauty, the romance, the independence offered, all the things a horse does for a boy is amplified if you are a girl. They allow girls to go places on their own they might not risk going on foot, into the wild, say. And as a boy rider, some of that good feeling is reflected back at you.

In your middle years, when you are wrestling with work and marriage and children, the horse is still there, still your friend, still able to bind up your wounds and make you feel good about yourself, remind you of the boy you once were.

But it's when you are old that the value of a good horse is beyond compare. You may have a bad heart, be unable to walk very well, troubled by hip and knee pain, damaged in so many ways, physically and mentally – the walking wounded as they say in the army. Yet when you get on your horse's back, the years fall away, lift from your shoulders in an instant and you are twenty years old again. You ride almost the same as when you were a teenager. To people you pass, you are not an old man, you are a horse rider.

And the horse does this all without speech, silently. In fact the essence of a horse would make for an amazing man, if a man could embody all that a horse is.

And that is only the beginning of the story of why I love horses.

MY HORSE'S LOVING TREE

There is a particular oak tree on Ashdown Forest that my horse Callum is extremely fond of. I call it his 'Loving Tree', as he always stops by it and will rub his long, elegant neck on it and then stand lost in admiration of the view. It's not a particularly old or noble oak tree, but it does command a view across the valley that is home to King's Standing Riding Stables, and on the valley crest opposite, the small copse of signature pines that marks King's Standing itself – just by the car park that holds an ice cream truck in summer.

This slightly magical place lies on a stony path that runs down the hill to neighbours of ours and our own home beyond and Callum's stable at the DIY yard that is his home. If you continue in the opposite direction up the hill, you pass another farm of neighbours and then the wide-open heathlands of the Forest itself.

King's Standing is so named as it was the place that Henry VIII came to shoot deer driven past his hide. It is a place famous for the wooing of Anne Boleyn who accompanied him on his hunts and whose family seat, the pocket-sized Hever Castle, is just five miles up the road.

So, as Callum and I stand there enjoying the view, in my mind's eye I stare back 500 years and see sturdy, leather-jerkined yeomen herding deer to be shot at by King Henry having a day out from kingly duties. It is a beguiling place.

For Callum, the interest is more complex and more mundane. He must pick up all sorts of scents wafting across the valley and on the skyline opposite he can see walkers with their dogs, and, of more interest, the odd solo rider like me or sometimes a group from the riding stable. Then that long neck shoots up to a point at around 25 hands, with ears as erect and quivering as exclamation marks.

I grip his sides then, for I know what is coming. It begins with a huge inhalation of air that threatens his girth strap, followed by a sort of trembling rumble that precedes a screaming neigh which is an unmistakeable challenge to those far-off horses. It's an impressive, distance-covering roar that causes geese to change their flight path and on occasion a squirrel to fall dead from fright right at our feet (just kidding). Callum is not messing about now. He wishes to be heard in as much of a royal way as did old King Henry across the valley.

I brace, as they tell you on aircraft facing turbulence, for I know that a violent Callum shoulder-dropping whip-round may well be coming, followed by an attempt to gallop up the hill to go check out the horses on the far hill. Sometimes it takes all the limited strength that remains in my arthritic hands, arms and shoulders to control the lunatic warmblood. If I am lucky, I win, the moment passes and Callum returns to caressing the loving oak with his neck.

Sometimes that damn tree is more trouble than it's worth.

TURNIP THE 'TOE-RAG'

There is a woman at my stable yard named Caroline, who owns a stunningly handsome dapple-grey Irish Draught x Thoroughbred gelding named Parsnip, a rather unfortunate name I think for one so lovely.

I always enjoy having a chat to her because she is very funny, calls a spade a spade, and doesn't stand for any nonsense from anyone. But her heart is pure gold.

Now at this point let me admit that I write about horses in a fairly loving, sometime even a spiritual way, as they have shown me the way through the magic door into a natural kingdom that I would never have known but for them. But after 70 years of riding, I know to my cost that they are not cuddly toys and in fact one misstep and they can kill you, as happened just a month ago to my American friend, Jan Alexander, another horse-loving writer, who was out for a quiet ride with a friend in the US when death came calling. What makes her death doubly tragic is that she had waited half a lifetime before being able to buy her own horse.

So these so-called 'heart horses' - my own Callum among them - can have a sting in their tail, as so many of us know to our cost.

This morning, as Caroline was mucking out, I passed by and asked after her horse.

'Oh, that toerag gave me a ride to remember yesterday,' she said, grimacing. She and Parsnip were out hacking solo when it came to her that she had passed the time for his feed and felt that he was a bit 'antsy' about this oversight on her part, but she thought he could wait another 20 minutes, surely?

Just then she and Parsnip spotted the roof of a tractor some way off moving fast behind a hedgerow. Parsnip planted and Caroline let him stand watching the tractor which then came into full view barrelling along at a good pace towards them. At this Parsnip felt that enough was enough and supper was waiting in his cosy stable, dropped a shoulder, whipped round, bucked and set off for home. But Caroline, a professional horsewoman, was still firmly in the saddle and was having none of this, and stopped him after some yards, at which point Parsnip backed himself into a tall overgrown hedgerow.

Caroline wisely decided that maybe discretion was the better part of valour and agreed to set off for home. But now Parsnip was bucking at every second stride. It says much for Caroline's horsemanship that the two were still one on reaching the stables. But now truly annoyed with her 'bastard horse' she headed for the sand school, much to Parsnip's annoyance. He proceeded to buck, but Caroline got him into the sand and a short unhappy lesson was had.

At this point a passing rider called out: 'Do you know there is a bramble on your horse's belly and between his hind legs?'

A rather shame-faced Caroline dismounted and removed the bramble, which must have been picked up by Parsnip when he backed his bottom deep into the hedgerow earlier. She walked him into his stable and after he'd finished his supper, he came over to her and gave her a loving lick and cuddle, the Irish Draught now once more in charge of the Thoroughbred side.

'You shit-head,' said Caroline, rubbing his ears, half angry with him for his bad behaviour, and half cross with herself about the bramble. Yes, horses are our blessing and on occasion our curse. The following old English nursery rhyme comes to mind:

Into the Enchanted Forest with Callum

> What are little boys made of?
> What are little boys made of?
> Frogs and snails,
> And puppy-dogs' tails;
> That's what little boys are made of.
> What are little girls made of?
> What are little girls made of?
> Sugar and spice,
> And all that's nice;
> That's what little girls are made of.

I think maybe that all horses, male or female, are made of things much akin to little boys, with a good dollop of devilry thrown in. Caroline adds: 'Yes, I suppose you could say that Parsnip is a very opinionated young man!' Then she leaned in conspiratorially and whispered: 'But I do so love him!'

Maybe the time has come to change Parsnip's name to Turnip the Toe-Rag!

Bloody horses!

IN PRAISE OF GROOMS AND STABLE HANDS

There is an army of young women and men, barely noticed, seldom acknowledged, a silent presence, who keep the whole horse world turning - they are the grooms and stable hands. These are the unsung heroes of the horse business, who get up each morning, often before dawn, to feed, water, muck out and groom their charges, very often for a pittance, earning wages that would not get most of us out of bed. But without them, the whole shebang would grind to a halt.

As someone who has been a beneficiary of their work, their advice, their help and their friendship, I want to take a moment to salute them. I know my voice will be joined by a mighty chorus of riders who agree that this is necessary and perhaps long overdue. These people are the muscle and bone that keeps the body of the horse world ticking smoothly.

For many years now, I have looked after my own horses and at 73, find it an increasing strain, emphasising just how physical and relentless this never-ending task is. So, my respect, gratitude and heartfelt thanks to those many thousands of boys and girls, men and women who are almost never seen without a pitchfork, a stable broom or a wheelbarrow in hand.

If the two Covid years taught us anything, it is how reliant we are on the army of supermarket shelf-stackers, delivery drivers, doctors, nurses and cleaners. They keep the world turning. The stable crews are the same. Without them, many older folks would simply not be able to keep a horse or ride, most riding stables would close and it would mean the end of the horse racing industry.

Let me choose one person to stand as a symbol for thousands, Christine, who helped to look after our horses in the small East Sussex village of Horsted Keynes when we first arrived in England from South Africa, when we were most in need of help and advice. She sadly died too young, still in her teens, in a motorcycle accident. She had such an affinity with horses, this English rose, and just being around her added to the pleasure of each day. Even at her very young age the professional horse woman was much in evidence, things were done 'just so'! And then she was gone.

Christine, we remember and miss you.

There are grooms, too, whose memory lives on in my mind these many long years, men I came across in the stables of the Cape in South Africa where I grew up. When I was a boy of 13, living in Cape Town, I had a bay pony called Don Juan that was stabled at Bobby Salkinder's yard next to the polo grounds alongside the Kenilworth Racecourse. The stables housed some thirty horses which were looked after by a staff of black men, Zulus and Xhosas, who lived on site in a small, whitewashed house, cooking for themselves on an open fire. The two I remember best were Banana and Long One. Even as I write those names now, I feel a sense of shame wash over me. These men in their 30s and 40s were Zulus I believe, tall, powerfully built men with fine, strong faces, who barely spoke to us. How is it that we were so at ease addressing them as Banana and Long One? How? But we did.

Thinking about it now, exactly sixty years later, it comes to me belatedly that Banana would have been a jokey misunderstanding of the Zulu word for boy, Bafana. This was a word that years later would resonate with white and black crowds who followed the South African football team known as Bafana Bafana – the boys, the boys. So 'Banana' would in fact have started off as Bafana – 'Boy,' as so many black men were addressed by whites. And if that was not sufficient insult, this name Bafana became the derogatory Banana. And Banana answered to it, always with a smile and with grace. How is it that I never asked him his real name?

And then there was 'Long One', God forgive us, a tall raw-boned black man who was virtually silent. How did these men live? They were far from home with no family to support them working at the most menial of jobs, mucking out our stables. The muckheap sat alongside their rooms. For this was the reality of apartheid, which Nelson Mandela was fighting to overthrow and spent 27 years on Robben Island for his trouble. My father had a bakery nearby and once in a while I would bring these men some pies or biscuits which they would receive with cupped hands and a bobbing of the head, like children. It bothered me then as it does now, but I lived with it. It was just the way things were. And if you were white and privileged, it did not keep you awake at night.

It is so easy to imagine how it must have been to live in times of slavery at the Cape. It would have been the same, simply the way things were. We are an endlessly adaptable species, most of us comfortable with the misfortune of others.

One thing I recall about these men and others like them was their great affection, kindness and rapport with the horses. They were superb horsemen, a skill they may have picked up as boys riding among the hills of Natal where they hailed from, 1,000 miles to the north. I recall them riding three horses at a time over to the polo fields when the games were on, riding long-legged and on the buckle of the reins, on the middle horse, leading one on each side.

In the summer, we lived at our seaside house in Bloubergstrand, outside Cape Town and on the way home from school in the afternoons, we often passed strings of racehorses being ridden out at the walk by their black grooms from the stables at the Milnerton Racecourse. The horses walked calmly, the grooms sitting relaxed and often smoking pipes, the strings, some thirty horses long, ambled along in the deep sand tracks among the Port Jackson scrub, blacks, greys, bays, chestnuts, each one groomed to perfection, their long-legged thoroughbred quality oozing from them, aristocrats of the horse world. For the grooms, it must have felt like time out in the warm afternoon sunlight, with the scent of the sea flooding in over the dunes, and the onshore breeze ruffling the horses' tails and manes.

Who were these men? I knew them not. They were as unknown to me as an Egyptian frieze of horsemen, figures in a landscape. We inhabited two different worlds – and I was the poorer for it. Banana, Long-One, I remember you. I remember you. Forgive me for not knowing your true names.

CALLUM'S CALMING FOUR-HILL RIDE

Spring 2024

There are times when spring grass leaves Callum almost beside himself with pent-up energy that is just too much for this warmblood. After the endless winter he is fit too, from all the exercise, as he's had to be kept off waterlogged fields. So, the quiet ride round the lake I had planned for us this morning is scrubbed and other plans are quickly made – plans that include hills.

He stands well enough while I mount, but then the huffing and puffing begins as soon as we leave the yard and I know it's the dragon version of my horse that I'm on this fine morning. A quick shoulder-dropping whip-round when a wood pigeon takes off in its wing-clapping way, confirms my fears and plans for the lake are definitely put aside. It is going to be one of those mornings if I don't take charge and smartish too.

When he is like this, it's a case of him or me, and while I am still up to it, only just, mind you, it's always going to be me I choose, rather than him, who gets to be top dog. A lifetime of riding blood horses has shown me that there is only peace when you are the boss, not the horse. Once he accepts you as his leader there is space for mutual respect, affection, even love, to enter the equation. At my age, Callum could so easily kill me, while I'd need a gun to kill him. So, in the 'live-or-die' stakes, for now, I've chosen me. This means some fast work up four stiff hills lie ahead and thank God for those hills! What do you do when your riding country is dead flat? Lunging, I suppose. Lots of lunging.

Something in my manner telegraphs itself to Callum who, as we descend the first hill from the stable, has the advantage over me, and he dances down ducking and diving at squirrels or nodding wind-rustled branches, or deer he's spotted, moving in the woods alongside us. I let him get on with it, secure in the knowledge that all I need do, if needs must, is make a U-turn and gallop him back up the hill to take some of the nonsense out of him. So down the hill we go, crab-like at times, or with moves that a Bolshoi ballet dancer would be proud to perform. The intricate patterns of Callum's legwork and dance moves would bring an audience to its feet, but I sit tight and wait it out.

Soon enough the trail levels off and we cross the old Victorian stone bridge. Now it's time for a loosening up trot, and we do it in ten-league strides, Callum's neck quivering with barely suppressed eagerness to take flight. Then the first hill is here finally, and I put him into a collected canter on the compacted dirt road, his hooves making a nice drum roll as effortlessly we rise and rise through stands of pine to one side and beech trees on the other. Nearing the top, I give him rein and in one bound he is free and into his ground-devouring gallop. At the top we flash through the mountains of stacked lumber as we approach the lumber yard and breathing hard, he pulls up, a little reluctantly. I turn him round and panting a bit, he is happy to walk normally now for the first time on this ride without prancing and we retrace our steps back down the hill.

At the bottom we turn left, away from the path home, to Callum's disgust, and squirming, his legs go left but his body is still committed to going right. My spurs win the day and left it is, towards another hill, with quite boggy going this time. I am out of the saddle now and once more we cruise up a hill. The hysterical barking of two dogs in the beechwood nearby adds its own incentive to Callum to shift his ass and he makes light work of this hill: boggy bits be damned.

Now he does have a blow and drops his head for the first time. I give him rein and check my watch; we've been out half an hour now. There is a lovely piece of woodland ahead that we thread our way through, taking in the sight and scent of bluebells at their very best in this late spring. It gives the big horse a chance to catch his breath. The longed-for sunlight is among the trees and seemingly shining out of the green neon of new leaf on the beech trees too. It is a blue-green world in the wood and the place is alive with birdsong, robins, thrushes, blackbirds, wrens and probably a dozen more varieties.

There is a glow on Callum's neck that tells me he is working up a sweat. Excellent. He really needs the exercise.

Now we ride over the little bump between two silver birch trees that marks the exit from Hundred Acre Wood and across the valley I can see Ghylls Lap and the Enchanted Place of Pooh Bear fame. But today we are not playing tourist and I lift Callum once more into a canter, his ears twitch back and forth making sure that I and my squeezing legs really mean it, but he goes on willingly enough, back on his haunches, working well from behind, the little round pond on our right where he likes to paddle flashes by and we are once more on the level, but I keep him at it more and more collectedly.

We flow along, effortlessly rising once more up the grass slopes, and it here on this good going that I really open him up and let him have the gallop he has been desperate to have. And as ever, the sheer power and speed of this magnificent animal takes me by surprise. We have become the wind, a one-horse cavalry charge, the speed is sheer exhilaration. I am mainlining my drug of choice and am high as a kite. With some difficulty I pull him up just in time to take the turn into Wood Reeves car park. We cross the road and head down the woodland path that will bring us to the carp fishing lake and then the final home hill.

Now at last, Callum is properly relaxed and he does not even fuss too much about the midges that are much in evidence. As usual, the swallows flying the 6,000 miles from Africa have judged it right while on the wing, knowing just when dinner is served in Britain. It's an annual miracle to me which chokes me up just a little bit each Spring when they start arriving in waves from my former home. Generations of swallows have been born in our old stables.

Callum swings along happily now, no more ducking and diving. We make the obligatory stop at the 'Loving Tree' where as usual he rubs his neck on the oak bark and inspects the valley and the views to the south, France invisible beyond the Channel.

Soon enough, we reach the base of the home valley and cross the two stone bridges through which the streams keep the lake topped up.

And then it's into a last canter up the long hill home and Callum makes light of it too, but it feels more effortful, he is having to work. Almost at the top, a big red dog fox bolts across our path but the horse barely gives it a glance. He is no longer anywhere near as 'above-himself' as he was at the outset of this ride. The hills have done their stuff once more.

I glance at my watch again and see we've been out an hour and twenty minutes and have covered some miles, but have not passed a single soul.

As we reach the hilltop and the lane we live on, Callum spots an orange traffic cone that was not there yesterday and gives a nice little sashay as if to say, 'There is plenty more in the tank, Mister!' There is no end to this horse – his energy is truly bottomless. And that is a good feeling, knowing he is carrying a 200lb, 6ft 2in man, plus tack.

After all my exertions, holding, controlling, collecting Callum, I am pretty much all in. Getting off at the mounting block is a slow and careful process. As I hobble up the stable yard, I think I hear what sounds like a snigger. I whip round but Callum is all innocence, but maybe there is more of a twinkle in those wise and knowing eyes, nothing more. My Lord, what a horse! I Think I may rename him: Callum, Four Hills. I take another hard look at him, and I swear the devil gives me a wink! It may have been a midge in his eye, but with this guy there is just no way of knowing. We may have to do the four-hill ride again tomorrow!

MORE CONFESSIONS OF A HALF-ASSED HORSEMAN

Spring 2024

As a man stabling among a largely female group, it would be wise at times to be cautious. And as it happens I am somewhat cautious by nature. On the Normandy Landing beaches of the Second World War, I suspect my approach might just have led me to stand aside, saying, 'After you, chaps,' to the more gung-ho of my regiment. Manners maketh the man, after all.

In my previous entry on the subject, I may have gone a bit over the top about the criticism I get for my slapdash horse-care style and even a bit of bullying from my female-horse-expert-neighbours at the DIY yard that Callum and I grace with our presence – the only man and oldest rider there. But in fact the situation is more complex, more nuanced than that. In fact it is not as bad as I may have intimated. There are in fact some very nice people there.

One who I will refer to as the 'Iced Danish', to protect her identity – although she is Scandinavian and decidedly Viking-like in her approach to riding – is a case in point. In fact I am very fond of her. She would have made an amazing hospital matron who didn't stand for any nonsense. But there is a twinkle in her eye which gives the lie to her rigorous manner, to which I warm. To further protect her identity let's call her Lene and the black 15.2 cob she rides Mickey

Mouse.

The thing about Lene that gets my goat, that yanks my chain, is that she and Mickey ride out in good weather and bad, religiously. Now when I say bad weather, I don't just mean a spot of rain, I mean sheets, bucketing down, I mean wind howling, I mean snow and ice. Lene and Mickey march out into it like Shackleton of the Antarctic. The difference is that Lene and Mickey don't get stuck out there in the ice for 400 days, after an hour or a two they saunter back into the yard, happy as Larry.

Having consulted with Callum at the start of the day, I find we are mostly in agreement as to the viability of a hack in inclement weather. A spot of rain at a push is OK, but anything more than that doesn't really float our boat. So I feel a bit undercut by Lene, a woman, showing me up. I can hear the matron-like timbre in her voice saying in a Great War nursing station, 'Oh for heaven's sake man, you've only lost one arm. You have another. And one doesn't really need both eyes!' That's how I feel when I see her and Mickey heading out of the yard into a storm with not a backward glance.

Now Lene is a few years younger than me and that I feel gives me some wiggle room. But this mad bravery in the face of storms is not the only thing that gets me going. Lene is never less than immaculately turned out, whatever the time of day, while I slouch over from my cottage next door in carpet slippers and anything really, other than pyjamas. Not Lene. She could be going to a show, she is on point always! And always in good humour too.

Now to aggravate me further, she has a friend, who to protect her identity we shall call Bev, who is about my age, I reckon. And she rides a grey 15hh horse whom we shall call Bear. Bev and Bear often join forces with Lene and Mickey and out into the torrents they go – leaving me absolutely no wiggle room whatsoever. The thing is I like, admire and respect these women but they have no concern for my feelings, as Callum and I cower in his stable, peeking out at the lashing rain. I stand there in my suede cowboy chaps and anorak, looking sheepish as they wave goodbye.

And what really rubs salt into my wounds is the fact that not once has Lene ever said anything about me being a half-assed horseman. Not once. In fact, recently she said: 'Don't be so hard on yourself, you are quite nice – for a man!'

Sometimes it's just hard being a man among women. Yup!

My Riding Horse is 'Just a Hack'

Spring 2024

A good riding horse, or hack, as they are known here in England, is rarer than chicken's teeth and as valuable as gold dust. Their status? Zero. How strange.

I cannot tell you how often an advert in Horse Quest or Horse & Hound will state, 'He-she does not like to hack alone, prefers to hack in company.' So, for me, that rules the horse out, as I prefer to ride on my own. It's not that I'm anti-social, I enjoy company. But a ride in company is a horse-borne conversation, it's not what I would call riding.

In company I find the meditative quality of riding is lost, the stuff that refreshes the soul. In company, you miss half of what is to be seen out there and you are more focused on the humans than your horse. That is not what I enjoy when getting my horse out for some miles.

For some older people, riding alone is not an option, I understand that, and if one day that is forced on me by issues of age or health or vulnerability I will take it, half a loaf is better than none. But it isn't riding in my book.

The ponies and horses bought for me when I was a boy, and those I have bought myself in my years of riding have not always been perfect hacks. In my early days, some came directly from the racetrack, others have been showing horses that had never seen wide open spaces, or tackled a mountain or the seaside. I've often, more often than not, had to put in many hours and many miles to produce the finished article, a riding horse that is almost an extension of my body.

This is a horse who will help me to open and close gates with no fuss, will stop and stand when I want him to, will stand for me to dismount and mount in all weathers and all situations, will not mind wind, rain, hail, lightning, or thunder. Will not object to crossing rivers, roads, forests, or wide-open spaces. He will not be bothered by other horses coming or going around him, as he is focussed on me and my plans for our ride.

He is not bothered by backfiring cars or bridges, by dogs or walkers, by blown plastic bags or pheasants exploding right under his feet. He will jump a log or a hedge or a fence to help him stay on our line of travel. He will not object to my taking a phone call, or a photo, or changing out of my jersey or coat while on his back. He will not mind carrying a rolled-up raincoat or saddle bags behind the saddle. And if needs be, he won't mind me carrying a second person if the occasion demands it, riding pillion behind the saddle.

He will not jibe at leaving the stable, not once, even if I need to come and go from the stable multiple times in a day if that is what the day demands. He will box and unbox for transport with no fuss and will be happy to stand tied up, with or without a hay net. He will stand to be groomed, shod, clipped, vetted or simply to be 'loved-on' a little.

This paragon of a horse is what is known as a riding horse or hack and believe me they are worth their weight in gold. But they do not have one per cent of the perceived value of a showjumper or dressage horse or eventer or even a hunter. They are seen as the bottom of the pile – just a hack.

Maybe it says something of what is seen as important these days, and generally that thing will involve competition of some kind. But when horses were our means of transport, our way of getting around the country, or going on a journey, the good riding horse was valued above all else. Not so today. There must be show horses, hunters, eventers, or showjumpers who are also good hacks, but experience and those telling adverts tell you something else. Not many of them will double as good hacks.

And getting back to riding in company, a good hack will go at the pace of those you are riding with, will stay at the back if so required or set the pace in the lead for the others, will nanny the unruly and give a wide berth to the kickers and biters. He will have impeccable manners. It goes without saying that he will not buck, rear, whip round, or shy. But he remains in the eyes of the majority I fear, just a hack. How very, very strange.

Hacking is an art and a discipline all of its own and to have a horse that truly qualifies as a hack with all that this implies is to be blessed. Then you can truly call yourself or your horse a 'happy hacker'. Maybe the time has come to discard this somewhat pejorative term in favour of 'The Riding Horse'.

I wish I could claim for Callum that he was the perfect hack, the finished article, but I would be lying through my teeth. He is a marvellous horse in so many ways, and is indeed a wonderful hack, but his occasional whip-rounds or high-performance drama means he is not the finished article. He is not a horse I would feel confident offering to anyone to hack out on.

But with Traveller, an Irish Sports Horse, a chestnut and white skewbald that Jan and I shared for many years, it was truly a partnership in which a conversation of sort took place, the language being landscape. I would note his response to something, a change in the weather, a worrying noise in the woods, distant horse riders, and would respond by avoiding them, or reassure him that all was well. In turn, he would note my route planning and he'd 'say' 'Oh, this way today!' or 'Really, you sure you want me to go straight down this crumbly riverbank?' and I would rethink my route. It was an unspoken but subtle communication, which enriched each and every ride. One of his unfailing qualities was his enthusiastic temperament. He was always up for a ride and would stride out from the stable with a will, filled with a zest for life that was contagious. And if he could sing, it would be 'Here we go, here we go, here we go!' And coming home was filled with just as much 'joie de vivre' and vigour. As they say here, he was a good egg.

For someone like me, in love with landscape with peace and quiet, with adventure on horseback, with a passion for forest bathing and nature cures, with a love of disappearing for hours or days into the deep woods, give me my trusty hack, my riding horse.

He is not for sale, nor ever will be, but if you did ask his price, it would shock you. And don't tell me: 'But he's just a hack!' Don't!

CALLUM, MY IRISH WATER HORSE

Spring 2024

Of all the many things that will startle Callum, water is not one of them, which is just as well as we live in soggy England. Here in East Sussex, we have lakes, rivers and ponds, some of them quiet, some gurgling, some of them roaring with floodwater after days or weeks of rain. Callum is not bothered. Water does not count as one of the Yikes! Gadzooks! Horrors! that he is subject to – unless it is solidifying into snow or hail. His first four years growing up on Ireland's Atlantic coast probably inured him to all things wet. Just as well.

The one thing I've not done with him is to take him down to the sea, some 33 miles from us at Camber Sands on the East Sussex coast. Taking Callum to the sea may be tempting fate, given his enjoyment of water. I have never forgotten the story that the local horse guru, Richard Wilkinson, tells of a Thoroughbred he took to the sea who, once into swimming depth could not be turned back, striking strongly out to sea, heading for France. It took enormous effort to turn the would-be Channel swimmer round and back to the beach. As Callum is rather taller than that Thoroughbred and I am the wrong side of 70, I'm not sure I'd manage to turn him, once he had the wind in his sails, set fair for France. So, for Callum and me it's just small streams, water holes and maybe the odd lake.

As a child, I used to love riding my horses to the sea at Muizenberg on Cape Town's False Bay coast, to swim them bareback. Back then, I had no idea that there were Great White Sharks patrolling just beyond the surf line. Hanging onto my horse's tail as we surfed in, it was probably just as well that I was unaware of the danger. Ignorance was bliss. And besides, the next landfall was Perth, Australia, 5,400 miles away, too far to tempt even the bravest horse.

Maybe it is this African history, a profound connection of birth and blood with the soil of that hot dry land, that gives water its importance to me, as well as its link to change, to the sacred. Water so often denotes boundaries, sometimes between countries, and of course the ancient belief that to reach the afterlife, you had to cross the River Styx.

The two bridges that I cross to leave the farmland of my home behind and to enter the wilds of the Forest are a kind of border crossing from the ordinary to the extraordinary. In a way, you could say I live on an island hill encircled by streams that in winter turn into roaring torrents. So it was a lucky day that I found my water horse.

When I enter water, its temperature is forever benchmarked against the cold of the South Atlantic sea of my boyhood – so cold it would knot tendons in my neck and shoulders and where getting in without a wetsuit was no small act of courage. So it suits me well that it is Callum, not I, who steps into the cold rivers.

Entering water on horseback is rather different, but it bears with it something akin to baptism, an act of changing oneself, of moving from the solid to the liquid, a rite of transformation. To be in the flow of things, with a potential for change.

Maybe it is just as well that Callum is unaware of this freight, this extra weight, this baggage, of thoughts about water that flood my mind. And just as well that he seems happy to stand in water and bathe his feet, dreaming of who knows what? Water; it seems unites us, him and me, in a liquid, making us brothers of sorts, crossing the species barrier as we commune with each other among the ripples and eddies. He is my water horse, my border crosser.

AN OLD HORSEMAN AWAITS WINTER'S END

Spring 2024

At my age now, each winter is an ever-greater challenge to look after my horse. The time may be coming when I am forced to outsource the grunt work. That is not something I look forward to, not only because of the additional cost, but because mucking out, grooming and feeding helps to keep me fit.

Riding these days is a fairly sedate perambulation around the Forest, mostly walking with the odd sitting trot (as my knees are shot) and brief canters where the going is good. It's rather like a Rajah being carried round on a palanquin. Except that this palanquin, called Callum, will spin round now and then when he spots some horror, a fallen branch or something out of place that should not be there. So while it has its moments, riding is not going to be enough to keep me fit in future. But we will cross that bridge when we get there.

In the meantime, there is much to celebrate, as winter finally loosens its grip after six hard cold and wet months here in England. It's a bit like the Stations of the Cross, as spring announces its coming, first with snowdrops in January, a blessed sign that (fingers crossed) the worst is over. Then in February and March the daffodils add some yellow sunlight to the green. The primroses join them with their pink and yellow shyness among the grass. In April the tulips emerge with a stunning display of hot pink in our garden just behind the kitchen. I cook while looking at them dancing in the breeze and think of Paris fashion, Chanel and Schiaparelli. Finally, the neon green of new beech leaf in the woods and the beech hedgerows means that we can begin to hope that summer is not too far off. Adding to that hope, the bluebells finally arrive, azure armies in the woods, their scent beguiling the day, the sight of them lifting the heart.

The horse grows fat on the spring grass, which to him is rocket fuel, making him sharp as knives, and you have to keep your wits about you. That means a Chifney bit for walking the monster a quarter mile to his grass paddock, when really he would like to show that he is a marlin, full of fight and up on his tail.

The first morning when you can finally sit out in the garden in the steamer chairs and bask like a cat, eyes closed and sun-dazzle behind your eyelids, the creeping warmth igniting old bones with the promise of one more year, that is a very good moment.

The sound of birdsong – a full dawn chorus – wakens me each day and as I draw back the curtains, there is apple blossom to greet me. Now the Forest is drying out, the mud hardening, the dripping hedges sprouting leaf, and the bracken beginning to unfurl. The time has come to venture further afield out of the wind-sheltered woods into the open heathlands and rediscover the secret places I found last summer and the forty summers before that.

Riding becomes more social as you emerge from the depths, dog walkers greet you or simply nod – this is England after all – and wild displays of friendliness are not really our thing. But Callum helps to loosen things up, a sun-blazing chestnut of his size stops most dogs in their tracks and for any walker who ever rode, it's a chance for a pat and a chat.

Then we are away again, making good time, but keeping an eye out for newly released cattle and sheep on the Forest, a cause of much excitement to Callum in his early years up here, but now simply a chance to show he can still foxtrot and trip the light fantastic. He gets a word from me and a tighter hand on the reins for his trouble.

For the first time in months, I look down to see a sweaty neck. The big fella is getting some proper exercise at last! Summer is almost here.

Riding Among the Word Trees

Spring 2024

Sometimes I wonder why Callum puts up with my nonsense. As a writer, I find my inspiration out in nature as we criss-cross our riding country. Every now and then, a thought comes to me and after tasting it for flavour, listening to its cadences, I halt the horse and start furiously writing on my smartphone.

A word tree, a sentence bush, a stream of consciousness, a paragraphed hill and a valley that is pure metaphor, a huge rock full stop. My landscape as a writer is one of wordscapes and living vocabulary, a local patois particular to me.

As I ride, I connect words and find lanes of sentences, leaves of ideas fall off trees. I stop the horse who gorges on leaf and grass as I type frantically with thumbs too large for the keyboard. Then I click my tongue and off we go again on our storied ride, a circular fable that leaves its mark upon the earth first as hoofprints, and then as ink marks upon a page.

The two of us are consuming nature, each in our own way. His mouthfuls become sustaining mulch and mine turn into stories and books that I hope will offer sustenance of a different kind – after all, man does not live by bread alone.

As we make our way through the Forest, I brush my free hand through the leaves and now and then a story sticks to my fingers. It is the strangest thing. The colours, the textures, the shapes, and the smells, are all so well known to me, each particular to its season, unchanging, and yet they trigger fresh impressions that can only mean I am some kind of story receptor that those leaves wait to fall on with their fragment of rhyme and reason.

Why do I do this? There is no answer to that question. It just happens and its happening gives me pleasure so it becomes a self-fulfilling process. And I am not unique, nor alone, for here on the Forest with its views of the South Downs I walk with giants, wordsmith heroes, A.A. Milne, Sir Arthur Conan Doyle, Rudyard Kipling W.B. Yeats, Ezra Pound, Virginia Woolf, the Nicholsons, E.F. Benson of *Mapp & Lucia* fame and the poet Hilaire Belloc who called the South Downs 'the great hills of the South Country'. For Rudyard Kipling, 'Our blunt, bow-headed, whale-backed Downs.' When Nobel Laureate and author of *The Forsyte Saga* John Galsworthy died, he had his ashes scattered across them from a plane.

Virginia Woolf lived, walked and wrote on the South Downs, living in Monk's House in Rodmell from 1919 until her death in 1941. Monk's House and Woolf's sister's house in Charleston also served as retreats for much of the Bloomsbury group and its wider circle, including the likes of E.M. Forster, John Maynard Keynes, T.S. Eliot and Lytton Strachey. All of these people loved, worked, and wrote like fury within twenty miles of our cottage and many walked the South Downs and the Forest where I have ridden these past 45 years. It is a privilege to count them as former neighbours.

The poet Alfred Lord Tennyson might well have been standing on the Forest when he wrote: 'You came and looked and loved the view, long known and loved by me. Green Sussex fading into blue, with one grey glimpse of sea.'

So for a book-loving horseman like me I see two Sussexes as I ride, my own as well as the Sussex beloved by all these legendary writers. It is a humbling thing to be a wordsmith here, where giants have gone before.

And Callum? Callum is oblivious to it all. What grabs his attention are not the leaves of books but those of trees. So the two of us take from this place the sustenance we need and pass on, 'a horseman passing by', as the epitaph on W.B. Yeats' gravestone (from his poem *Under Ben Bulben*) reads:

> Cast a cold eye
> On life, on death.
> Horseman, pass by!

He is one of my literary heroes and so this line with its reference to a passing horseman touches me. Another poem of his has echoes for me in the woods as I ride.

> Had I the heavens' embroidered cloths
> Enwrought with golden and silver light
> The blue and the dim and the dark cloths
> Of night and light and the half-light
> I would spread the cloths under your feet
> But I, being poor, have only my dreams,
> I have spread my dreams under your feet,
> Tread softly because you tread on my dreams.

And by and large, Callum does tread softly. My dreams are frail things after all.

No-Mow May – A Life-Changing Decision

Spring 2024

As I sit tapping away on my laptop in the garden, there is half-wild lawn that surrounds me this Spring. And to my great surprise, I am loving it. After 44 years of mowing this hillside lawn into a quarter inch submission I have given up and feel as liberated as the grass, the insects, especially the bees, and the newly arrived swallows out of Africa who winnow the quarter acre of rampant garden with abandon, throwing curves and airborne wheelies. There is a kind of wild joy in the garden now that its manicured predecessor never knew. How did I not come to this decision years ago?

Three things helped me to make this call. The first was the endlessly wet Spring of 2024 that made lawn cutting impossible right into May. Then, adding to it was the fact that my old lawnmower has seen better days and struggled with the long grass when I gave it a go back in April. And finally, my age, which makes wrestling this hillside lawn under control once a week a horrible back breaking exercise. So when Jan said: 'Why not have a "No Mow-May"?' I needed no persuading. And the benefits were immediate.

I no longer watch the lengthening grass with trepidation; if I'm honest, it's always felt like a chore there was no escaping. Giving all that up was liberating. And then new wildflowers started to emerge, little white things, little blue things, little yellow things and something rosy too. A whole new world that had waited 44 years for my bones to age now exploded into life. I found that there were at least three different kinds of grass amid the rioting green herbage. Soon the grasses started budding seed heads and the butterflies arrived.

Dodging responsibility even more, I called on our neighbour, Robert Taylor, whom I turn to for all things practical in this house. I forgive and ignore his barely controlled amusement at my utter cack-handedness at all things practical. He is a poet and so forgives me mostly, I think. He brought his brute of a lawnmower round, a beast that brooks no opposition from any lawn be it at No.1, No.2, No 3, or No.10 in length, to use a barber's yardstick. It just ploughs through the trembling stalks like a German Tiger Tank.

Soon there were curving pathways through the rampant lawn and I could bring my breakfast and my laptop out here with my trousers and shoes remaining dry instead of wet from the dewy grasses. It was a revelation to have grass at knee height. Gus the dog loved it too, crapping on a new piece of the path-maze each day. Well, nothing is perfect, is it? But that was easily dealt with. And I love to see Gus come lobbing up the former lawn through the narrow, mown paths. He seems happy with it too.

So now I sit amid this grass maze or lie down to see it from the ground and it's a veritable Amazon. I think it has another benefit too – it sets off the old cottage to perfection. This wildness is a very fitting contrast to the white clapboard and stone of our 1760 home. It shouts Country now, instead of Suburb.

And there is no bloody work involved. The former lawn is the one doing all the work, lending charm to our home, a host of new perspectives, the sound of hoovering bees and buzzing insects, the swirl and skirl of the swallows and the white and blue butterflies dancing amid the green. It is almost as if the Forest has invaded our garden and it is no worse for that. After all, I am always escaping into the woods.

I am a late converter to this view of letting the lawn go wild, but in the best of company. I find I am now part of a practice known as 'the King Charles Mow' — cut one path through the rampaging lawn and otherwise let everything grow high. It earned its name after pictures of Charles's garden paths at Highgrove emerged. He practises the green ethos as much as he preaches it. The Charles Mow is much more about environmental concern, which allows me to feel good about my idleness. In this garden, the 400-year-old status symbol of a perfectly mown and rolled lawn is history. And it is just so liberating.

It may not be to everyone's taste. Our neighbour called over the hedge to ask if we'd maybe seen his sons' pet rabbit. I said we had not but that he should pop over to see why that may be. Terry is in his 30s and is not easily shocked but I could see that he was more than a little surprised. We trawled through the long grass but there was no sign of the missing rabbit. Later we found it crouched under my car in the driveway and carried it next door. I could not resist teasing Terry and said if he let his garden run wild too maybe the rabbit would not be so eager to do a runner. But I could see he wasn't buying it.

But I am so enamoured by this new look in the garden that I am going to seed the lawn with a mass of wildflowers once I have had Robert cut it right back come September. So the lawn will have had two haircuts this year, the making of the mazy paths that allow us to wander around it and the final hurrah in the autumn once all the new arrivals that have lain dormant for four decades have shown their heads, bloomed, blossomed and made seed. It is an alternative kind of garden now and I must say it feels great. And although I can't claim any credit for this transformation from manicured to rampant grass, I am as proud of it as any Chelsea Flower Show garden designer; more so, I'd say.

The Chinese Dogwood tree is just coming into its

white-green explosion that will soon turn cream and then pink and it looks lovelier than ever with the grasses crowding in at its base. The apple trees too look just so in their white blossom amid this expanse of green and yellow.

The kids came to visit on my birthday mid-May and the photos we took show them standing in a meadow with grass almost knee high.

It is an utter transformation. It feels and looks like a strait-laced teacher who has suddenly shed her black suit and donned a billowing green dress and a bandana, barefoot at a music festival.

This is how the world is meant to look, natural and wild. Wild is natural. It promises to be a summer of revelations amid the waving grasses at Home Farm Cottage up here on the Forest.

A Wood Reborn

Summer 2024

This week I noticed that the twenty acres of Blue Spruce in Tilhill Forest near our home, which the Foresters cut down this winter, is budding. It looks like a mix of deciduous tree planting has replaced the blue spruce. Hundreds of new saplings are putting out light green growth in the tall fenced-off enclosure that keeps the new trees safe from the marauding deer who would have the lot if they could.

Callum was as interested as I was and we stood a few minutes marvelling at the power of nature to regenerate, admittedly in this instance with some help from man. The Foresters had spent a week on the re-planting in mid-winter and I thought it would be years before I saw anything come of this work, and yet here before me stretched a tree nursery bursting with new life. The devastated acres were growing new ground cover amid the grey branches strewn about, stuff too small to bother clearing.

Then, to my surprise, I noticed a gate in the ten-foot fence. I urged Callum forward and I saw there was no lock, just a latch right at the top that I lifted and the gate swung open easily. The big horse and I went through and then turned to relatch the gate which took some doing as Callum was chary at first of this high gate swinging back into his face. But in the end we managed, with him standing side-on to the gate and my long arms having just sufficient reach to do the job of securing the latch. Once inside the enclosure, we looked more closely at the saplings which seemed in fine fettle and made our way on the path through them to the next gate at the top of the rising ground where we exited the area. This time Callum fussed less and I managed the gate opening and closing manoeuvre more easily. There are uses for an 18-hand horse and a 6ft 2in rider now and again.

I am still not sure if the story the Foresters offered while clear-cutting this hillside is true. They said that this stand of blue spruce was infested with a blue spruce beetle and hence had to come down. True or not, the trees came down, leaving a raw, devastated, gaping hole in the Forest that each time we rode past seemed to offer an accusation. But now there was life once again and as Callum and I stood there, happy with this new growth, it felt as though a wound was healing, both in me and in the forest cover.

I closed the gate carefully, making sure it was safely latched, and rode on into the sweet chestnut tunnel that slants up the hill, the going underfoot inviting enough for me to urge Callum to canter softly. We rolled uphill, looking about for the herd of deer that haunts this spot. All was silent but for birdsong. We found the deer a few hundred yards on in the huge 300-acre field that curves around the inner northwestern elbow of this valley. Some thirty animals grazed head down in the distance. They knew we were there at the fringe of the treeline, but we were far enough away not to bother them. Callum checked them out with all the attention of a 16-year-old lad hitting a beach dotted with bikinis. I watched too; they are my totem animal after all. With them I feel I am among friends, a friendship that has spanned three continents, Africa, Europe and America.

The cry of a buzzard makes Callum look up. He is not keen on these huge raptors who have a habit of 'buzzing' us, perching in a tree until we've passed and then swooping low over us once more. It took me a while to realise what was going on – they hope that we will flush out a rabbit or a pheasant or squirrel for them. So when Callum hears their cries, so common here in Tilhill and Five Hundred Acre Wood, he gets restive.

I lift the reins and we move on through a recently widened woodland path. This has encouraged the growth of foxgloves which mass to either side of us, here and there one or two white ones stand out. The place looks like a church, decorated for a spectacular June wedding. The groom's heart would be beating hard, appropriately enough, surrounded as he is by all this digitalis in bloom, a heart medicine he may need later in life.

In my mind's eye I think back to how different this place looked some months back when it was clothed in snow and the woods were a tracery of black tree skeletons, their spring and summer clothes turned to mulch by their feet. And a Robert Frost poem came to mind, *Stopping by Woods on a Snowy Evening*:

> ... To watch his woods fill up with snow.
>
> My horse must think it queer
> To stop without a farmhouse near
> Between the woods and frozen lake
> The darkest evening of the year. .
>
> The woods are lovely, dark and deep,
> But I have promises to keep,
> And miles to go before I sleep,
> And miles to go before I sleep.

Actually, in my case I do not have far to go, this wood is just half a mile from our cottage. So it takes just a few minutes to go from our hamlet to the splendour of the woods.

The growth and culling of trees on this Forest is like a slow motion tide that rises and falls every few years, instead of the twice daily occurrence on the seashores. The vast heathlands of Ashdown are kept open by grazing animals and some burning, but now and then the Forest team cuts back the silver birch that would take over if it was let loose and the billowing waves of prickly yellow gorse too. In the woods there is much evidence of wood coppicing, the chestnuts, which were traditionally used for stakes and staves and the multitude of light jobs that such wood can be turned to. However hard the chestnuts are cut back, the sprouting of new stems never fails and it's rather like cutting giant sticks of asparagus.

So Callum and I ride amid an ever-changing landscape of trees and bushes that clothe these high slopes in a variety of greens, browns, silvers and yellows, from lowly bracken and ferns to the giant oaks, beech, birch, chestnut and pines of many varieties. Each of them drawing water out of this rain and river-soaked region, taking the liquid high into branches 200 and 300 ft into the sky, secret, bark-clothed fountains whose rising and falling tides is utterly silent.

The horse and I turn for home, our forest bathing over for the day, the wood it seems is in good heart and for this reason so am I, and my horse too. Here on this Forest for a few centuries the partnership between man and nature has created a beauty that endures amid a world of troubles. And these replacements for the blue spruce, so recently felled are starting their climb into the sky – future perches for the buzzards.

The Road Less Travelled

Summer 2024

The road less travelled is always my choice. This morning's ride with Callum is a fine example of why that is.

After six months of hibernating like bears in the woods, Callum and I finally emerged this morning into the wide-open spaces of the Forest's miles of rolling heathlands. In winter they are quite exposed up here at 1,000 ft above sea level, but this morning it was glorious summer at its best and so Callum and I ventured out of the deep gloom of the Forests where we had spent the winter riding in densely wooded valleys to keep out of the worst of the weather. The time had come to risk the more public and peopled part of the Forest.

I had no sooner opened the gate onto the 'Big Bowl', as we call the central part of Ashdown, when a black cow came running towards us bellowing its lungs out. Callum wasn't impressed by this impertinence, but he was not too bothered, so off we went down the hill leaving the cow in our wake. About ten minutes later I felt him tense up, looking at the sky to his left. It was one of those huge radio-controlled planes doing rolls and dives, silently. Well, Callum wasn't having this silent death come anywhere near him and proceeded to do what felt like a cha-cha crossed with a tango – but still going sideways down the hill while looking at the strange object in the sky. Not surprisingly, now and then he stumbled.

Finally, we got far enough away from the model plane for him to calm down. But shortly after that it was a couple of madcap spaniels rushing out of the gorse bushes, their owners in hot pursuit, shouting apologies and waving dog leads as the spaniels danced and barked around us. I will spare you the rest of the two-hour ride, which was on the whole much calmer.

But one final issue was finding the cow herd lying down in the shade of Camp Hill Clump, (so named for the thousands of soldiers from both world wars who camped here before crossing the Channel to France). This stand of pines commands the highest point of the Big Bowl opposite Old Lodge, a stately home and nature reserve on the far side of this vast valley. Callum approached the cows lying amid the pine shadows cautiously, snorting. We circled round the cows in their pine copse and headed for home.

We had been out just two hours and yet the ride had been filled with alarms and excursions, some dancing, some snorting, some fear in my horse. All so very different from our usual forest bathing style rides in the woods. So, yes, give me the road less travelled. Always.

I am one of the many thousands of South Africans who left the country of our birth during the years of Apartheid, voting with our feet and seeking a better life in Europe. That decision came at some considerable cost. The loss of my culture, friends, family, landscapes and Cape Town, the city I loved, the soul food and the humour, the places I thought of as my spiritual and physical home. It took me more than a decade to accept that it was now in the past and there was no going back. The road less travelled can be bumpy and painful but it also holds rewards for those who venture down it. In my case my life has been hugely enriched by exposing me to the challenges, opportunities and stimulation of Europe's many rich cultures, from which my mother's family came to Africa nearly four centuries before and my father's family some 150 years ago.

And yet, and yet, when I fly into Cape Town even now, some 45 years after I turned my back on it, there are tears in my eyes. As I fly south some 6,000 miles, the anticipation builds and when I see the majesty of Table Mountain encircled by the deep blue of the South Atlantic the tears fall. I feel in some profound way that I am home once more, I am returned to the place that gave me life.

There is a poem by an Irish writer, Bernard O'Donoghue, who it has been my very great privilege to know slightly, which captures exquisitely this feeling of the journey home to a place long departed. It is called *Westering Home* and describes the road from Magdalen College Oxford where he teaches, west across Wales and the Irish sea to his birthplace, Ireland. It has a power to move me that I can hardly explain.

> Though you'd be pressed to say exactly where
> It first sets in, driving west through Wales
> Things start to feel like Ireland. It can't be
> The chapels with their clear grey windows,
>
> Or the buzzards menacing the scooped valleys.
> In April, have the blurred blackthorn hedges
>
> Something to do with it? Or possibly
> The motorway, which seems to lose its nerve
> Mile by mile. The houses, up to a point,
>
> With their masoned gables, each upper window
> A raised eyebrow. More though, than all of this.
> It's the architecture of the spirit:
> The old thin ache you thought that you'd forgotten.
>
> More smoke, admittedly, than flame:
> Less tears than rain. And the whole business
> Neither here nor there, and therefore home.

I love that and I feel I know what he means, 'Neither here nor there and therefore home'. Perhaps we can be at peace with being out of place, dislocated, neither here nor there. So it has been for me. Part of me, an essential part, has never left Africa and wishes to return, like the ache one feels in an amputated foot, long gone, but the ache of it tells you it is still there, still part of you. And the hell of it is that the road less travelled now, is the road home.

Apologies for getting maudlin, but that is where thoughts of the road less travelled take me. So maybe my choice to always choose the road less travelled, has some deep meaning? A search for my lost birthplace, a sense of adventure not yet quelled? The loneliness and aloneness of the road less travelled calls to me. Maybe it's the quiet promise of peace, far away from model aeroplanes, barking dogs and lowing cows, just an untrammelled lonely path beneath the trees, through a wood. And that is enough for me and my horse. It offers a form of consolation – it is our own form of Westering Home. A different continent and a different horse but still in the saddle, still on a horse. My truest home, when all is said and done.

MY FOREST HOME

When you have lived for as long as I have on Ashdown Forest, my feelings for it are as deep and profound as those I have for my actual home of stone and mortar, clapboard and tiles, maybe even more so. The Forest, 50 miles south east of London and 26 miles from the south coast with its white cliffs, has become a part of me.

Not everyone who visits the Forest falls in love with it. In 1822, the political writer William Cobbett whose book *Rural Rides* was an investigation into the state of farming in England, came upon the Forest and described it thus: 'Ashdown Forest – the most villainously ugly spot in England.' Truly, beauty is in the eye of the beholder. One can only wonder what was bugging Mr Cobbett on that day. The Forest is an ancient area of open heathland occupying the highest sandy ridge-top of the High Weald Area of Outstanding Natural Beauty.

There must be some twenty or thirty riding stables sprinkled around the Forest, private ones and those that are in the business of offering livery to those of us who wish to ride its miles. There are as many pubs in and around the Forest and there are farms that border it. The Forest provides a home to a shifting number of sheep, cattle and ponies. It is not one continuous forest, but criss-crossed by a number of roads that offer car access and the car parks that serve visitors. There are ice-cream vans in a few strategic places. The Forest is totally unlike some I have visited in South Africa or France, where you find mile after mile of untouched deep wood that is very little tampered with by the hand of man. Ashdown survives despite the presence of man. It is more of a forest garden than a forest fastness, and like all gardens it is a place of pleasure. But here and there, hidden in its depths, are places of utter silence, of deep contemplation, where the presence of man is barely felt or acknowledged. It is to these that I am drawn again and again and to which I direct my horse's step when setting out for a ride.

Callum has an increasing say in our destinations and routes. Ever since he injured his check ligament, I limit the miles we do. In the past, I would happily be gone for a whole morning or afternoon, or a ride at dusk that lasts many hours. Now I tend to keep it to under two hours. It suits him and it suits my knees and hips too. The two of us are getting old together, two old soldiers leaning on each other as we make our way.

But for the purposes of this story, this visit to the Forest rooms that have held my riding life, I will rely on those earlier days, when Callum and I travelled many miles in the spirit of adventure and curiosity.

Leaving the DIY yard next door to our hill-top cottage, I have two options to reach the Forest, one that takes me downhill and then up, due south to Wood Reeves car park and one that takes me north, downhill and then up to the Church Hill Car Park. The latter gives access to Five Hundred and One Hundred Acre Woods, the first one private and the second, part of Ashdown. Riding in both is my small act of defiance that does no harm to anyone, not to the woods or the animals who make it their home. I love it for the utter peace and privacy I find there. Very few people find their way here. The 'Private: Keep Out' signs make sure of that I feel strongly that the tiny eight per cent of England that the public has access to is profoundly wrong, unfair, and keeps citizens as serfs of a kind in their own country. I would dearly love to see a law that offers a free right to roam on designated paths, as in Scotland.

The Forest is like a piece of paper that has been crumpled up a bit and then allowed to open up and spread out, leaving endless peaks and troughs, hills and valleys holding innumerable streams and the odd lake or pond. It is ideal for exercising an energetic horse.

The Wood Reeves car park gives access to the first open heathland 'room' which includes two valleys, one that runs down to a stream and then rises to Ghylls Lap, the Enchanted Place and then west of these, it drops down to a second valley that bottoms out at a road with a 'splash' (a stream crossing) at one end and the car park for Pooh Sticks Bridge at the other. There are some lovely homes, some with stables, on the small country lane that runs for half a mile between the two.

Depending on the time of day, the footpath for visitors down to Pooh Sticks Bridge can be busy with people coming to see this iconic sight that has enthralled children for a century. The new bridge was paid for by Disney, local building firms and the public. The old one was repaired and sold to the 11th Earl De La Warr, William Sackville, in 2021 for £131,625, and put up near its original home on his estate. The Forest's link to the gentry goes back many centuries. It was at one point the property of John of Gaunt, Duke of Lancaster, as a hunting forest from 1372.

These days, children leave jars of honey at the door of Pooh's house. I tend to avoid this place, as Callum is not always keen on pushchairs or lines of children laden with backpacks. Recently, riding down there, he got quite lit up even with nobody around, for reasons only known to him and he took a hold and was a bit snorty until we made it back up the hill to the Enchanted Place.

There is a wood in this 'room' that has a twisty path through a deciduous Forest which is a lovely place in summer. And the long canters on the grassed paths make it good place to visit. The Enchanted Place itself holds a commemorative block of granite bearing a bronze plaque with the names of the two creative geniuses who collaborated

Into the Enchanted Forest with Callum

to give us the Pooh Bear books, A.A. Milne and E.H. Shepard. Callum enjoys a bit of standing and staring at the views to the north that the Enchanted Place offers, taking in parts of Kent, Sussex and Surrey. But he has also been known to bolt out of this tree encircled spot when a dog arrives unexpectedly or a rustle he can't place upsets his equilibrium. One never quite knows which it will be when edging inside this tree circle with its narrow entrance – the 'view gazer' or the 'bolter'; it's best to be prepared for both.

Quite often, we find walkers here and leave them to pay their respects, giving them space to enjoy the end point of their pilgrimage. Countless numbers of people from every part of the world make their way here to see for themselves the place that provided the inspiration for the Pooh Bear books. They don't need to share it with a somewhat bolshie horse. So, more often than not, we pass on by.

If you drop down to the splash at the bottom of the almost perpendicular Kidd's Hill, you will be close to The Hatch Inn, which dates back to 1430. Its low doors and ceilings add to its charm alongside the draft bitter beer on tap. Originally a row of three cottages, legend has it that the pub was a haven for smugglers, with rum as its speciality and Captain Kidd as its reputed mastermind, though little evidence supports this claim. But the place does seem to hide secrets in its cool dim interior.

Halfway down Kidd's Hill on the southern side of the road, there is an entrance to a huge private off-limits area of army land that runs all the way cross country to Pippingford Manor close to the village of Nutley. Much as I enjoy a spot of trespassing, this is an area that remains terra incognita.

If you take a path to your left lower down the hill as you approach the Hatch, it will bring you to another room on the Forest. This one offers another beech wood as well as more open heathland, the Ashdown Park Hotel, the Ashdown Forest Centre opposite the hotel and then a valley dropping down to the Royal Ashdown Forest Golf course, through which you can ride on a bridlepath, then cross the road and find your way to the old railway line that ran from Tunbridge Wells to East Grinstead, before it was axed. Today the rails and the wooden ties are long gone and the ash bed provides an excellent base for a long slow canter.

Returning to my point of entry onto the Forest at Wood Reeves car park, there are routes into four separate rooms. Turning left, you ride past the Black Hill car park, then cross the road onto the room dominated by King Standing clump at the summit of the hill and in the valley north of it is the Ashdown Forest Riding Centre. Here there are a number of cantering tracks to choose from and one that invites a gallop up rising ground, if clear of dog walkers. If you ride due east, you will come up the back of the Crow & Gate Pub on the A26.

Do a U-turn there and you have another rising ground canter up to another of the signature pine clumps. Next to it is a vast underground complex which during WW2 served as a military black ops propaganda operation. The King's Standing Transmitter Station based at Duddleswell (on the way to Crowborough) was used during the Second World War for the transmission of black propaganda broadcasts to Germany. From May 1941 to October 1942, the programme succeeded in catching German attention by a mixture of lascivious stories and crude anti-British propaganda; Winston Churchill, for example, was described as 'a flat-footed bastard son of a drunk'. Having thus gained the confidence of their German audience, the broadcasters were able to deliberate on the incompetence of the Fuhrer's advisers, who were also accused of all manner of sexual perversions. Callum and I skirt this massive hole in the ground dug by 600 Canadian soldiers to house the vast transmitter.

If this facility was aimed at unsettling German plans to invade England, then just a hundred yards away are the remains of an earlier successful invasion. Across the road and into another room. The Big Bowl as I call it, there is another construction, this one linked to the successful invasion of

43AD by the Romans under the leadership of Vespasian, whose army of 45,000 successfully subdued the local tribes. The remains of the Roman road are still in place and Callum and I cross it regularly, thoughts of Romans and Germans much in mind. It amazes me that the Second World War architects of the underground transmitter complex did not get the heebie-jeebies, thinking how close the Roman invasion road was? It would have bothered me no end to site it so close to a symbol of successful invasion.

The Big Bowl, with its two pine clumps commanding the high points, Friends Clump on the southern fringe and Camphill Clump which overlooks a view of the best galloping track on the Forest, has long been a favourite of mine. If Callum or his predecessors started getting 'above themselves' we would head for this galloping hill and give them a pipe-opener that was brisk enough to promptly shut down the naughty behaviour. The journey home was always much calmer.

Before setting off at a gallop it's advisable to look up the hill to check for dog walkers or other horse riders heading down. Most dog walkers seeing you start up the hill will leash their dogs and stand to one side to enjoy the spectacle of a big blood horse doing what he does best – gallop. The trick for the rider is to stay on board if the horse decides to jink or shy when passing the walkers. It has been known to happen.

Once at the top, you are alongside Camp Hill Clump of pine trees. From here you can ride south, downhill to Ellison's Pond (hearsay has it that it is a famous dogging site), and from there, uphill once more to Friends Clump with its views north across the Big Bowl and south to the South Downs. To exit this room, you can either cross the road into the fourth room, the southern flank of the Forest, with the Airman's Grave on one of the four paths that take you down to Cackle Street on the southern extremity of the Forest and the option of four uphill runs on the way home. I recall riding a chestnut Irish horse named Max with Jan on Kesh in the 1980s, overfed, fit and wanting to run, this room was a favourite place to really open the horses' lungs and stretch their legs. We flew up this hill many a day before breakfast and work.

An alternate loop on the Forest takes you into another 'room', east across the Duddleswell-Fairwarp Road. This ride enters a steep dip to a stream and then swings north on a gently rising hill behind the old tearoom, making for one of the best grassed canter tracks on the Forest. On a hot day, it's worth riding into Fairwarp Village for a pint at the Foresters Arms.

Once you are back at the top of the hill after that canter, cross the road once more and head west past the Nutley Windmill, and you enter the fifth room, Mill Hill, which houses Pippingford Manor with its stableyard at one end, and Londonderry Farm stables at the Nutley end, below the windmill. Once again, this room offers a long canter track that carries you up to the car and truck parking area on the brow of the hill on the road from East Grinstead to Forest Row, Wych Cross and Nutley.

Every now and again, Pippingford hosts a music festival with hundreds of white bell tents looking like a field of mushrooms that popped up after a night of rain.

One of the pleasures of riding a beautiful horse like Callum is the compliments he attracts, something he understands and approves of, knowing as he does that it is his due and may often come with a mint, his favourite thing after carrots. And it must be said that his rider is not immune to this pleasure – the appreciation of others who know beauty when they see it. I admit it freely; it's one of my failings.

I blame my mother for this inherited trait. She was one of those people who loved beauty in all its forms, be it food, flowers, furnishing, men, women or indeed clothes, her speciality subject about which she knew much, and even more about what and how to wear them. Her life consisted in no small measure – for reasons both obvious and less so – in shopping for clothes. On the subject of living beauty in men or women she would advise her sons and daughter in

Into the Enchanted Forest with Callum

her Afrikaans mother-tongue, 'Jy moet ook iets vir die oog hê.' You must also have something that pleases the eye. And in my mind, she was right.

But the wise say: never judge a book by its cover, and in Callum's case, how right that is. His beauty is skin-deep, for under that golden hide hides a veritable demon of fear and temperament and other things that I am still discovering after living with him for six years. He wants to be good. I am sure of that, but his demons get the better of him all too often. A bird flying suddenly out of a hedge is in his mind the equivalent of the Hindenburg bursting into flames right next to him and his evasive action is explosive.

He is, in truth, not an old man's ideal horse. But pride you see, pride cometh before a fall. And I admit to pride in him. He is like a Ferrari, beautiful but not always reliable or practical. So the admiring glances and the appreciative comments are balm to the soul, my soul. 'What a beautiful horse!' If I've heard that once in six years, I've heard it a thousand times or more. And the comment allows me in all good conscience to pull up and have a brief conversation about horses and riding and in this way, I have met many charming people in my time. Usually it is a woman with a dog and a man, or a woman alone with a dog.

I thank them for the kind comment and ask them if they ride. I tell them their appreciation is appreciated and as for Callum, he thinks he believes he knows it is only his due. And so a brief but satisfactory conversation ensues, one that leaves both me and the walker the happier for it. For it is as much a pleasure to give a gift as it is to receive it.

So after 45 years of riding these miles, my own efforts at storytelling have added a new pleasure to the Forest – compliments for my horse and sometimes for my writing. It is an irresistible combination for any man, not least this easily flattered man. So these days, Callum and my perambulations about the Forest have a very human pleasure to add to the many other pleasures of the place.

Moving on west under the flight path of aircraft heading for Gatwick Airport, you cross the road and you are in Chelwood Vachery country, another room in the Forest with the remains of the long clay emergency aircraft landing strip for planes in trouble returning from bombing raids in Germany. For such a quiet, bucolic area there is much evidence of war here, from Roman roads to hidden transmitters, from bomb holes and the Airman's Grave to emergency runways.

There are too, here and there, if you know where to look, enormous grassed-over craters where the V-1 and V-2 German flying rockets or buzzbombs falling short of London or shot down by Spitfires or anti-aircraft guns, left their marks on the ground. There are many hammer ponds in the area too, places where iron was mined to make cannon or the fittings for the ships of the Royal Navy. The Forest has seen it all in its last 2,000 years. History might be said to form a haze over the region from Hastings to London.

In this part of the Forest, you will also find a couple of cricket pitches near Birch Grove, once the home of former prime minister, Harold Macmillan. In 1963, the area was turned upside down for a visit by the American President John F. Kennedy in June, high summer, just five months before he was shot dead in Dallas, Texas.

Writing for the local paper, the *Brighton Evening Argus*, Bill Gardiner describes the visit of Kennedy to Macmillan, who with true patrician arrogance, famously told Britain, 'You've never had it so good!'

> At the height of the Cold War, the eyes of the world turned briefly to this quiet corner of the Sussex countryside. On 29 June 1963, America's youthful and charismatic president John F Kennedy paid a flying visit to meet Prime Minister Harold Macmillan at his country house, Birch Grove. Kennedy was on his way to Italy and the final leg of his historic four-nation European tour.

Into the Enchanted Forest with Callum

Kennedy came to Sussex for crucial Cold War talks with Macmillan, but also because he wanted to see the English countryside – and he didn't come alone. The **Sussex Police** files from the time show almost every hotel in the area was booked up as far as Brighton. The world's press stayed in Brighton, at the Metropole Hotel, while American government officials and the crew of Air Force One stayed at The Grand.

There were helicopter shuttles to and from Hove Lawns to Birch Grove House, with officials scurrying to JFK's every beck and call. In nearby Chelwood Gate, the landlord of the Red Lion pub was besieged by reporters – some of whom even asked if they could sleep in the attic.

Days before the president arrived, Secret Service agents had swarmed into tiny Horsted Keynes village to set up a base in the Crown Inn. According to locals, their powerful security transmitters put every television in the area out of action for the entire weekend.

If you ride past Birch Grove House, you will come across a grove of pines known as the Kennedy Clump which commemorate the presidential visit. A few hundred yards further west, just past the small cricket field, you can descend through woods and farmland, an area adjacent to the Forest proper, which brings you out on the Wych Cross Road to Sharpthorne and on to Turners Hill, one of the routes to Gatwick Airport. This is a little-known loop, which is a well-kept secret held by a few local riders and a small number of adventurous spirits. If your horse is traffic-proof, you can take the route back to Pippingford from the Roebuck Hotel at Wych Cross, which will give you a mile-long canter track that runs just a 100ft from the road south to Nutley.

As you pass Pippingford on the way back to the Big Bowl you can, in summer, take the lower path through the woods by the river and come out below Friends Clump which you put behind you as you head north, with the majestic manor of Old Lodge on your left.

It was here that an English bull terrier tried to latch onto Jan's horse's nose many years ago and got short shrift and a broken leg when the horse not surprisingly reared up and struck out at her. The dog's owners were understandably upset as was Jan, but what they failed to grasp was that if their dog had managed to latch onto Sebastian's nose, chances are Jan might have been killed and the horse seriously injured too. Horses and dogs don't always mix well if the dog owners are unaware of the potential dangers posed when the two meet.

By this point on such a gallivanting ride, Callum will be well and truly ready for his stable, which lies some two miles northeast. There is a last canter up the hill from the stream and its Garden of Eden waterfall. Once you have crossed the plank bridge, it is a few hundred yards to the top of the hill and the gate that gives access to the Big Bowl. Then it is half a mile to the Wood Reeves car park and down the hill through the woods, to the lake and home.

Callum has earned his oats for this outing and for me there is a drink or two and a slap-up dinner. The rooms of our cottage provide a well-earned rest from Callum's canters and gallops and mile long cooling down walks through the rooms of my other home, the Forest. But just as the stable comes in sight, a pheasant erupts out of the long grass and Callum leaps away from the noise as if electrified. It is more by luck and instinct that I stay with him. There is no way of getting to the bottom of these Irish horses, they always have something more in the tank, and one had best be aware of that and ride with respect for the beast beneath your saddle.

Any ride on the Forest offers peace and the chance for contemplation, but just below the surface there is the barely audible babble of men and women who called this place home for thousands of years, shooting deer, tending cattle, shepherding sheep, cutting bracken for animal bedding, raising children. And one can hear too, amid the call of the skylarks who haunt this place, the blare of Roman war trumpets and the marching of a thousand legionnaires. In its own way, the Forest carries its past and its present lightly. It welcomes everyone from prime ministers to presidents, Caesars to celebrities and ordinary dog walkers and the odd horse rider too. It's all one to the Forest, which is why I and so many are proud to call it home.

END TIMES, BUT SOLDIERING ON

Summer 2024

Callum and I have a weird kind of synchronicity in our downward spiral, and I am fighting a rear-guard action against gravity and pain that is dragging us both down. I am 74 and he is 16, no great age in his case, but in mine, old enough.

I am battling two shot knees that need replacing, a right hip that is also beginning to fail, a heart that has seen better days and is shored up with two stents, and that is it for now, but for how long no one knows. But these, to quote the writer Peter Godwin, are just 'exit wounds' that point the way off the stage of life.

Callum has given me five years of fantastic trail riding or hacking as we say this side of the pond. During that time he has won out against a nail in his right front foot and a damaged check ligament. And more recently there are changes in his navicular and pedal bones of that same foot, where internal bony growths are trying and failing to shore things up. I am keeping an eye on that with our vet.

I noticed that after a ride he would lift that right front leg that had the nail and then ligament issue and naturally thought, here we go again. But Duncan our vet reassured me that the ligament was well mended. This looked like something else entirely. And so the X-rays proved. There were arthritic changes in the eleven bones of his hoof. We tried a number of things, but none worked. I asked around the yard and also did some reading and a potential answer, it seemed, lay with an Arthramid injection. Such an injection had helped the horse of a show jumping friend regain soundness so with the vet's encouragement we went ahead. It did the trick. And at £1,000 a pop, it's just as well.

That Arthramid injection plus remedial shoeing, continues to work miracles (touch wood) and he is sound as a bell, although on our vet's advice we limit our rides to walking with short bouts of trotting. And I am letting him wander at will rather than lunging him in the round sand pen as it's easier on his joints – something that seems to meet with his approval.

Keeping the big guy going is as much in his interest as it is in my own. I doubt that there is another horse in my future, so keeping Callum going is something of a priority.

The two of us are crocks and should be put out of our misery, but we soldier on, the walking wounded, not ready for the 'Rainbow Bridge' to the great beyond just yet. Our local woods call to us still with their beguiling beauty. And thus far we go to them almost daily, slowly, carefully, but we manage. And as we move through the trees it is as though we are already gone and this ride is a forerunner of ghostly rides to come. I see with trifocal eyes – the past is here, all 45 years of it in this place, and so is the present, and I also get a strong intimation of the future, when we will be gone, but maybe not entirely. Loving my early morning and evening rides, with luck we will give the odd dog walker a proper fright, a ghost rider on a ghostly horse.

Getting old is a bitch. There is no 'Golden Years' nonsense. People we love and respect are dying around us, and at the funerals you note with foreboding that you are one of the oldest there. This ageing business does mess with your head. A few days ago, I did a head count of friends and family who had passed on and the total gave me pause, as they outnumbered the people who inhabit my life now. Among those missing in action is a schoolfriend who took his own life at 15 by jumping off a multi-storey building in Cape Town

Into the Enchanted Forest with Callum

back in the 1960s, and a brilliant young nephew who took his life at 26, just as he was finishing his doctorate in Ornithology. This year, I lost two old friends. So, Golden Years it ain't. But I hang on in here.

As I hobble back from the stables, trying my best to disguise my limp, I think of all the many men and women I watched over the years, walking with odd gaits, some of them barely able to move. At the time I felt a mix of pity and mystification. I wondered why they clung to life when they were so physically compromised? Now I know, life is precious and there is a beauty and sweetness to these end times, despite the dead who haunt me, despite the physical pain, despite the knowledge that I am living in the last chance corral. Now the thought of facing the stairs gives me pause. Do I really need that book, that handkerchief, my laptop, my phone, a jersey? It is a humbling business, this getting old malarkey. And the enemy within, that two faced friend asks: 'If the stairs are too much, how are you going to cope with Callum this winter now that you hobble on those pins and one hard pull on the lead rope will send you flying?'

It is a day at a time business this eighth decade hustle. But life is precious and made more so by the little wisdom and education gathered on the way, picked up from school and university, from family and friends, from the thousands of books read, the movies. I see now with the most educated eye I have ever had, and it casts a bittersweet glow on things.

So, I bring to Callum a compassion that I may not have had in years gone by. I see him as a fellow soldier, a friend and companion. I am more concerned for his wellbeing than I am for my own, if truth be told. My health issues just irritate or scare me, but I really don't feel I deserve better. I have been blessed in this life more than most. But Callum cannot call the shots, or the vets; I have to do that for him.

I have him on shoes with pads and back crossbar supports that are helping significantly, and that shot of Arthramid has been a game changer. He spent last night in his paddock as usual during the summer and this morning I came down to a head tossing, foot stamping, trotting up and down horse that was back to his old self. I was glad of the Chifney bit I use to keep him civil as we walk the half mile up the hill to the stable yard. Long may this last.

Callum is not just a horse. He is my gym instructor, my doctor, my shrink, my life coach. He is pretty much irreplaceable and so I am buoyed up by this new incarnation of my horse as he dances beneath me once we are out in the woods again. He does his little Oldenburg two-step now and then, an incredibly rapid movement you'd swear is motivated by a red-hot branding iron applied to his more delicate parts. All it takes is a rustle in the bushes. But now I smile to feel this energy and light footedness.

When I dismount, I will be 74 again, but for now I am 20 in that saddle and my own failing body is forgotten, totally forgotten. How can I ever repay that gift? So don't count us out just yet. Thank God for horses!

Horse, Spirit, Earth – The Sacred Landscape

Autumn 2024

The horse offers a key to something profound, the understanding that we inhabit a sacred landscape, to which our future is linked.

The truth that horses can lead us to, that will set us free, was known to every tribe, every people who lived before us, who lived in harmony and in sympathy with their land, the San Bushmen of Africa, the Australian Aborigines, the Amazonian Indians, and so many more, our own forbears among them..

What has this got to do with horses, you ask? Well, it has a great deal to do with horses, in my case. I have spent seven decades outside, riding in landscapes as varied as possible, beaches, mountains, prairies, forests. It is hard to describe what I found out there. The trouble is finding the language, the words, to describe this thing that is almost beyond comprehension and beyond words.

The key phrase in the paragraphs above is: 'I have spent seven decades outside'. I know that any hope of salvation does not occur inside buildings, but outside. One cannot spend so much time under the open sky, close to nature, observing the slow turn of the seasons, too hot and too cold by turn, by day and by night under the wheeling constellations, not to have picked up on something special.

You can do this perfectly well on foot, but in my experience doing it on horseback adds a whole new dimension of awareness, of sensitivity, of openness, and yes, some fear, that peels back the layers of civilization that are actually thinner than onion skin.

For those of us who ride horses, not for sport, but to simply disappear into the landscape, as far from humanity as it is possible to get, in our wildly overpopulated world, will have stumbled across some aspect of this thing I talk about. What have I found out there that now compels me to write? And there is the rub. There is no easy way to show you. You would need to repeat my experience, and only then, and only dimly, as dimly as I see or sense it, will this thing manifest itself in a ghostly way.

If I've heard it once, I've heard it a thousand times – horses bring healing. That is true, and I know this, too, that if you partner with a horse in solo rides into nature something of the great universality of nature, something of the Divine, manifests itself to you. It has something to do with the horse being a prey animal; it is as nervous as hell about everything out there. It places a lot of trust in you to even venture into the wild with you, without the company of other horses. And as you sit perched on this nervy thing, the horse, you would have to be the most insensitive human on earth not to be aware that your own security is now partly in the care of this creature on whose back you sit. It is a humbling thing. And it opens your mind to a kind of thinking that our ancient ancestors, hunters and gatherers, themselves preyed upon animals, would have felt keenly, a sense of some inexplicable 'otherness' out there.

Sitting quietly on your horse in the silence of a wood, listening intently to the movement of the wind and the creaking of branches, the thread of birdsong or the sudden shock of a crow's harsh 'craaaaaack', there comes upon you a sense of worshipfulness in ways I've not experienced in the humblest church or the greatest cathedral. How could they? They are made of stone or brick that hold the world of nature at bay.

Given the threats we face as a species, this is a time to think more deeply about life and its meaning beyond the constraints and demands of the everyday. If we are not thinking now about the meaning of our lives, our world, our future, then we are truly lost. And horses are a great help on this journey of discovery.

We are like ants crawling over the face of God, blindly unaware of the sacred nature of our journey. I am talking of what our ancestors took for granted, a sense of wonder, of magic, of spiritual power that was invested in us and in our physical reality. The landscape was alive for them, inhabited by explicable and inexplicable powers. The rivers sang, the trees whispered, and the very stones had stories to tell, if only one would sit in quiet contemplation and listen!

This is not a plea for a return to a world filled with superstition, though that is part of the lost magic; some of its loss is for the good. It is also not a plea for turning our backs on science or technology, or education. These need to be embraced, for in them lie part of our possible salvation. But they are also responsible for the culture of greed, of dominance over the natural world, of taking for granted everything given to us on this earth. Our intellect has poisoned us and our world.

Environmentalism has at its core an understanding that everything is linked, and that we need once more to worship the world, to treat it as sacred, because it is our only real heritage, our inheritance and the basis of life on earth, not only for us but for every living thing now and in the future, if there is to be a future.

We need to stop long enough to come to understand how such a belief enriches everything in our lives. For if the most mundane thing, the most abject material, is filled with spirit, then we have a better understanding of ourselves as sacred animals moving through a sacred landscape. That belief makes it much more difficult to damage or destroy anything.

When I was a boy, growing up at the foot of Table Mountain in Cape Town, at the southernmost tip of Africa, it was no great feat of the imagination to see the mountain as holy, sacred, a spiritual place, the home of those who had gone before. In my dreams I circled it flying as freely as a bird, experiencing that most powerful feeling of unassisted flight. No wonder then, that as I rode my horse in the woods and streams near my home, I was filled with a sense of wonder, by the presence of an unseen 'Other' that has never entirely left me. It is, I believe, the oldest known truth, that in ways we cannot comprehend, we are not alone. That we are observed, and the good and evil we do is noted. And that help is at hand if only we would ask for it.

Mankind cannot and does not entirely live by bread alone. We want more. We want to return to Eden, to innocence, to a life lived with meaning in harmony with the universe. And it is for this that I seek. There is a gypsy in all of us. We walked as a species out of Africa and colonised the world. By walking, we took ownership of the earth. In walking lies a sort of redemption, and thus the pilgrimage was born.

Today, we are tethered to our homes as never before; fear of the world keeps us there, as do the warmth, security, TV and computers. For many children and adults, the landscape is terra incognita. For many the world beyond their street or town is an unknown world, and this at a time of the greatest social and geographic mobility man has ever experienced. So many of us live within the blaring noise of our culture and its total lack of contemplation, of veneration for silence.

Where is all this taking me? I don't know. Maybe nowhere. But as I grow older, I am in search of something to help me understand my life's journey. I sense that I have missed much, that I am impoverished with the richness of the twentieth and twenty-first centuries. I would like to get a greater glimpse of our connection to the earth before I pass into the silence of death. I would like to be more than an unthinking ant. The closest I can get to this undefinable thing is on horseback.

So, even as we are held hostage by the world, I listen to the call of the wild, to the song of birds, the rush of water, the wind in the trees. I stop and look into the gloom of the woods and note the new growth, the slow silent turning of the world. I pick up stones and caress them. For in doing these things I am honouring the world and healing myself and giving a chance for the 'Other' to manifest itself. It may take a lifetime, it may never happen, but at least I would not have travelled unaware, blind to what lies about me, to beauty.

A door has to be opened if one is to receive a visitor. All one can do is to wait and listen and be ready by the open door to offer a welcome. And for us, the horse riders, our horses hold the key to this new old thinking. If you ride into the wild you are a figure in a sacred landscape, whether you know it or not.

NO MORE LONELY

Autumn 2024

There is an epidemic of loneliness in the world right now and it is growing. Its impact on our health is serious. Loneliness can increase the risk for premature death to levels comparable to smoking fifteen cigarettes a day, according to the US Surgeon General. The physical results of loneliness can be devastating – a 29 per cent increased risk of heart disease; a 32 per cent increased risk of stroke; and a 50 per cent increased risk of developing dementia for older adults.

Each of us lives alone with ourselves, to a greater or lesser extent, and most of us struggle with this issue. For those of us who are privileged to ride, we know that a horse can change the dynamics of loneliness just as much as a dog does, although in different ways. A horse adds to your peace, calm and identity in ways that are hard to explain.

When that lonely ache in your chest and stomach is hard to shift and tablets and booze and shrinks don't cut it by much, go stand among horses and breathe them in. Take in their quiet silence, their patience, their beauty, their seeming meditative messages: 'Just be', 'Just keep on', 'You are good enough', 'You matter'. And when a little spark of hope is lit in you, then, if you can, saddle up and go. The person who returns will be a different, happier you. And then repeat and never stop. The prize is getting your life back. And no more lonely.

Into the Enchanted Forest with Callum

For so many people, a horse is a ticket to a world of connections. It starts by getting you out of the house. The horse needs to be fed, mucked out exercised, taken to its field and brought back in. Owning one connects you to a community, farriers, food merchants, hay suppliers, dentists, physiotherapists, grooms, other riders, and yard owners. You are part of a tribe. Loneliness is less of an issue now.

And if the loneliness is the result of bereavement, a lost job, a new town, kids leaving home, or a failing relationship, the horse can and will take on the role of your best friend and significant other. With a horse in your life, there is no more loneliness, or significantly less. A much-loved horse will give you a reason to get up in the morning, a reason to go to work (to pay its bills), and a reason to live. It's more of a reason than many people have. And yet few acknowledge this. Horses are not just for riding. They can be and often are the reason to live.

A horse will fill your life in so many ways: with beauty, with physical and spiritual pleasure, with the grit and grind of mucking out, with grooming, with planning, with sharing your stories, building a relationship with it. And this is all before you even start riding. No wonder that the loss of a horse can be as hard to bear as the loss of a human loved one. The sudden absence of a loved horse hollows out your life just as much as the loss of a partner. But horses are like love; that well is never empty, there are always other horses, new loves.

When you ride out alone or in company, you are no longer lonely, you are with your partner. And if you have a new human partner, they'd best understand that they are now part of a three-way relationship with split loyalties and a shared or unshared passion. Often the horse is a deal breaker, just too much competition, too much emotional support.

A horse will teach you the difference between lonely and alone. Your understanding of the joys of solitude will take on a whole new meaning. Being by yourself with your horse will be peace-inducing, not stressful. And if your horse is a handful, that too will keep the horrors of loneliness at bay. There is no space for loneliness when you have a horse performing beneath you, throwing curves.

Out there in the woods or the vast open spaces, you will run into walkers or other horse people and you will stop and talk and exchange pleasantries, and now and again, once in a while, you will meet someone who becomes a new friend, another gift of your horse.

What else can give you such a legal high as a horse, can make you smile, sing, and shout with joy as this beautiful creature carries you away into the wilds, with no need for a human minder or chaperone or protector? What else can bear you into the magic of nature in the way that a horse can, with you six feet off the ground, floating on a magic carpet?

If you are in the least bit creative or artistic, the horse will trigger all your creative juices and you will write or paint or sing or dance with new energy and vitality. You will be high on life. If a horse was a substance, it would have to be banned. The stuff can make you crazy. But really, what it does do, is make you sane, connects you to the earth, to the world, to nature, to life. And the next morning there is no hangover. Or if there is, it's with a surfeit of joy.

With a horse in your life there is much less lonely.

SUSSEX AUTUMN FASHION SHOW

Autumn 2024

Callum and I were out hacking this morning, and a friend from the stable yard, Katie, walking her lovely dog Willow, stopped for a chat and took a photo of us with the huge oak in the background. When I look at this image and think of the alternative, had the Arthramid shot not worked - the end of this horse who has given me so much joy - I can hardly bear the thought.

I went over to the stables at 8am, fed him, tacked him up and off we went into the mist-shrouded woods, all silent but for the rustling of squirrels hard at work laying in supplies of nuts and acorns to see them through the winter. We weren't half a mile from home when I spotted a tiny muntjac dear standing watching us from among the trees.

We have been making our rides last no longer than an hour or an hour fifteen minutes and just walking round the lake, but yesterday Callum took himself down a different path and I realised he was getting bored with the same old lake ride, so this morning I pointed him to the path that leads up to the open Forest and he stepped out with a will.

For some reason, the song California Dreaming was playing in my head, maybe because the skies were grey, and I thought I'd be safe and warm if I was in LA where we are heading this Christmas. But soon enough the evident pleasure Callum was feeling, being once more out in the woods, brought me back to this landscape that I love. We headed into Five Hundred Acre Wood then Hundred Acre Wood then Wood Reeves and then the path home via the two old Victorian bridges over the stream, past the Candelabra oak and the lake with not a single ripple on its glassy surface.

Callum looked about him as usual, not missing a thing, hearing things lost on me and now and then doing a brisk little sashay or a tiny jerk just to check that I was awake and on my toes. He was on his toes, that's for sure, and the thought brought another rush of joy.

There was a sort of very muted English sexiness in the woods, if that's the right phrase. The oak and beech trees are dressed in moss green, velvet lingerie and ivy suspenders, for this year's Sussex Autumn Fashion Show.

The clocks went back this Sunday, and it had the usual spirit-dousing effect on me. We are entered into the dark wet tunnel of an interminable English winter. But in the woods I noticed something that spiced up my rides – there is an erotic charge among the trees who've welcomed the early dark with a spot of dressing up.

It's driving the holly and birches green with envy, though truth be told the oaks and beeches slip into this underwear each October and it sees them through the winter. It has caught Callum's eye too and he likes a bite of the moss now and again, so he seems to get it.

And it wasn't just the vegetation looking frisky! One of the joys of riding this week is seeing the number of bucks out for the rut. One stood his ground till Callum and I were about thirty yards from him and then he just languidly turned and walked off into the brush. The deer rut seemed to be getting into gear with stags much in evidence and in no hurry to give way to us, pumped up as they are just now. One of them was so tardy to slip off the path that I managed a few pics of him. Long may this last.

It has been very mixed weather over the last couple of

weeks and Callum continued to go out to pasture during the day, staying in when the showers turned to downpours. And coming in at night.

This morning I saddled Callum up for a slow walk round the hill. We left the yard with him at his 'looky-looky' best and making soft snorts. I worked to keep him collected and moving forward. He felt well and strode out with a will; the plan was a 30-minute ride at the walk down to the lake and back.

After some minutes he began to work into the bridle, and I started to look around me. The bracken was a mix of umber and old blood, the beech trees gold and green and leaves carpeting the ground. It had rained all night and alongside the path little rivulets and steams trickled and tinkled, but the woods looked strangely deserted like a house the morning after a party.

Callum looked about him too. Autumn had advanced considerably. It was so good to be out on the big fella feeling well in himself and walking out strongly, now and then breaking into a jog. Each time I brought him back to a walk and by the time we reached the lake he'd got the message. This was to be a sedate stroll, not a pipe-opening gallop.

I sang to him in Afrikaans, my old favourite, Sarie Marais, an old Boer War song from 120 years ago. What might Rudyard Kipling or Sir Arthur Conan Doyle, two local Victorian literary giants, have made of the song, I wondered.

As we came through the gate by the lake and turned up the hill for home we found our way blocked by an enormous beech tree that had fallen some time before but had not as yet been cleared. There was nothing for it but to circle back the way we had come.

Callum seemed a bit nonplussed by this U-turn, but went on happily enough. Back at the yard after 40 minutes, he seemed his old self and I said a silent prayer of thanks.

As we walked down to his paddock I felt a bit wobbly, perhaps all that mossy fecundity and rutting randiness was just too much for me? But no, probably just the mud-slicked ground was making me wobbly. I kept wiping drops of water off my face, falling from the bushes I suppose. I was in a much a worse state than the horse who had just one thought in his head – grass, get me to the grass!

A HORSE MIRACLE AND WEATHER FORECASTING

Winter 2024

The first icy weather of the English winter is here once again and Callum is back into being a fire-breathing-dragon, so full of himself that he broke free of the lunge rein in the indoor school and did some free schooling for a few minutes till I could catch him. Horses are so affected by weather.

There is a side to riding that is not too much discussed but underlies every aspect of the sport, hobby, lifestyle, call it what you will. Namely. the weather.

Do you, like me, on waking up at 6am, poke your head out the bathroom or bedroom window first thing, to see if the Meteorological Office has got it right or wrong? And is your own forecast more or less accurate than that of the professionals?

By the time I've downed my first life restoring mug of Italian, Moroccan or Brazilian coffee, I've run a computation of the plan for the day in my mind. Too cold with icy paths, forget it. Have another coffee. Too wet, just horrible and Callum will have conniptions – go back to bed for half an hour. Too windy, doable if I stay in the woods and don't venture out to the high points of the Forest. Both windy and wet, back to bed. Sunny and mild, get yourself out of bed - fast!

Clothes are the next issue. Comfort before style is my watchword. I've never heard Callum complain. 'Oh, Lord, Julian; that colour does you no favours!' He just wants his breakfast – and be damn quick about it too! And on the rare and infrequent occasions that we go out to dinner, people are pleasantly surprised by how neat I look with hair brushed, a clean pair of jeans, and polished moccasins. I tend to agree with them. I am not yet utterly devoid of all vanity – even at my age. And why not? I still have my own teeth, even if the knees are about to be thrown out. In fact I'm thinking of getting extra-large knees which will give me back some of the inches I've lost in height.

Now that I'm tacking up, if it's a warm day, I do a review of the local insect life. What is the midge, fly and stinging pest situation? Does one spray or not? Sunglasses? Fly mask for Callum?

The really weird thing about all this stuff is that it's not idle nonsense or over thinking or fussing. Your life could depend on getting it right.

Who else is riding, and which way are they heading? I may need to reroute. How recently has your horse been clipped? A fresh wind and a just-clipped horse? Beware.

I must admit I read the runes closely and take note. It's something I do almost subconsciously these days. Seventy years in the saddle gives you a PhD in horse management and survival skills. It's a bit pitiful really, I must admit.

And of course, age changes how we compute this stuff. When I was 18, hail, lightning, thunder, rain bucketing down – nothing, but nothing, not Hell nor high water would have kept me out of the saddle. These days, I'm much more of a fair-weather rider. It's really all about kindness, to the horse as much as to myself. One has to take the horse's feelings into account, after all! Callum could go off me if I was too gung-ho. I don't want Callum turning cartwheels in the air. That would never do.

And with that happy thought I throw a leg over and we

are off into the wild, chancing it once more, gambling just one more time.

RIDING THROUGH THE PAIN

Winter 2024

My mornings start at around 6am, give or take a few minutes on either side, due to the level of light hammering or caressing the curtains, and whether it's summertime or wintertime. At the age of 74, with two stents in my heart and crocked knees awaiting replacement and a right hip that is beginning to gnaw at me because of the knee problem, I'm always reasonably happy to find I am still here when I open my eyes. Living in Sniper's Alley as I am, the fact that I am still breathing is a head start to the day.

I check the day's weather with the Met Office website for my hilltop town. Usually, it is remarkably accurate. Depending on what I find there, my day's plans will be decided, to put my horse out to grass for the day, or for a few hours, or to ride or not to ride. The Met Office helps me decide these things.

Then pulling the duvet back, I see how easily I will be able to stand up - will the crocked knees support me one more day? They are always a bit shaky, so I don't rush it, I use the wait to put on a zipped jumper and then I try out a few steps. If all is well, and that is a relative phrase, I head downstairs to make my first essential coffee of the day. Going downstairs is a cautious business, with my back to the wall and my hands on the banister rail. If the knees give way at this point, I will at least have back friction and handgrip to slow any collapse.

Arriving on the entrance lobby's red tiles is another small achievement. Then I walk almost normally through the TV room and into the kitchen, stroke the cat Coco, feed her, put the kettle on and find my favourite china mug decorated with blue irises. Once the coffee is made, I trek back upstairs to bed. There I briefly check the morning's news and when I can't take any more, I switch to my Facebook page to read any comments sent to me. Then I check Amazon for any new reviews of my books and I may read a few pages of whatever book I am currently into.

Just before 8am I shower and dress cautiously, and with my legs feeling much more limber than two hours before, I make my way to the DIY livery yard next door. A kindly friend who is up at the crack of dawn to do her own horse has already given Callum his breakfast, something she offered to do which I accepted with alacrity and much gratitude as it gives me some extra time in bed each morning.

The walk over to the stable involves stepping over our 2ft high back garden fence and then a little wood to negotiate and a split-pole fence to duck through. In the past all of this would have been done on automatic and I would not even have noticed the actions required to negotiate these obstacles. Today, however, I have to think each action through and then help my body as much as I can. Yep, getting old sucks, but it beats the other option hands down.

I get Callum his hay and while he munches, I muck out and water him and remove his rugs if I am riding, as I will be this morning as it's a glorious spring day, which is going to go to 8 degrees by noon. It's been minus 2 Celsius overnight but the March sun has melted the frost and the water buckets are ice free.

I leave the horse to his hay and make my way home for my own breakfast, legs working almost normally, but I keep a sharp lookout for obstacles. If my right foot strikes a rock sticking out of the ground, it forces my lower leg back just far enough to create an agonising shooting pain that leaves me gasping for air as it shoots through my leg right up to the right hip. I hang onto whatever is to hand, a wall or tree, whatever, if there is something to lean on, if not I just bend over and hold my knees, breathing shallowly.

Breakfast is the same each day; my second mug of coffee and toast, butter and marmalade. It never fails to give me a shot in the arm. Then it's back to the stables, being careful of all obstacles.

It takes a little longer to tack Callum up than it did some years back but then it's done and I hobble alongside him to the mounting block. He stands like a Trojan while I mount, which is just as well. I lean down and tighten the girths one hole now that he has let himself breathe out. I gather the reins and off we go. In the 50 feet to the yard gate a small miracle occurs which never ceases to amaze me, in those few short strides I've lost 55 years and am 20 once again. I breathe the spring morning air in deep and look around me as if for the first time that morning. Everything is now on automatic once more, thanks to the horse doing the grunt work of moving me. And people wonder why oldies keep on riding. If they had one of my mornings, they would not wonder at all, they would understand profoundly just what a gift a horse is to an old rider.

Yes, riding could kill you, but if you are half-dead already and unlikely to improve in any miraculous way soon, what the hell!

We make our way down the hill through the streaming sun into the gloom of the pine woods, stippled with sunlight where it's been able to penetrate the tree canopy. Callum being Callum, there are small jerks of alarm and excitement at birds coming out of hedges or untoward sounds that only he can hear, my own hearing being as compromised as my knees and heart. These little jigs and jinks don't worry me, Callum is not a bolter, though on one or two occasions he has given it a good shot.

I lift both my legs alongside his neck to protect my knees as we edge our way through the Forest gate and for my pains there is some discomfort in doing this, but soon enough my legs are back where they should be. When he reaches level ground, I put him into a slow jog that he will hold for miles if need be, a very comfortable gait on this long-backed beast. My knees are not up to posting at the trot, though if needs be, I can manage a few yards of it. So, these days it's just walk, jog and very occasionally a short canter on grass or the soft going of the canter track behind the cottage..

It is still cold enough despite the sunshine that my arthritic hands are sore. So I put each one in my jacket pockets alternately to warm up as we jog our way alongside the stream that runs through the deciduous woods on the valley floor, oaks, chestnuts, beech in the main, with some silver birth and holly thrown in for good measure.

Just then Callum does a little sideways move to avoid a rock and I feel it sharply in my right hip. I slow him to a walk and lay my torso along his neck, a move that eases my hip and we continue for a few strides. To any observer it will look as if I am having a little cuddle with my horse but in fact it's the easiest way to relieve the stress on my hip.

None of this physical stuff detracts from the joy of being in the woods on this magnificent blood horse, a horse I have come to love and cherish for all his foibles. I can't be sure if it's my imagination or if Callum is going about his rides these days with more care for my wellbeing? He does far fewer of his mad whirls away from real or imagined horrors in the woods. Maybe he realises I am more fragile than some years ago?

An hour and a half sees us back at the stables and I am filled with the natural high of endorphins, buzzing. At the mounting block, Callum stands like a statue as I dismount. Once off his back, the full weight of those discarded 55 years returns with a thump, as though my old army sergeant has loaded my backpack with rocks once again for a spot of punishment drill. It takes me a full minute to adjust to the change and then I cautiously dismount the three steps of the block. My knees need some real mental and physical energy to control as I hobble up the yard to Callum's stable.

Carefully, I untack him, rub him down, and check his hay and water. My legs are loose and easier now though the old knees are burning. They will ease once I put them up on a sofa back at the cottage where I will have a third coffee of the morning and rerun the ride through my head. Then it's time for some writing work; thank God my brain has no need of knees!

Not one word of this is a complaint. I am only too aware what a privilege it is to ride, at this age more than any other. I think it a miracle that with my 75th birthday a few months off I am still able to ride. I do worry though about what will happen when I can no longer swing a leg across Callum's back. When my deepest held image of myself as a horseman is no longer something I can claim to be, what will that do to my head?

I have known one or two athletes and rugby players who are washed up at 30. It is a brutal end for them. Some have not been able to cope and have gone on to live a sort of twilight life and one has actually ended his life tragically. I have nothing to complain of, nothing. Seventy years of riding has given me golden memories that I have already started mining in my writing. Maybe that will be enough?

When Is It Time to Call Time on Riding?

Winter 2025

It is that time of year again, the end of January with half the winter done and another half to get through. It takes some grit to survive the English winter, especially as my first 30 years of life was spent in the sunshine of the southern hemisphere. This is a time to ask oneself questions.

Each morning and evening as I feed, water and muck Callum out, I inch closer to a decision about when to call time on this lifestyle choice of mine. I am giving this some serious thought. I have a knee replacement operation to get through this year. If all goes well that could be a game changer, and if so, I will soldier on till I just cannot throw a leg over my horse anymore.

But a small, nagging part of my brain argues for an end to the horse shenanigans. After all, I've now had 70 years in the saddle, surely that is enough for anyone? Currently I'm not riding, thanks to a broken rib that is taking some time to heal – six weeks, they say. I don't want to risk a punctured lung by riding my less than bombproof horse. I had one ride with the damaged rib and the odd jiggle had me gasping in the saddle. So now some kind of frustrated patience prevails.

All of this – winter blues and chest pain – is focusing my mind on a life without horses and as yet I cannot look this future is the eyes. I drop my gaze or glance away. It is a thought too horrible to contemplate. If someone asked me who I was, I could give many answers – media consultant, writer, husband, father, but my self-image is most wedded to that of being a horseman. That is who and what I most truly am, the rest are bolt on personas.

The longer I keep riding, the greater is the danger that I will end my life in a wheelchair. I know the odds, for I am less elastic, less fit, less robust than I once was and a fall now from my tall horse could well be catastrophic.

So I know in my very bones that the smart thing would be to quit while I am still ahead. And yet, and yet, the pull of the woods, the smell of spring, the dance of a fine horse beneath me, the feeling of being twenty again that comes to me in that deep comfortable saddle that has been home to me for so long. It is hard to give it all up.

A week ago, nursing that damn rib, I threw caution to the wind and gave Callum his head up the home hill. Those few hundred yards between the winter naked trees, rising, rising, up the hill, with that old rhythm of a cantering horse coursing through my veins, left me elated and filled with joy. My back was straight, my swing in the saddle still there, my eyes still focused on the path between those pointing ears. In that moment I once more tasted the honey of life and I am reluctant to give it up. Stupid? Maybe?

When you know that soon you will no longer be riding these trails and then, finally, you will not be here at all to make hoofprints in the dust or mud of home, the place takes on a kind of sanctity and each ride becomes a ritual not unlike a mass. The horse is in my blood, and the land will soon accept my body. We have made it ours by our co-operative venture here, covering each corner of this our hunting ground in fine straight and curving lines at walk, trot and canter with the odd burst of a gallop in special stretches where the going allows for such high jinks.

There is a beauty and bitter sweetness to this process that so appeals to one who loves marmalade. I am like one of those ancient beetles encasing itself in amber as its own memento-mori, a soul encased in eternal sunshine in this place I called my own.

We know the streams, the pines, the birch, the beech and the oak trees, the silver birch and the holly too, we know the gorse and the language of those who went before us memorialising this place in their own unique way – A.A. Milne sanctified it forever as a children's dream landscape with Winnie the Pooh and Christopher Robin, Eeyore and Piglet: Sir Arthur Conan Doyle used its mists and fogs to infuse the world of Sherlock Holmes with mystery; and the poet W.B. Yeats found here the 'bee-loud glades and the evenings filled with linnet's wings' that he'd been hunting ever since escaping London's pavements grey.

This place cupped its arms around me when, like a human fruit plucked from its tree too soon, I found myself adrift in the world, an unhappy exile from Africa. Slowly the gentle magic of this place soothed that hurt and helped me see that this too could be a home. Horses carried me hither and yon and like a frantic spider I rebuilt my web, destroyed by the 6,000 miles move north. These faithful horse friends carried a rider who no longer quite knew who he was. But the trees comforted me, the mosses smoothed my way, the streams accepted my tears and the northern summer sun warmed me. My riding was a displacement activity holding fear at bay.

So now in these last rides I have much to be grateful for and a landscape to thank, alongside the horses that rocked me as in a waking dream through, over and around this place, this second-chance-place that is now become my home, the second chamber of my heart, the first being the Cape, the second Sussex.

As I ride it now, I am become a part of it, now and forever, and I see that it is good. The last ride when it comes will have no special significance other than to paint the last stroke on a canvas that illustrates a life spent with horses. Who could ask for more?

I will be sorry when riding ends; but if that end is not

also my own, what golden seams of memory I will mine. No squirrel seeking his winter hoard will find greater riches. I will remember the horses on quiet nights as the winter land lies stilled, and summer friends long gone. Horses bedded on straw and cats lying quiet on corduroy. Pheasants strutting the lanes away from huntsmen-haunted woods, stored chestnuts and leaves that rustled, fermenting now on forest floors. The sun will be gone and with it work.

The winter land is still. And finally, so am I.

Snowdrops Signal the End of Winter

Winter 2024

Soon, soon, the woods will once more welcome the sound of Callum's hoofbeats between the beech, the birch and the oak. I know this thanks to the smallest white flower, the snowdrop, a flag of surrender from Old Man Frost, that winter has had its time.

No storm-tossed, seasick sailor after a journey of months at sea welcomes the sight of land as much as I'm heartened by the sight of snowdrops in January and February here in England. They say to me that the end of winter is in sight and that soon the mud, the ice and the cold will be but a memory and my horse and I can once more enter the verdant woody cloisters of Spring.

For me, a wild African violet, transplanted 6,000 miles north, the most spectacular fynbos landscape, filled with proteas, cannot hold the freight of joy and hope that this small pure shivery white bell holds within its delicate elegance.

D.H. Lawrence wrote in *Firelight and Nightfall*, 'Here lamps are white like snowdrops in the grass.' And truly, these pure white heads on grass-green stems are truly a light in the dark of an early winter evening, they nod in the wind and carry a freight of dew or rain, but there they are. Their message says to me that this northern earth is once more

opening up for the business of life.
    And Callum and I will be out there soon. Soon.

A LIFE SPENT WITH HORSES ON TWO CONTINENTS

Now and then, someone will ask me about the horses that have so enriched my life, and if there is a common thread that binds the disparate characters and experiences.

As I began writing, it was an unconscious exploration of those things that had meant most to me growing up, sea fishing and horse riding, two activities that took me deep into nature and solitude and self-exploration, a form of meditation, though at the time I would not have known that word or its meaning as I lost myself in the landscapes of the Cape in South Africa.

Later I would come to read and love nature writers like Richard Mabey, Roger Deakin, Robert Macfarlane, Barry Lopez, and travel writers Jonathan Raban and Paul Theroux, Paddy Leigh Fermor, whose travels on foot or by sea or by train was another way of exploring our world and its landscapes. Later I discovered the writers I have shared Sussex with, Rudyard Kipling, Arthur Conan Doyle, E.F. Benson, Virginia Woolf, W.B. Yeats, Ezra Pound, Hillaire Belloc and the Charleston Farmhouse gang.

I came to see, looking back at my course, my spoor, as they say in Africa, my birthplace, that there was indeed a pattern. It was a pilgrimage, in search of identity. My own, at birth, being two complex threads of very different peoples; the Jews of Lithuania, the Litvaks and the Protestant French

Dutch settlers in South Africa, two tribes in search of a new place to call home. I too have wandered the earth in search of a place, a landscape, to call my own. I can say now that I have two. Africa made me and England has added the rest.

I observed how the spirits of place impose their own colouring on one's identity. If there are figures in my landscapes, they are there not so much for themselves, but to illustrate the landscape within them.

Before I understood the terms forest bathing or the nature cure, or the sanctity of landscape ascribed to it by early man, I sensed something of this 'other' as I moved through the fynbos in South Africa and the woods and heathland, rarer than rainforest, that I found in East Sussex, England. And it was always on horses that I travelled these landscapes.

I searched and if I found a place for myself in this world, it was in Nature that I found the clearest answer, the greatest sense of being at home. That I was of a place I loved and that spoke to me and that in Nature I found my reason for being, the stringing together of worlds that attempts to explain the importance of Mother Earth to us humans and how our forgetting that has almost led to our annihilation as a species.

Looking back at the course my life has taken, I can clearly see the huge cost of emigration, of leaving the land of my birth and the pain of that irreplaceable loss of culture, of the shared humour of home cooking, of the lost landscapes that housed my soul and the many friendships left behind.

Someone once asked what it was like to emigrate at the age of 30, to start all over again. I flippantly replied that it was like having your legs cut off but you could still feel them through the pain.

When I visited South Africa years later to research a book, an academic asked me bitterly if I was back in the country to try to fill the 'hole in my soul'. He had a point. Maybe my writing is an attempt to find my amputated cultural legs. And my riding through Sussex landscapes a communing meditation with the landscape I have come to love so deeply.

It was my horses that carried me on this pilgrimage to find myself and my place in the world, it was horses that provided the door to a wider world and it was with horses that I rejoiced and it was horses that mended me when I felt broken. Horses have been the common thread that runs through the cloth of my life – like gold.

Hombre and Army Days Revisited

One of the joys of visiting family are the photographic memories that emerge after gathering dust for more than half a century.

This morning my brother placed in my hands a small plastic fold-out photo album the size of a wallet and suddenly I was back in 1969, in the army, with shaved head and my five-gaited American Saddler, Hombre, who accompanied me. I was suddenly transported back into the dustbowl cauldron of Oudtshoorn, home to a million ostriches, the Cango Caves and not much else besides the small town and the huge army barracks 300 miles north of my parents' home in Cape Town.

I was an unworldly 19-year-old, rather dazed by the heat and the army life. But twice a week, Wednesday and Saturday afternoons, I was allowed out past the guard posts and barbed wire to go and exercise my horse. I'd struck a deal with the local traffic cop to look after my horse at the small local showground stables. He rode a massive Harley Davidson and had an elderly horse that now and then he would take out for a meander in the dusty hills.

The sense of wild freedom that accompanied my own rides, away from the choking army discipline was intoxicating. Hombre and I would set off for the farms that spread thinly into the hills.

Sitting deep in the saddle, I would give him his head

and off we'd go at a brisk rolling gait which ate up the miles. It was almost impossible to pass any of the farm homesteads where Hombre's good looks were soon noted among the horse-loving farmers, and we would be hailed. 'Kerel Kom drink koffie!' 'Hey, young man, come and drink coffee!' Unable to resist, I would urge Hombre into his show-stopping rack and with front hooves flying, we'd make our entry into the farmyard.

I would either hitch the horse to a post or one of the farm labourers would take him off to eat lucerne (alfalfa) in the cool of some whitewashed stone stable. It suited him well. I would be shown to a rocking chair or rawhide strip bench on the stoep (veranda) and one of the shy daughters of the house would bring coffee and koeksisters, sweet pastries.

Horse talk would keep us going until the sun began to set and I would make my thanks and set off back to the showgrounds and then on to my own barrack quarters.

Those rides in the hills among the ostriches were 'time out' in the most profound sense of that phrase. I had been treated as an honoured guest, a fellow horseman. My army status as the lowest of the low, a squaddie, grunt, infantryman in basics was briefly forgotten in those few hours. And the sometimes shy, sometimes bold stares of the daughters of the house would add a thrill – a possible promise of more than pastries. It was all rather bewitching. Then, like Cinderella's coach and horses turning into a pumpkin, I would re-enter the army camp and become once more a half-baked trainee soldier, not sure of his ass or his elbow.

I looked intently at these two small photographs from 1969 and a small pain filled me. Sitting here today in California sunshine with the sounds of breaking surf below the sea cliff, I could once more taste the red African dust and smell the kakiebos as the years rolled back.

But I also recall the gaits of that magnificent horse and the joy of escaping the army for a few hours. Wherever you are, Hombre, may you have the sweetest grass, crystal clear water and kind memories of that bewildered boy who loved you, trying to puzzle out this damn business called life.

After nine months of my national service, I walked through those army gates for the last time. Hombre was on a train headed home to Cape Town. There was a thin rain falling, settling the dust. And as I drove my grandmother's old car she'd given me out of Oudtshoorn, hundreds upon hundreds of ostriches were dancing in the rain, wings outstretched, doing a stately minuet as though to celebrate my release. I rolled down the car windows, gave a rebel yell and at a steady 80mph raced the train bearing my horse home.

Slip Sliding Away

I'm writing this having just got back from an eventful hour and a half ride and am enjoying a belated breakfast – coffee and white sourdough toast with marmalade as usual. My pleasure in the meal is added to by the feeling that it is good to be alive. Is that too dramatic? Not really, but you decide once you've heard my story.

I did not ride this weekend as the weather was miserable and I did not fancy getting wet. So this morning I decided I must get Callum out. He was calm as I saddled up after he'd had his breakfast some time before. We headed out, down the hill and into the woods. At our first grassy slope I felt just how wet it was, with Callum slip-sliding even on the way uphill.

The Forest paths were boggy and covered in the huge leaf-fall, making it difficult to see the worst parts beneath. When riding Callum, a long-backed horse, I have to work hard to keep his back end engaged and doing its fair share of work. He is only too happy to slop along on the forehand, losing his rear end in anything slippery. A year or two back, he fell down flat on a hard dry gravel path we were riding, so I know he lacks something in the footwork department. And not wanting a 1,500lb horse rolling on me, I am very aware of giving him the right aids.

But this morning the muddy going disguised beneath leaves made things trickier than usual. At one point he slipped badly when he stood on an unseen log under the leaf mould and his feet skated over the wood's slimy hard surface, almost causing him to land on his nose.

After that, we went even more cautiously, the going reminding me of driving on black ice, only nominally in charge of my vehicle. Now and then, despite having my legs on him firmly, he lost his rear end and felt as though he might be going down. But each time he found a 'fifth leg' and we soldiered on through the woods, skeletal now and bare of all leaf.

It was beautiful in its own stripped back way, the woods black and brown and grey against a pale sky. Slowly we made our way into Five Hundred Acre Wood. I kept a sharp eye out for the camber of the paths as I know in this slippery going, the slightest slope just adds to the potential for disaster. Callum wasn't much fazed by any of this but I certainly was aware of the constant tension of looking out for him. Despite my best efforts, now and then he would hit a really boggy bit and would slip or stumble. I was heading for a part of the Forest where gravel paths would make for much safer going, but we had to cut through this wood first.

But Callum being Callum every now and then he would jerk or shake or jump at a wood pigeon flapping too close or a squirrel hurtling through the canopy or scuttling up a tree trunk. Each time I would collect him again and speak quietly, encouraging him.

Finally, we broke free of this morass and jogged a bit out into the sunshine on the heather and bracken heights. I stopped him by a rivulet and let him have his regulation drink, one for the road as it were, and we went on our way.

We crossed the B2028 road at Wood Reeves and headed down the hill that leads home. For reasons best known to himself, the big fella decided to get a bit lit up and we sashayed down the hill, with me keeping him on a firm rein. As we crossed the two old stone bridges on the valley floor there was some head tossing and small leaps – the horse wanted to gallop up the home hill. So when his energy seemed liable to explode, I just circled him time and again and in this odd way we made our way relatively slowly up the hill. As the stable yard came in sight, he relaxed and went back into slopping along mode. I relaxed too. Too soon.

Just then, I spotted a neighbour with one of her huge Great Danes off the lead. Just the week before, one of her dogs had run at Callum, causing him to gallop off down the hill. So I collected him sharply, which was just as well, as the second Great Dane came dashing round the corner, oblivious to the owner's shouts. Callum dropped his left shoulder, whirled round and headed off downhill at a flat out run on a badly rutted surface. It took me the best part of 100 yards to stop him and turn him back up the hill.

All the while the owner of the dogs was shouting and cussing at her dogs. I was furious but said nothing in response to her apologies. This was the second time in ten days that this had happened. What would make her realise that walking two huge pony-sized dogs, off the lead, in a horse-riding area was not a great idea? I said nothing but looked daggers.

Two minutes later I dismounted at the stable yard, happy to be home safe. And back at the cottage, the toast and coffee tasted better than usual. It had been just an hour and a half in the woods, but I felt as though I had been on a mini-Odyssey.

RIDING AS ART

When I was very young, the beauty of the world overwhelmed me and I wanted to be a painter, an artist. I drew and painted endlessly, Table Mountain, flowers, trees, seashells, horses, people's faces. But life had something else in store for me, a passion for horses and landscape and stories. And now at the tail end of my life, I find myself to be a writer, an author of stories about landscapes and horses and people.

I have ridden the landscapes of three continents, Africa, Europe and America, and I belatedly came to see and to appreciate that my twisty, bushwhacking, 'bundu-bashing' trails in the African metaphor, were my canvas and my horses my brushes. When the works of land artists like Richard Long's Stone Circles, Andy Galsworthy's 'Sand Edges' on a beach, Maya Lin's grassed 'Earthwaves', Robert Smithson's 'Spiral Jetty', became recognised and established, it struck me that I too had been creating art of a sort in my criss-cross hatching of trails across the countrysides I have loved, the Cape, East Sussex, California.

And then I put those trails into tales and into books so that any reader who rode with me would have access to the places and people and horses who made drumbeats on the earth, imprinting hoof marks, leaving a soft soundscape of our passing amid the birds and the squirrels, the Port Jackson scrub, the dunes, beaches, marram grasses of the Cape, the deciduous oak, beech, chestnut, holly and birch woods of East Sussex, and the burnt umber rolling grasslands, hills and vineyards of California.

My art is even more ephemeral than that of the land artists, theirs lasts for weeks and months, mine is gone in my passing through, but an echo dimly repeats on the pages of my books. Maybe photos shot from a drone would offer an image not unlike the wild cohesion of a Jackson Pollock painting, capturing my crawls, canters and gallops like the frantic or quiet contemplative movement of an ant crawling across a landscape.

For those of us who ride amid heart stopping beauty, this thought of mine must surely too have crossed your minds. We are making art of our lives on horseback, alone out there amid creation, quiet and at peace or filled with wonder and joy, inspired by creation we cut our own engravings on the earth, and find them beautiful.

The Message of an English Winter

Winter 2024

It's that time of the year again. A time when one has to stiffen one's sinews, boost morale and brace up generally. It's winter in England with a horse to keep going through to Spring.

Last week Callum lost a shoe in his field, one of the new circular expensive ones with rubber pads and putty beneath it. I took a long walking stick down to the paddock and squelched about in my wellies poking into each deep imprint in search of that damn shoe. But no joy, sadly. It's just another reminder that easeful summer is gone and a harder season is with us once more.

As I ride through the woods with Callum, I notice here and there a message I missed in sunnier times. Crocked, fallen, broken trees that have not given up the ghost but are still growing, soldiering on – and it speaks to my heart. As an old crock myself, their message seems to be, 'Endure; this too shall pass'. Your shape and litheness may have gone, but this soil is still feeding you. Carry on carrying on!

And I do. It gives me a shot in the arm to see oaks upended with half their root systems exposed, but still in leaf from the summer past. There are any number of beech trees lying parallel to the earth that have shot a new trunk skywards. A one-time branch that is now the new trunk, vertical and bonny looking. Coppiced chestnuts that now sprout four trunks where previously there was just one. It is a small everyday wooden miracle and a clear message for this old man and his horse, both a bit broken but not giving up.

    Not yet.
    Not yet.

A Spring in Callum's Step

Winter 2025

This grey February morning, Callum and I left the stable yard early to avoid the rain that had been forecast and we had an hour-long ride, staying dry, with the heavens opening just as I got off at the mounting block back at the yard.

What made this a really lovely ride was the gladdening sight of the first daffodils, sunshine on green stems and the shy purity of snowdrops. The crocuses and primroses are up as well. It seems like we've come through another winter in England. Though I'm not kidding myself that it's the end of the rain and storms. We've had snow in May here many a time.

The old ribs are mended, and Callum is going sound. When I urged him forward on the canter-track up the back hill through the woods, he was more than happy to shake a leg, despite the mud. We were heading home, after all.

At the yard as I was dismounting, there was a welcome surprise: Julie, a near neighbour and a nurse for forty years, appeared on her new purchase, Olive, a 6-year-old 16-hand dark bay Thoroughbred mare off the racetrack. A perfect example of a light-boned ladies' hack. She has the nicest nature and a very elegant blood Arab head.

Julie lives with her husband Maurice on a small farm up the hill from us, where they have raised four sons and keep some pigs and a couple of beef bullocks, all destined

Into the Enchanted Forest with Callum

for their deep freeze. For some years now, she has been saying that when she retires from nursing she was going to buy a horse and ride the Forest again as she did in her youth. Frankly I had wondered if this was just a pipe dream, but here was proof that dreams can and do come true. She found Olive on Horsequest among the increasing numbers of former Thoroughbred racehorses for sale at prices more affordable than most. At present, Olive needs some building up, but once she has a summer at grass under her belt, she will blossom into a lovely horse.

Callum was gagging to say hello, but we just allowed the two to nod a greeting to each other and then I stabled my lad. Enough excitement for one morning – flowers, woodland canters and a new horse friend!

Back home, having breakfast in the warm, the promised rain let rip and I congratulated myself on our dry ride amid the daffodils.

CALLUM AND THE WHITE CLIFFS OF DOVER

Spring 2025

Life throws you some curve balls that's for sure. And with age they come thick and fast, many more curve balls than usual. Forgive me if I get a bit dark here for a bit. As the writer Meera Syal named her TV series: *Life isn't all Ha Ha Hee Hee.*

A medical friend described life after sixty as living in 'Snipers Alley' and never a truer word was said on this subject. You begin to lose friends and relatives, and it is borne in on you that you too are getting close to the jumping-off point.

With this realisation comes the question of putting your affairs in order, wills, living wills etc. And then one day it strikes you that your dog and cat and horse could possibly outlive you if they are relatively young. And you realise there are hard decisions to make about their future.

So, what to do with Callum? Jan is ten years younger than me so the cat and dog are sorted with luck, but she would not want to ride Callum; he is just too big and has already managed to break her shoulder in that unscheduled dismount some years back. Despite this, they are fond of each other. But, that said, Jan is big on forgiveness; I have been a beneficiary of this quality of hers, so Callum will be OK. And what if we both go at once? Our animals are all written into our wills, so it's reassuring to know that our family will either take them in or find them good new homes.

It would be so helpful to know just how long this riding lark will last, with me still able to throw a leg over the horse's back. And even more useful to know when 'Joe Black' is going to arrive with an invitation that there is no saying no to. But there is just no knowing. Callum is 16 and I am about to be 75. In my dreams I think I might just about push it to 80, God willing. That would mean Callum is 21 when he marches in my funeral procession. A fairly old horse for a monster with arthritis.

Living less than an hour's drive from the White Cliffs of Dover, it has struck me on occasion that a last wild gallop on the South Downs which run along the top of the famous cliffs that face across the Channel to France, might solve my and Callum's problems. Imagine that run and final parabola out into the sky and then into the sea. What a way to go! What an entrance we'd make at the Gates of Hell!

The irony of all this malarkey is that six years ago at the age of 69 I bought Callum as my last horse, my 'Old Man's Horse'. The deal was that this giant warmblood would plant me somewhere out on the Forest, avoiding all need of hospitals and old age homes and diapers. But though on occasion I thought it was coming, he has not carried out his part of the bargain, so this is why I am stuck considering my options.

These are not happy thoughts, they give me no joy, but there is no escaping them. They are part of the rich tapestry that comes with age, while taking part in a dangerous sport. Life no doubt will sort it out one way or another.

Just then Callum snuffles my hair and I know I just don't have it in me to destroy this horse. He has become my literary partner, my writing pal, my fellow Forest wanderer. The great lump has become my friend.

But do keep an eye on the White Cliffs of Dover!

TROUBLE AT DINGLY DELL

Spring 2025

If you've ridden horses for any length of time, you know in your bones that this is a risky hobby that you are embarked on. And the older you get the greater the risks and the shorter the odds.

A good example of what can happen out of the blue, bit me in the butt this morning, on what was a perfect spring day, 9 March 2025, my late father's birthday.

The sun was shining, the birds were singing and all suggested a good time for a ride. An hour after he'd had his breakfast, Callum and I headed out into the woods at 8.30am. We sloped down to the lake, then cut across the hill and down to the little river crossing known as Dingly Dell by the riders from our yard. I must have been through it hundreds of times over the 40-plus years we've lived here and it's no big deal. There is a gentle slope down to the stream on either side and it is just 3ft across, a rivulet really, at this time of the year. In summer, it almost dries up.

We crossed the stream and chose one of the ways up the far side, heading for the open fields beyond. The path up narrowed to a deep muddy cut just wide enough for a horse to get through. But since I'd ridden this path, a small 2ft high gorse bush had spread halfway across the path. Gorse is immensely prickly, and horses don't like going through it. But I figured Callum wouldn't mind a slight brush of it against his legs as we passed. I judged wrong. Callum swung away from the gorse bush, intent on lifting himself out of the cut and onto a parallel path, but in doing so lost his footing and fell down flat on his face. For a second, my feet in the stirrups touched the ground.

Then with one immense heave the big horse got himself out of that like a cat and we were onto the dry grass fields. Both of us had quite a fright – for a second it felt as if a shadow had crossed the sun. It might have ended so differently had he hurt or broken a leg or struggled to right himself but slipped sideways, trapping me beneath him. It could so easily have ended in hospital or worse.

As we moved off, I checked his stride. He seemed fine, so we made our way slowly to a lovely pool at another river crossing a little further down the valley, where I let him cool his legs in the water for ten minutes. All seemed sorted, so we walked on home, and he was sound. When we got to the yard I led him out to a grass paddock for a roll and watched him closely to see if he was favouring a leg, or if his back muscles were sore. But all appeared well. I ran my hands over his legs and his back and his neck, but all felt fine. I then hosed him down in the warm sunshine, scraped the water off his gleaming gold coat and put him in his box with his huge hay net for the day.

I will only truly know if there is any damage this evening when I take him out of his box to check on his legs and back. If there is stiffness, I will give him some Bute in his feed and check him tomorrow morning again. This unfortunate fall is not the first. Callum is a very stumbly horse, partly due to flat feet I think, and partly due to the fact that he does not watch where he is going, his mind and eyes are always up ahead, looking for monsters. It has never stopped me riding him and this latest fall won't either, but it does remind me how close the line is between safety and disaster. There must be some pretty damn powerful drug that keeps us riding.

Some hours later I'm just back from the evening feed and muck out. All is well. Callum hoovered his food up as usual and then strolled round the indoor with no sign of anything amiss. We live to ride another day!

Out There Again

Spring 2025

I found myself feeling decidedly twitchy this morning. I'd done Callum, feeding him his breakfast, mucking out, letting him have a leg stretch in the indoor. Not that he did much but womble about, smelling the sand in places. And doing some standing and staring.

I went back to the cottage and did all my work stuff, and suddenly it was noon. The weather was grey and overcast as it's been for days, and more days of it yet to come, but no rain or wind,. Quite a still day and not freezing, nor particularly cold. My ribs were virtually healed after three weeks, allowing me to roll over in bed without wincing.

During the past weeks I had watched endless horse programmes on YouTube, as well as sailing in every part of the globe, and enough food programmes to sate even my endless greed for great grub. I had read so many books and watched what seems the whole of the Netflix offering. I'd had enough of being a spectator!

It came to me that I could go for a ride, the first in two months, the time off due to holiday and business travel and those damn ribs. And that is when the magical thinking nonsense kicked in. Should I risk it before the two important doctors' appointments in a few days? The annual heart check-up, and a first meeting with my knee surgeon. Maybe better to wait till after those were done.

Callum has been out in his field on and off these past

two months, depending on just how bad the weather's been and been lunged in the round pen and in the indoor school. And when sent in there loose for a run round, he has barely got out of a walk. He was pig fat and lazy and not at all crazy for lack of exercise. So why the magical thinking and a touch of the collywobbles? Well two months off is two months off and at this age it takes a little impetus to get back in the saddle again. I told myself not to be a wuss. And one more day on the couch and I'd be climbing the walls. Go ride! So I did.

Callum saw me coming with his saddle and bridle and pawed the ground and drummed his knees on the stable door. I had the slightest of wobbles but pushed past it. Body protector on, riding helmet on. Back into the waxed jacket and then saddle the lad up. The girth leathers were damp and slippery, and I struggled to get them to the seventh hole. He really had piled the pounds on. Finally, I mounted at the block, and we were out of the yard heading down the hill to the woods and I felt my spirits begin to rise.

We walked and jogged and had one short canter. Callum was as good as gold. I need not have concerned myself. The woods were sodden, so we stayed on the gravel paths as much as possible. There were a number of trees down since my last ride pre-California.

There were faint traces of birdsong, the hand-clapping sound of wood pigeons taking off and in the distance, the first woodpecker of spring hammering away. A fox crossed our path some hundred yards ahead of us and I saw a solitary deer halfway up a wooded hill.

Callum checked slightly when he spotted a carp fisherman down by the lake. I greeted the man and he called a cheery hello back and on we went. At the second old Victorian bridge, just before the home hill, the horse checked slightly again, as half the path was cordoned off by orange plastic tape. The bridge had crumbled a little on the left. We walked past swiftly, not wanting to test the bridge too long with the weight of this horse. And then it was a nice jog up the hill home.

Sitting here at home once more on my cosy blanketed couch with a coffee and a sandwich, I count the little victories and am well pleased with both my horse and me. Back in the saddle again. Tonight I will clean my tack and oil it and let it dry out properly. Tomorrow I plan to be out again.

CALLUM'S COMING OF AGE?

Spring 2025

May I brag about my horse a little? (Knowing full well that pride cometh before a fall).

I'm aware that I'm not always Callum's biggest fan. He stumbles, he falls down, he whirls away 180 degrees and gallops off. He is a bit of a bloody prima donna. When it rains and the wind blows, he wants to come in immediately. But there is another side to the big lad.

We've had a number of really good days recently with some testing stuff for him to deal with and he has been more than good; he has come through them all with flags flying and a red rosette from me.

Two weeks ago, I was exiting the Forest at Wood Reeves, about to cross the road and head home down the green tree tunnel when a low rumbling noise and an odd tarry smell stopped Callum dead. Just up ahead, outside the black and white house, was the most enormous road tarring machine, the size of a combine harvester, with two guys up in the glassed-in cabin.

Callum and I stood watching it at work for a full minute and as we did, I was mentally whisked 6,000 miles south to my 7-year-old self, walking in the soft tar being laid down on our suburban road in Newlands, Cape Town. I also recalled walking the melting tar roads around our summer house at Bloubergstrand, my feet so hard from a summer barefoot on the ocean rocks that I felt nothing but a gentle warmth from the oozy blackness.

To my surprise, Callum seemed more intrigued than freaked out by the huge contraption and having had a good gander at the machine, calmly crossed the road and we headed home. His early years from 4 to 11 on a busy farm stands him in good stead.

It must be said that this good behaviour and general helpfulness is not that rare. Just last week riding up the hill to access the Forest, I reached a neighbour's house in the woods only to find red and white tape cordoning off the path ahead, past their home. A tree surgeon was 100ft up in a cherry-picker among the canopy, lopping chunks off an oak tree that was endangering the telephone cables strung between poles. Yes, we still use landlines in the UK from time to time.

Callum took a keen interest in the goings on as huge lengths of oak descended with a thump, hitting the ground right in front of us. Eventually Ed, the neighbour who was directing operations, saw us and called a halt to the proceedings, just long enough to let us through. Callum sashayed past the cherry-picker's engine without turning a hair! To say I was astonished about sums it up. He was as cool as a cucumber.

All this good behaviour is making me a bit suspicious and wanting to find answers. I wondered about a young lad who visits the stables from time to time to feed mints to the horses. Was he giving them something different? Maybe Callum was getting a weekly doses of CBD gummies and was high as a kite!?

Today, I decided to ride early and then put him out for a few hours on the spring grass till lunchtime when I had an errand to run. So, after a brief one-hour ride round the hill, past the lake and home, I had a brainwave – I would ride him down the quarter mile to his field and leave his tack there and later on ride him back to the stable yard to save myself time, and my knees some aggravation.

Now I know that what follows is absolutely no big deal if you're a fit teen or 20-year-old, but for a 74-year-old, semi cripple, it took some doing I can tell you and my horse helped me do it every step of the way.

We got to the top gate, a solid wooden five-bar affair, which was closed of course. I struggled to lift the latch and push the gate open with one hand, my left, but the latch kept falling back. And in struggling I was all over Callum's neck. He stood firm. I then realised I should use my left hand to undo the latch and push the gate open with my right hand which meant leaving the reins completely. After a couple of tries I managed, and Callum pushed the gate wide open with his chest.

We then rode down to his own paddock, and I dismounted, using the steel five-bar gate, while he stood alongside it. Jumping down, or sliding off, this big horse is pure torture for my knees, so I need a mounting block, or a makeshift mounting block, and the gate worked great, thanks to Callum standing like one of those black chargers on guard outside Buckingham Palace.

I untacked him and rubbed his ears and sent him on his way, telling him what a good boy he was. Just before lunch I went down to get him. I tacked him up, fully prepared to lead him up the hill if I could not mount. Long gone are my vaulting days. But once more he stood where I needed him to, next to the five-bar gate again which I struggled up, bracing myself against the horse's neck and the saddle. I had left the top gate open so that was no problem, and then we were back in the stable yard alongside the mounting block. The whole thing took ten minutes.

To say I was pleased does not do justice to how warmly I felt towards Callum. I know only too well how some horses would have fussed, bobbed, ducked and weaved through any and all of these manoeuvres. Callum was like an old war horse, a proper soldier. Tonight, he is getting double rations and I'm having steak!

Maybe at 17 the great lump is finally growing up!

My Riding Dreamspace

As I criss-cross the Forest on Callum I'm aware that I ride on the dreams of many. So it is for us, as we make our way through this enchanted place. All about us, like the scattered, layered leaves of autumn, lie the dreams of those who walked and rode here before us.

This is a place apart. It is a few miles square of dreamspace set down in Sussex. To the north is the mad heaving of London, filled with ten million struggling lives. To the south is bustling Brighton, sedate Eastbourne and Hastings where life remains a battle. To the west are Gatwick and Heathrow airports with Slough beyond, where the poet John Betjeman's bombs have yet to drop. To the east is open country all the way to Canterbury and its tourist coaches. Above us the groan of heavy-laden planes, their noise like the lions roaring through my childhood in Africa.

Amid all this busyness, the Forest is a sanctuary. Here business has no remit, nor work, nor want. Here there is peace, not a lot, but enough. It is a fragile peace, one easily disturbed, by fire, by rain, by wind, by noise. But for now it holds the line – for dreams and dreamers. They pass by softly, their thoughts add meaning to these acres, they hang on trees and cover bushes, they settle gently to the ground, covering paths and gorse and bracken, loading all, lightly as snow, with feeling.

I ride among them. What thoughts, what fantasies. Here are trees as well as serried ranks of prayerful thanks. Here are ponds, and thoughts, reflecting God. Here be distant views and yet more distant hopes. Earth, wind and fire, each and every element is here, and so is man, but gentle with it, seeking solace.

I came to this place with little and it has given generously. I have a blood tie to it now. Here it was I first held my son and saw my daughter walk. There is a link of birth and blood now. This is a landscape of dreams fulfilled, and dreams to be, with luck.

Ashdown dreamspace. The horse knows it well. It's why his ears are pricked and his steps light. He knows that here is both a world and intimations of worlds beyond. I heed him well. Together we dream this place as it dreams us.

LOVE AMONG THE TREES

Spring 2025

I have ridden in South Africa's beautiful Cape for 30 years, the magical Ashdown Forest for 45 years and had the odd ride in California, in the rolling hill country back of Santa Barbara. All have offered beauty, peace and the odd excitement.

But the Forest is different in one respect. After dark, when the dog walkers and most horse riders have gone home for supper, a new group, courting couples, take ownership of these woods and heathlands. They don't bother Callum, or me for that matter, most of them don't even see us, so wrapped up are they in each other.

One of the little understood or appreciated benefits of the twenty-first century is that most lovemaking occurs in the comfort of a bed, a room, a home – or at least a place with a roof and a floor. It was not always so. In past centuries, when mankind lived in small groups as hunter gatherers or subsistence farmers, we lived cheek by jowl – there was virtually no privacy. So married or courting couples found comfort, solace and pleasure in the woods and fields, far from prying eyes. Babies were made at the foot of a tree or in the long grass.

And this particular pleasure – the call of the wild in the wild – lives on in places like this, one of the last places in the southeast to be tamed and Christianised. It was a rough old place until very recently, the home of outlaws, highwaymen,

Into the Enchanted Forest with Callum

gypsies. It came late into the fold of so-called civilisation and that is one of its great appeals.

This place remains a magnet for lovers whose living arrangements make beds, floors and roofs a luxury not at their disposal. How do I know this? Well, from first-hand observation over 45 years. As I ride its 6,500 acres by day and by night, it is perfectly obvious to me and my horse that this largest of the great open spaces left in crowded South East England continues to attract lovers. So Callum and I tread discreetly, and detour when necessary.

You have only to think back to the lockdowns of the Covid pandemic years, when the Forest car parks were rammed as never before with people desperate for some space, some fresh air, some reconnection with nature, and to escape the close confines of their homes. And maybe to find some privacy in the woods where love might bloom?

Each and every Forest car park has its appeal, from the excitements of Box Park near Ellison's Ponds to the more discreet charms of Wood Reeves or Gills Lap car park near The Enchanted Place. While the pubs, the night clubs and the discos have their own appeal to lovers, there is a breed of nature lovers, couples who mimic our forebears and find Eden and ecstasy on Ashdown Forest. The Old Pagan Gods are smiling, the Green Man of the Woods too, and our mother Gaia knows it of old.

There is a nice symmetry to Ashdown after dark, for here too you will find the dead, their ashes spread in much-loved spots, one of them a friend of mine, and one day soon, my own too maybe. So here we have both the living and the dead, some restless, some at rest. It is fitting, for you can't just have the making of life without the breaking.

Love is all around you here; even as the incoming aircraft headed for Gatwick groan and roar overhead, they find an echo amid the bracken. Long may it be so. Sheets, beds, roofs and floors may be very well on a cold winter's night, but in the warmth of a blue summer dusk, the Forest has a far greater magic.

As my horse and I head home, my thoughts turn back fifty-five years to my own memories of love amid the salt wind and marram grasses of a distant shore. And I smile, happy that in some respects, the world is unchanged.

A Spring of Yellow Gorse and Lemon Sunshine

Spring 2025

As Callum and I meander between massed yellow displays of gorse bushes on Ashdown Forest I think of Pooh Bear's issue with the prickly plant. His experience with gorse bushes was not a happy one, having once fallen from a tree and found himself stuck in a bush, which led to him saying that a gorse bush had sprung at him suddenly and that it took him six days to get all the prickles out of himself. He described the prickly yellow plant as an 'am-bush'. Spot on, they are prickly.

Callum is blithely unbothered by the prickles, eating the flowers delicately but with relish, the smell of coconut is quite intoxicating. As he munches, we are surrounded by an orchestral symphony of birdsong, with the drumroll of woodpeckers as a backdrop, and the cuckoo's call the soloist. The land may be dry, but this sound-a-round Niagara offers a multiplicity of notes that mimic falling rain.

It is now the first week of April, the fifth week without rain in this unusually dry spring of 2025. We could actually do with some rain to help the spring grass come on. In the paddocks the horses have eaten the grass down to the roots among the ankle-turning hoof imprints in what was mud just six weeks ago. Now the fields are dusty.

The sun is like a honeyed benediction and my horse

and I move through it with all the ease and pleasure of a dolphin surfing. The sun at 16 degrees is warm enough to lift the spirits and massage old bones, without any of the red chilli heat of the summer to come. It is a blessing, warm day following warm day, with none of the turmoil of the usual English spring - wet, windy, cold and sunny by turns, repeated endlessly. There is just this still, calm sunshine which seems as if it might go on forever. And billowing waves of yellow gorse, as though the sunshine is now also erupting from the earth. What would Pooh Bear say to all this? Callum likes it and so do I.

We leave the Forest's open heathland, a blazing golden horse amid the blazing yellow gorse and enter the cool woods again, heading home. Movement in the trees catch my eye. It's a squirrel racing up a birch like a thermometer dipped in hot water, sending the silver mercury racing to the top. Mercurial squirrels, the comparison is so apt, I smile. By the time we reach the lake, Callum and I have sent three other squirrels reaching for the sky. Silver grey streaks up mottled trunks.

And as if all this were not enough, the swallows have just arrived from Africa! They are cleaning out their nests in the stable rafters, their 6,000-mile journey over at last, till September anyway. Born in Africa myself, this is my annual opportunity to show I've learned something here in England - this annual arrival is always an emotional moment, but my upper lip is holding firm, with just the odd quiver.

So now it's official, spring is here!

A dry spell lasting weeks through all of March and half of April is a first for all our 45 years in East Sussex. It has shortened the interminable English winter considerably this year. However, the weather forecasters are predicting rain this weekend - and it will be welcome, as it is now much needed to bring on the spring grass. The ground is like iron. Callum cannot believe his good fortune to have had weeks of sunshine on his back. It's done him the world of good and he is looking very well.

We were out early this morning for a ride through the woods and then out onto the open heathland of the Forest itself. Callum has sussed that there is a smorgasbord of yellow gorse flowers available for his delectation and when I let him, he strolls from bush to bush, snacking as we go.

We took a semi-secret route this morning to one of his favourite lookout spots in the elbow of the valley in which we live. It is home to a spectacular farm in a sylvan setting. Callum likes to stand and stare for as long as I will let him, and this morning we spotted a herd of deer and a single buzzard quartering the fields, for rabbits I expect.

Out on the heathland a few minutes later, we were hailed by a couple of riders on a grey and a bay coming out of Hundred Acre Wood who asked if it would be OK to canter off ahead of us. I said it would be fine and off they went. Just to settle Callum I steered him to a snacking distance of a gorse bush and he was happy with the deal, rather to my surprise.

We then took a slightly different path to that of the horses and Callum slopped along. He still surprises me from time to time – I am never sure if it's the tiger or the pussycat I will be getting on any given day.

A Farewell Foretold

I was riding past the lake at the bottom of our hill in bright sunlight, the images of the fringing trees reflected as if in a mirror. Callum was finally calm after a 40-minute ride up and down some hills and strode along, casting a look at the ducks on the lake now and then. He knows that they can take off with an explosion of noise, so keeps an eye on their antics.

And then, suddenly, without warning it was as if I had ridden into another dimension, a place where past, present, and future were one. I was no longer only riding the horse but was also some way back and above the horse and rider, observing myself on Callum. It was disconcerting until it came to me that I was a ghost seeing my past self on the horse in a landscape that had been my home for 45 years, or was it the horse and rider who were the ghosts? A deep calm settled on me as I watched the movements of the horse and my figure from the back, the passing trees, and the shadows across the path. The sunlight on the water and its passage through the winter trees.

I felt a great affection for horse and rider and a sadness too, seeing how ephemeral they were, a horseman passing by. I was being given an insight into my own passing. The knowledge that I would not be riding for much longer has been ever present in my mind and maybe this powered my subconscious to produce this strange, elegiac moment. I looked fondly on the figure of a horseman moving through a landscape as familiar to him as his own hands.

And then, as suddenly as I had departed my body, I was once more physically back on the horse with all the intensity that comes with riding. It was all distinctly strange. But I felt it as a gift too, a chance to say goodbye before my actual departure. Rather like an airport farewell to friends before going through customs and the departure lounge.

It came to me then how swiftly the four and a half decades had passed and the preceding three as well. A lifetime measured out in hoofbeats. At the stables some minutes later, three men got off the horse, the man present, the man past and the future man, no longer riding. It was a bittersweet gift, but a gift all the same. As a horseman, I know you don't look a gift horse in the mouth.

The Forest is waiting for me to leave, to become a little wilder again, a little less visited in its dark green heart. It won't miss me or my horse, forever touching bark, breaking branches, eating leaves, churning up soil, leaving hoofprints. It will return to its primordial sleep with the rising and falling of water columns in its many trunks, a silent unheard breathing, undisturbed in what passes for peace in this pastoral setting.

But I like to think that some form of wood memory, of fungal brain, has somehow registered my presence and maybe my passing too. That vegetative memory held within a forest floor and 100-ton beech trunks will do me for a marker; that a horseman visited this place for a few years and then was gone.

FRIENDS IN NEED

Spring 2025

The DIY livery yard next door where Callum has lived this past six years is closing down, prior to its sale along with the farm. The date of its closure has coincided with my first knee replacement on 30 April 2025, so it's been a bit of a scramble to get something set up for Callum while I'm hors de combat.

Luckily, a big stable has suddenly come free at the yard where Jan boards Traveller – just ten minutes from home and right in the heart of the Forest. So that is where we moved him this morning with the help of Sophie's horsebox driven by her dad, Brett. Thanks guys!

Callum has not been in a horsebox for six years, when he was delivered to us, but he strolled onto the lorry like an old hand, travelled well and then moseyed down the drive at the new yard, looking about him with great interest and grabbing grass as he went. So that is Callum sorted. Isn't it strange how the Universe (and friends) provide help when help is much needed.

My only concern about this arrangement is whether Callum will be happy leaving his friend Traveller and other new friends to return to our own stables in the garden on his own when I am recovered from my knee replacement. He was given a very warm welcome at his new digs from Jane, Rachel and Rowena and looks most content.

When I am fully recovered, a near neighbour has

kindly offered a field just across the lane from our cottage and another friend has offered two hardy ponies to keep Callum company when he is out grazing. And there is a huge seven-acre field in reserve, just down the lane at Barry Shaw's, next door to Kim Sibson's ponies, if needed.

So my cup, and Callum's, is overflowing. Thanks one and all.

A New Knee, A New Day, A New Dawn

Spring 2025

The knee replacement surgery this week went well, thanks to the wonderful team at the Horder Centre, five minutes from home – and now I am back at the cottage again after a three-day stay in the medical world. My worst fear – finding myself awake and able to hear what was going on during the operation in theatre – did not occur. The anaesthetist did me proud; the epidural and sedation kept me out of it until I came round in recovery.

The early physio and stair climbing passed without incident, other than a slight bleed in the wound, and I find myself managing well on elbow-crutches at home. Now the really hard part begins, thrice daily exercises aimed at boosting knee flexion to a good 90 degrees or an outstanding 120 degrees, which allows you to tuck your feet under a chair. My pride in my progress was cut short when I had the lowest score for flexion among my five fellow patients – 70 degrees against 80, 85, 90, and even 102. I can see that my intolerance of pain is going to hold me back.

Jan is, as ever, at her best in a crisis, and has been endlessly patient and caring, lugging Zimmer frames, crutches, and the rest of the stuff needed, including a waterproof leg protector for use while showering. And organising the myriad different medications needed, for use twice and three times a day. And delicious food, which I'm not doing justice to, as I've rather lost my appetite. Maybe it's my body's response: 'You bastard, what have you done to me?' I can see that it's going to be a long haul, and six months will need to pass before I can think of having the left knee done.

This whole knee saga was brought about by my own impatience, when at the age of 20, after a long day in the saddle, my horse wanted to jog home and I wanted him to walk. The yank that I gave the reins brought him up on his hind legs and he toppled backwards onto me. As a result of that one moment of madness, I've had knee pain and countless arthroscopies over the past 55 years. A hard lesson learned.

Meanwhile, Callum is lapping up the luxury of full livery in his new yard, spending most days in a paddock at grass in this record-breaking warm spring, and nights in a stable so clean I'd happily eat off the floor. And he senses that he is among horse lovers, as he is more chilled that I have ever seen him.

I'm pushing through the pain of the flexion exercises, wanting to be able once more to put the full pressure of my legs on his flanks to collect him and drive the beast from behind. I'm coming for you, lazy bones!

Well, nobody said it was going to be a doddle, did they? Everyone did their level best, in a discreet way, to warn me that this was not going to be a picnic. Against a background chorus of 'Do your exercises', I went ahead.

The surgeon, a month out from the op, warned me that the total knee joint replacement procedure had a 90 per cent success rate, but there was a slim chance, a very slim chance, that I risked meeting my Maker. This was just before asking me to sign a waiver of any and all blame on the hospital if things went belly up. I didn't recognise my signature. But I signed.

The pre-op briefing was equally alarming. A German

anaesthetist revealed that the operation would not take place under a general anaesthetic, but using an epidural and sedation. She advised me to I bring headphones and music to drown out the sound of the surgeons talking and laughing in theatre and (more troublingly) the sounds of sawing, banging and drilling. It was at that point that I found myself mentally hobbling home as fast as I could, but somehow my feet would not obey me, and when I came to, I was still in the consulting room with the anaesthetist and Jan.

Well, so far so good; I lived to tell this tale. Though in a post-op physio session one patient revealed that she had come round enough to hear the sounds of the surgeons talking and laughing and some scary sounds of carpentry. Dear God, thank you that I was spared that. I told my surgeon prior to the op that this was my worst nightmare and he pooh-poohed my fears and bless him, I came round in the recovery room and talked to a horse-riding nurse with the most enormous sense of relief.

As someone once said: 'I don't mind dying, I just don't want to be there when it happens!' Then the really hard work began. I soon realised that the op was the easy part. The recovery, rather worryingly, was partly in my own hands. Those damn exercises faced me as challengingly as the twenty-six hedges of the Grand National, one of which is tellingly named 'the coffin'.

Family and friends were told of my miraculous survival and good wishes poured in. So now I had an audience for my own hobble-on part of this play. I came out of theatre at 3pm and had a night from hell before being helped out of bed to walk a dozen steps. To my utter astonishment, the leg did not buckle, and I was soon back in the bed, with Jan and the nurses making encouraging noises.

Three nights in the hospital and I was just getting comfortable with the routine, if not with my leg, and I was sent packing into the tender loving care of my other half. Those who know me well know that I'm not the cloth that heroes are cut from. In fact, I am the Life Chairman of the esteemed body known as The International Society for Committed Cowards, a charity that does sterling work amongst the faint of heart and the those who quail at life's rigours. And now suddenly I was required to be brave. Dear Lord.

My nights are haunted by thoughts of the bloody chorus of 'Are you doing the exercises?' as I toss and turn on my bed of pain. And yes, I am doing the bloody exercises, just as much as they are doing me right back! If I took the number of pain-killing pills that I have, most doctors would describe me not unfairly as a junkie. But painkillers are now my best friends.

The real hero in all of this has been Jan who provides me with pills, delicious food, clean clothing, moral support and every kind of encouragement, just short of offering to do my exercises for me. Mother Teresa has competition. And I wouldn't describe myself as a good patient. Say a little prayer for my partner of 45 years, she is dealing with one of the greatest challenges of our marriage, and there have been more than a few.

Yesterday evening, after a day in the garden admiring our no-mow-May lawn and its sprinkling of white cuckoo flowers, she hauled me off to see Callum for the first time in twelve days. The lad is looking in astonishingly good shape, not surprising with no exercise and the life of Reilly on spring grass. He looks like a show hunter and in show hunter condition. If ever I needed a slap about the chops, a kick in the butt and a long drink of motivation cocktail this was it! Onwards and upwards. But I am writing! And Callum is chilling.

Into the Enchanted Forest with Callum

HORSES WILL BE MY SALVATION

Spring 2025

In England, the good dinner guest is advised to avoid the subjects of sex, religion and politics – to limit the risk of giving offence. But as these are subjects close to my heart, I have tended to ignore the advice. Dinner parties and life generally are the poorer without these topics being on the menu. And besides, I've spent half a lifetime writing books about religion and politics, besides horses and landscapes. And in this benighted year of 2025 when the world of politics seems to have gone mad this must surely be a time to look hard at it.

In writing what follows, I have once again taken my own line across country and would like to speak of current politics. It may be that when the dust settles, those of us who have survived this time will have our horses to thank for our sanity. I expect so, just as they got us through Covid. We are, I fear, in a time of another plague. This time, it may well manage to damage us beyond repair.

Maybe this is a time for another horseman, a latter-day Paul Revere, immortalised by the poet Longfellow, to ride again – to warn against what is coming. Whatever your politics, I am sure we can agree that we are in an unprecedented place and none of us knows how and when it will end.

Why should a wild colonial boy from South Africa living in England be writing about this, knowing it will give offence? Well, what else is there to write about that is more important? And besides, when America sneezes, the rest of the world catches cold. So, I think it's fair to add my tuppence to the debate.

Listening to the news, I feel an overwhelming need to muck Callum out; shifting horse manure puts me strangely in a better frame of mind. And then a ride in the woods adds to my calm. The world seems to me to have become a darker, more dangerous place this year, but in the woods, the wild garlic is blooming and the beech trees are about to explode into their neon spring green. The birds are wild with song from 5am in the morning and the breeze carries scents of pine and a growing, stirring earth. Nature is oblivious to man's madness and the worst we are capable of. With or without us, it will continue giving life to this world. The sun brings my horse's coat to a gleaming gold and warms my bones. By the time I reach home, I am at peace.

If this is going to be Armageddon, I intend to ride my way through it and meet whatever horror is slouching its way towards us, on horseback. Thank God for horses! This is not a time to be silent. As the priest, Pastor Niemöller wrote so movingly:

> First they came for the Communists
> And I did not speak out
> Because I was not a Communist.
> Then they came for the Socialists
> And I did not speak out
> Because I was not a Socialist.
> Then they came for the trade unionists
> And I did not speak out
> Because I was not a trade unionist.
> Then they came for the Jews
> And I did not speak out
> Because I was not a Jew.
> Then they came for me
> And there was no one left

Into the Enchanted Forest with Callum

To speak out for me.

Callum is not the most demonstrative horse, but that is not to say he is not sensitive or intuitive. Maybe he picks up more about me than he lets on. Perhaps sensing my distress and anxiety, even fear, at what is happening to the world, this morning he nuzzled right into my ear and shoulder as we stood by the door on the indoor school.

A friend from the stable-yard, Katie Lowe, was passing and she was touched by Callum's loving on me and captured some images of us at the gate. Callum whispered in my ear: 'Old man, can I get back to my breakfast hay now, please? I've walked round the indoor twice!'

Looking at the images that Katie mailed to me later, the a few words from the song by Sammy Fain, *Love is a Many-Splendored Thing*, came to mind: . 'The golden crown/That makes a man a king.' Callum is indeed the 'golden crown' that makes this old man a king.. Later on, walking in brilliant sunshine zinging off the bright yellow gorse bushes, heavy with blossom, the thought came to me that despite the darkness of the world just now, it is a marmalade spring of yellow gorse bathed in sunshine that we are having, and that is reason to celebrate.

A Time to Mend

Summer 2025

This past month of recovering from my knee replacement, impatient at times, in pain at times, grateful at times, the words in Ecclesiastes 3:1 came to mind, 'For everything there is a season, and a time for every activity under heaven'. Words I love and that move me still:

> There is a time for everything, and a season for every activity under the heavens: a time to be born and a time to die, a time to plant and a time to uproot, a time to kill and a time to heal, a time to tear down and a time to build, a time to weep and a time to laugh, a time to mourn and a time to dance, a time to scatter stones and a time to gather them, a time to embrace and a time to refrain from embracing, a time to search and a time to give up, a time to keep and a time to throw away, a time to tear and a time to mend, a time to be silent and a time to speak, a time to love and a time to hate, a time for war and a time for peace.

For me, the replacement of my old knee has been followed by a time for mending. And it has had its challenges. I am impatient by nature, and much wedded to my independence, so to find myself a little bit helpless and dependent has not been easy. The operation and recovery could not have gone better and thanks to Jan, I have lacked for nothing. And once beyond the first painful days, it has been a time for reflection between the ongoing demands of my working life which continued unabated, promoting clients in the media.

There have been moments of profound joy and gratitude that despite my squeamish and somewhat cowardly nature, I finally screwed up the gumption to get this operation done. Living half-crippled by arthritis is no way to exist, if there is a way out. Lying in bed at 6am listening to the birds' May-morning chorus, broadcast from our 20ft tall beech hedges that encircle the cottage like green battlements, has been blissful. And last thing at night, the call of the barn owls flying over the surrounding fields was the happiest sound to slip the lines of consciousness for the darkness of sleep.

The weather – eleven weeks of unbroken sunshine from March through to the third week of May – has been a blessing too. But I would not be human and a horseman if this perfection of the weather did not constantly remind me of the riding time lost. At 75, there is much to be grateful for, but not an abundance of time left. The feeling called up in me came from my teens when I stood fishing, rod in hand, knee deep in the bracing cold of the Cape surf in and around Cape Town, waiting for fish to bite as those around me hauled in kabeljou, sand shark, blacktail and musselcracker. Patience hard learned, but never quite mastered.

A time to mend is an exercise in patience, fortitude and gratitude in equal measure. There came a moment when Jan drove me to see how Callum was doing at his new digs, and wobbling toward my horse on crutches to give him a carrot left me breathless with longing. And a couple of weeks later when I had driven my car up the lane, just for the hell of it, when Jan was out, I felt a wild desire to keep going to the stables down the A26 and across the Forest. But Jan had warned me that until the hospital signed me off as fit to rejoin the working world, I was uninsured to drive.

This took me back to the top of the garden, where with our rescue dog Gus by my side, I read, wrote and dreamed of times past when alone with pony or horse I was free to explore the world of my youth. I revisited the beaches of the Cape where we left galloping hoofprints in the sand, bioluminescence in the sea, puffs of dust as we made our way up the fire crew roads that climb the back of Table Mountain, the deep cool pine forest of Tokai and the vineyards of Groot Constantia, the first vineyard In the Cape, established in the seventeenth century when my mother's people, the Afrikaners, had been in Africa a century already. Then back to the coast at Bloubergstrand, with its view over the bay to Robben Island, before Mandela arrived a decade later, and the flat-topped mountain that stood four- square across the bay. These rides seemed to push our East Sussex garden's green imprisoning walls away from me for a while.

Just beyond them, however, lies Ashdown Forest and Tilhill Forest – Hundred Acre Wood and 500 Acre wood – where I had not set foot for a month. And beyond them, Callum grazing and getting fat in his field and far too friendly with the resident peacock. The itch to ride was on me, but I had to say, be calm, be quiet and mend, you bloody fool. Enjoy the enforced leisure, the peace and the quiet. Take your time. But as I sit there, the lawn, uncut for months, is now knee high, and the thought comes to me that if I sit here another few weeks I may never be found, engulfed by green.

Jan, who has walked and ridden by my side for almost 50 years, knew instinctively what I was feeling and organised short drives to see Callum and to eat at Babylon café on the Forest, and the Hatch Inn nearby. The days multiplied and passed like the beads on a rosary, went round, came round, and then went round again, interminably.

And then, one day I had no need of pain killers, ice packs or crutches, and I began to plan some lunging work for my grass-fat friend, that would take the edge off his warmblood temperament. Soon, soon, soon, we will disappear once more into the beech, oak, birch, and holly crowded woods, where trails are so narrow you need to lift your legs forward under your horse's neck to avoid injuries to your knees from the tree trunks. And via these paths, by and by, we will emerge into the secret cathedrals far from the beaten paths which it's taken me 45 years of exploring to find. And there I know the hairs on my arms and the back of my neck will lift briefly as we meet the spirit of the woods once more, come to inspect a newly healed rider and his shining chestnut horse.

Today, 28 May 2025, I walked up the lane to the 20-acre cross-country field with the three bay brood mares who have been there through the winter. They look astoundingly fat, fit and well. The boss mare came over to sniff and inspect me and Gus. He slipped back under the five-bar gate, not welcoming this nosy impertinence, and watched her from the safety of the lane.

This tranquil, everyday countryside scene, was miraculous in one respect – 28 days ago, my right knee was replaced with a titanium joint and a plastic knee cap. The fact that I was able to do this 200-yard stroll and stand once more among horses in a field and then stroll back home, on my own, with just the dog for company, without crutches, without pain killers, was indeed miraculous to me. Thank God for modern medicine. The scar is quite healed.

In two weeks' time, a very proper sort of Englishman, my surgeon, is going to experience something that will no doubt embarrass him. He is going to be hugged and kissed on both cheeks. The shock may well unhinge him, if it does not kill him outright. But he deserves it. He has transformed my life – walking for the first time in years without pain, climbing stairs, getting up off a low couch with ease.

I am just sorry that lack of courage on my part prevented me from having this done years ago. But in my sixties, I was warned by a surgeon who had done several arthroscopies on my knees, that artificial knees were only good for ten to fifteen years, and that I did not want to have to have the knee replaced twice. I took his advice, in the hopeful belief that I might make old bones.

When I got home from the horses' field this morning, still without pain, I made a celebratory cup of coffee and drank it with my legs up on the sofa in the living room, basking in warm sunshine. I pushed the boat out even further and had a two-finger KitKat chocolate wafer as part of this knees-up party.

Now I have two more weeks to be signed off as fit to rejoin the working world, the driving world and best of all, the horse-riding world. I aim to ride Callum back from the livery yard where he has been coddled like a precious egg. Now that will be a real cause for celebration.

The next full moon night I will stand by his shoulder in his plush hedgerowed field and watch the summer moon rise over Crowborough Hill, my independence and mobility restored. And when I go back inside, I will hug Jan who has carried me on her hands as they say; I've been more coddled than Callum, much more so. I suspect she could do with a hug and kisses on both cheeks too.

As I stroll up the lane, the sights and sounds engulf me after so much time inside - the foxgloves are at their best and the honeysuckle is coming on nicely, the birds are in full orchestral mode, and was that a cuckoo? This has been a spring like no other, three months of sun from March to May, more like Cape Town than Crowborough. And in my head I hear The Spinners singing that old Seventies song, *Working My Way Back to You*, (Callum)!

BACK IN THE SADDLE

Summer 2025

Today was the 48th day since my knee replacement surgery. It was a warm summer's evening, and the third time I've lunged Callum since I'd become more mobile on the new knee. He was lethargic with heat and a day out at grass and could barely bother to lift into a trot in the indoor school at the livery yard where he has been boarding.

I'd saddled him intending to ride after 15 minutes on the lunge, but he was so chilled that I called time on the indoor exercises. Despite my butterflies, I took him to the mounting block and gingerly lifted my newly fixed right leg over his quarters and settled in the saddle. I let out a deep breath. I was back in my favourite place in all the world.

All we did was amble and jog up the long drive to the road that bisects the Forest, make a U-turn and came back down again. He was a bit sticky going past a white plastic pig on a pole, and unusually for him ,did not want to stop to graze. I could feel a slight edge. He did a few headshakes. Jan kindly filmed our first outing.

We then rode down to the small gate that gives access to the Forest and stopped there and took in the view. I sensed that he now knew where he had been for the past seven weeks. I said a small prayer of thanks for my surgeon, his team, the nurses and the NHS, and for Jan who had helped me back from crippling pain and my limited ability to walk. And I thanked my lucky stars for this horse of mine.

I dismounted carefully, untacked Callum and took off my helmet and body protector, the little breeze cooling me down. Tomorrow we may venture a little further. Fifty days on from my full knee replacement operation I can walk up a flight of stairs, alternating feet like a normal person, I can get off a low sofa in one easy movement, instead of having to push myself up from the armrest, I am walking about a mile a day and I can get in and out of my car in one fluid movement. I am able to wash, dress, drive and sleep in comfort. And all of this without painkillers. I've even now had that brief 15-minute ride on Callum, who is summer-fat and very laid back. It is all something of a miracle.

Why, I wonder, did I not do this years ago? The answer is simple; my level of incapacity had crept up on me so slowly – like the frog in the pot of warming water – that I barely noticed it at first and had time to get almost comfortable with being somewhat crippled.

I had feared the operation. I had two neighbours who'd not had a happy outcome with this op. So I soldiered on. It had been 55 years since the horse-riding accident that kick-started the knee problems.

And then one day I'd just had enough of being so physically limited. I was helped in this decision by an Arthramid injection I arranged for Callum, to help him with arthritic changes to the bones of his hoof. It had been transformative. So now Callum and I have been given a new lease of life. I would not say I am now like a spring chicken, though Callum on occasion feels rather like one!

In the late afternoon heat of yesterday I took Callum out for an hour, solo on the Forest. We went down to the splash below Friends Clump and then along the little stream north and then swung a right up the hill to Camp Hill Clump, jogging. Then down to Ellison's Ponds and up the hill to Friends Clump, down past the Nutley Windmill and back to the livery yard. Callum didn't put a foot wrong. My knee was fine throughout. But when I got home, I felt exhausted –

from age, heat, tension and loss of fitness. But we are getting there. Together, we are putting one foot in front of the other and building up strength, and the hope in my heart is that we have a few more years of trail-riding in us, now he is 16 and I am 75. Time will tell.

A New Lease of Life for Callum and Me

Summer 2025

The reversal of the ageing process promised by scientists is going to be too late for me, but I have some idea how it will feel. You see, with my brand-new knee I am celebrating my own new lease of life. For it is allowing me to take stairs in my stride once more, and best of all, keep my big horse collected and moving forward with impulsion.

This morning we set off on our ride with hearts high and a real swing in Callum's step. He was on the bit, head tossing a little, breaking into a trot here and there, and for the first time in years I was able to post at the trot, easily and with no pain in my right knee.

Our recent rides have been a bit of a challenge as the woodsmen are thinning out the pine plantations near our home, making a right mess of sections of the woods, requiring us to make U-turns and do some bushwhacking to get around locked gates and blocked paths. My arms are black and blue with bruises and a few cuts from whipping branches and wood spikes. But Callum has taken it all in his stride. He thinks his way through these obstacles and pauses in narrow places to help me lift my legs out of the way.

As I write this, I am watching him graze in the four-acre field in front of our cottage and I am not ashamed to admit to feelings of love for this horse who can on occasion be such a prima donna. We may not have got all of our youth back, but our moxie is back, big time!

This morning I was just finishing my first coffee of the day in bed when a ringing neigh from outside my window rattled the panes of glass. I'd made the mistake of giving Cal his breakfast at 6am yesterday, and the big lad was not amused to be kept waiting till 7am today. Who says horses are stupid? They know the time, they know your and their routine, and they quite rightly feel that they have a stake in all this. It's lovely having him home again, we are now a couple once again since his return from full livery while I was recovering from surgery and he says he is depending on me – bugger lying in bed, new knee be damned!

We are living in a sea of grass, heat and horseflies. Callum's return from a two-month full livery stays at Londonderry Farm in Nutley while I had my knee replacement coincided with a summer heatwave here in East Sussex with temperatures up to 33 degrees. No bad thing maybe as it has kept Callum quiet; he was too hot by half to be performing.

He has now discovered the three brood mares in the adjacent 20-acre field, and he is doing his best to round them up, while standing at the gate, yelling instructions for them to come and attend to him. Thus far they are studiously ignoring his demands for attention. This may just be the moment when this horse remembers that both his sire and dam jumped internationally. I do hope that we can avoid this. It's not going to be pretty if he gets over that five-bar gate in among the mares, he may be in for a drubbing.

Toby, our farrier, arrived to give him his new shoes and at the end of the process Callum did something weird; he tried to lie down in the crossties, something he has never done in his six years with me. Toby and I struggled to keep him up and pull the three-legged iron smithing-stand out of his way. I undid the cross ties and led him around. Toby said he was walking fine after 100 yards, so I tacked him up and rode out for 40 minutes to get a feel of what might be wrong, but he was sound. Jan scolded me later for riding him after his attempt to lie down, and she was right of course. But like all husbands, I take it on myself to be wrong on occasion.

A friend who is a very insightful horsewoman with vast professional experience may have put her finger on the problem. She reckons Cal is not getting enough sleep currently, with the new regime out at grass 24/7 and the excitement of the mares next door. And maybe he simply felt that a snooze was in order after standing for an hour and a half on three legs while being shod? I suspect I will never truly know what was going on in his mind. We may be a 'couple' again, but like most such partnerships, 50% of the time you are in the dark.

We are coming up to September soon, the month he had the Arthramid shot last year. A week ago our vet said let's see how he does on Bute until September to keep him going sound. He is also getting Boswellia Serrata, a natural anti-inflammatory supplement, twice a day.

He has now discovered two gaps in the hedgerow between him and the mares, where the deer have scraped a way through at ground level. The mares have got over being coy and are now playing peek-a-boo with my lad, and I worry that he may try to tunnel through to them, following the lead of the deer. So I criss-crossed both gaps with electric tape and armloads of bramble cuttings, which seems to have dampened his ardour. Ah, horses!

I gave him two days off after his lie down and then had a lovely ride with him back to his long striding, swinging walk, lifting into a sound trot now and then. The Forest is looking its best just now with the purple heather beginning to bloom and in the shadier spots, the grass is lush.

I am liking this routine of having Callum home and out 24/7 as it means no mucking out and lower costs all round. I am not sure how he will take to this in the winter (I'm thinking perhaps a field shelter), but if the weather really throws the worst at us, he has a nice cozy stable waiting just behind the kitchen at the top of our garden.

Science may not be in time to turn back the clock for Callum and me to our peak of youth, but there is something about this new lease of life we've both been given, and back on our home turf, that is very special indeed.

With things so good, I'm reluctant to wish for more, but if my arm was twisted and I was told to make a wish that wish would be for land of our own.

My paternal grandfather, Herman Roup (after whom my younger brother is named), was a Lithuanian Jewish pedlar who created a business and a reputation for honesty based on selling horses, donkeys and mules in South Africa's Cape. He had a number of farms inland to which the horses he bred or imported by ship from Argentina in the 1920s would be gently herded from the Cape Town docks to graze at peace for some weeks to recover from their South Atlantic crossing.

My maternal grandfather, Anfries Abraham Louw, was the spoiled son of a wealthy farming family who inherited farms and lost them all to bad management. So land and the loss of land is a theme that runs through my family's history.

I grew up in suburban Cape Town and have ridden all my life, but my ponies and then my horses were kept at livery yards, full livery when I was young and later in DIY yards in England, when Jan and I did them, juggling work and horses around each other.

Eventually in Sussex, we erected a small stable block for our two horses and a children's pony with a tack room-feedstore at the top of the garden and hired a field for them to graze in during good weather. But in all these seven decades, I have never owned land. It has remained a dream.

At present, I am closer to having fulfilled that dream with Callum in the field right in front of our cottage. I can go to feed him his breakfast in my pyjamas if I like. But the land is rented from the farm we live on; it isn't ours.

I've always felt that land of one's own represented the truest, most valuable form of wealth, given its capacity to provide space, privacy, independence and food growing potential. For many complex reasons, the main one being financial resources, I've never had the wherewithal.

I have been thinking about this a lot recently. The fact that I am reading a fascinating book which is utterly transforming my understanding of human pre-history. The book is titled *The Dawn of Everything - A New History of Humanity*, by David Graeber, an anthropologist and David Wengrow, an archaeologist. Anthropology is a field in which I majored at university and which has always fascinated me, as has archaeology, maybe because my formative years were spent in Africa, mankind's original birthplace.

The book provides compelling evidence that our early history as hunter-gatherers, then farmers and later city dwellers is much more complex than previously understood. We were neither Jean-Jacques Rousseau's 'noble savage', nor was life 'nasty, brutish and short', as Thomas Hobbes argued. Early man, it appears, was extremely sophisticated about human politics; freedom and equality were everything to them and they set up social constructs to avoid having one man dominate another - chiefs and kings, they well understood, would lead them into a loss of personal freedom and in some instances, into chains.

Land was free when we lived in small groups or larger clusters of free ranging hunter gatherers. And the land belonged to all men and women too. They saw the land as their mother and something that could not be owned. In this, their egalitarian freedom was maintained and life was sustained.

How was the desire for dominance or status controlled? First of all, by controlling the distribution of meat, so that no one went hungry; sharing was ingrained as the rule of survival. Any animal brought to camp would be fairly apportioned by someone who was not the hunter responsible for the kill. Anyone who got too big for their boots and started to show signs of big-headedness or a wish to dominate would face the mocking songs of the women from the dark just beyond the light of the fires. Public shaming is not a new internet fad, it's as old as man. In good times the hunter-gatherer 'economy' required just three days 'work' of hunting and gathering a week to maintain a good life, leaving the rest of the time to play with the children, rest, tell stories and for romance. Today we see the remnant of such behaviour among the San Bushmen of the Kalahari and other African tribal groups. In South Africa the word 'Ubuntu' sums up this social reality – it means humanity towards others. 'I am, because we are.' It's a philosophy emphasising interconnectedness, compassion and community. It highlights that a person's humanity is inextricably linked to their relationships with others and the broader community.

This social security and freedom were lost with the coming of the agrarian revolution and its food surpluses in which relative wealth made you vulnerable to envy and attack and land became a form of slavery, as you were chained to it to make it provide. Later, the people who worked the land themselves became part of it as serfs and slaves controlled by landlords, aristocrats and kings. So, land in our history has represented both ends of life on earth, freedom and slavery.

Maybe it is understanding something of this strange duality of land for many years which added to the pull and the glamour of land, plus a powerful romantic, almost poetic attachment to the landscapes in which I have lived my life, both landscapes easy to fall in love with and to be bewitched by.

As I walk the field by our cottage, I am currently a sort of pretend landowner. It is just for a while, anyway until the farm finds a new owner. My age also means land ownership is just too late. At my age I am not about to take on the sometimes-onerous demands of keeping land in good order.

But as I saddle Callum up and head out into the woods for a spot of forest bathing, a little trespassing and some communing with the spirit of the land, I can imagine myself to be some kind of latter-day hunter gatherer and the land as far as I can see, is my land, mine by dint of the half-century I have lived on it, by it, with it. And a sense of freedom enters my soul.

NO FLIES ON WINNIE-THE-POOH

Summer 2025

Is this the most fly-riddled summer yet? Judging by the numbers of flies besieging our cottage and Callum's field opposite, I think it may very well be. The big lad is now living permanently in a fly mask which comes off at around 9pm and goes back on at around 8am, once he has had his breakfast. And for the first time ever, I rode him out in it yesterday and he was super-chilled in his new turquoise face protector. On top of it he also wore his lavender fly fringe with flopping strings. And of course, I whisked away errant flies with a trusty three-foot length of beech, stripped of most of its leaves with just three left at the tip.

The one thing I might have added if I had such a thing, was a plastic dragon fly on a three-inch length of stiff wire that attached to the top of the bridle just between the horse's ears. The effect of this insect predator is much the same as the shouted instruction from a beach lifeguard: "Great White approaching – clear the water!" But my threefold levels of protection worked pretty well, and it made our ride around the woods that much more pleasant.

As we made our way down the western side of Hundred Acre Wood, I saw a tall man walking a mid-sized black muzzled dog. He asked, 'Is your name Julian?' I replied that indeed it was. 'Julian Roup?' he added. I said that was correct. He said he had read my book about the time of Covid *(Life in a Time of Plague)*. "Did you enjoy it?" I asked.

And he said: "I did. I love jazz and I very much enjoy getting into the head of someone who can go off on riffs, like you do in your writing." I thanked him and told him that my new book would be out in the autumn. He said he would look out for it. And then, wishing him good day, Callum and I moved off down the hill. I felt buoyed up by the compliment and by the strange impact my writing was having on my riding.

After that, we crossed the bone-dry splash at the bottom of the hill, climbed the far side and crossed the Hartfield Road a little further on. As we rode on with the path down to Pooh Sticks Bridge on our right, I saw a horse and rider coming down the hill from Gills Lap. As we passed, we both nodded with all the formality of people meeting while waiting for a medal ceremony in a Buckingham Palace waiting room. Her horse was a lovely light bay, and she wore a Day-Glo fluorescent tabard.

I thought of following her after a few minutes grace down to the bridge, to see if I could just spot Christopher Robin and his friends as we crossed it, noting the small pots of honey left by visiting children for Pooh Bear at the base of an oak tree that holds a beautifully carved wooden front door. But I decided it was a loop too far and continued homeward.

We climbed the hill to the Enchanted Place and stopped for a moment there in the little tree-bound enclosure to take in the view. And whether it was a sign of respect, or whether the flies and horseflies didn't like the feel of heated bronze, there were no flies on Winnie the Pooh's memorial plaque. Protected perhaps by the power of the magic that emanates wordlessly from the best children's books.

A little further on, Callum pulled up to inspect the Exmoor ponies, earning their keep by keeping the brush under control. And looking tub-fat on it. These are the closest living relatives of the Wild Horse of Europe who found their way to Britain 130,000 years ago before the sea broke through the land bridge to the Continent and the English Channel cut off dry land access.

Into the Enchanted Forest with Callum

In a clearing near home we smelled fire, a worry in midsummer, but it was the Tilhill Foresters, clearing a river dell of selected pines and burning the offcuts. Callum kept a chary eye on the crackling fire until we were past. He had enjoyed our ride in the shade of the woods with me whisking flies away. I thought he must be squirming a bit at the thought of a return to his paddock. Now that he is part of the mare group who congregate on the other side of his gate in the far corner of his field, he needs protection as never before. Four horses in one group are such an invitation to every flying insect that a feast is at hand. Thank heavens for fly masks!

These rides of mine during the week are always accompanied by a small nagging sense of guilt, for they are indeed my guilty pleasure. At my age, and working from home, placing stories in the national and international media for art and antiques auction houses, you'd think I'd feel free to work for as long or as little as I like and relax for as long as I like, but no. If I have an early morning ride or a ride at lunchtime, I feel guilty if I'm not at my desk. It's the result of a lifetime of work-focused conditioning, I suppose. Ten years beyond the normal retirement age of 65, you'd think I'd have outgrown it, but I've not.

Weekends are no problem; I feel free as a bird to indulge. These days, of course I always carry a mobile phone which tracks my route in the sometimes-trackless parts of Ashdown Forest, just in case Callum goes home without me. And as a result of carrying the world with me, not surprisingly the world knocks on my door now and then. Because the global media never sleep, something surreal takes place. If I'm riding late afternoon or evening UK time it's not unusual to get a call from the *New York Times* or the *LA Times*, the *Washington Post* and most recently PBS, the TV network in the US wanting pictures of a sixteenth-century Italian painting depicting a woman in a blue denim dress – the first known sighting of this ubiquitous cloth.

Thanks to the needle-sharp mic in the phone the question inevitably comes up, 'Are those birds I can hear?

Are you outside?' I admit that I am but that the pics will be with them shortly. And then the question. 'You're not on a horse by any chance? I can hear clip clopping!' I curse inwardly and pull on the reins or try to steer Callum in the direction of some greenery to eat.

On more than one occasion, when I say I am out riding, my caller will admit to being a rider too, and where I am riding? I explain that I live in Winnie the Pooh Country, and am just passing the Enchanted Place, or have crossed Pooh Sticks Bridge a minute ago. And then the caller, the picture editor or the news editor or the journalist starts singing: "If you go down to the woods today........." Surreal, indeed! Bizarrely, Callum as my guilty pleasure has added warmth to what would otherwise have been a very straightforward business call. Sometimes a guilty pleasure comes with benefits! And the damn flies are just incidental.

AERIAL VISIONS AND DISASTER AVERTED

Summer 2025

It says much for my horse that despite seeing the saddle he strolls over to meet me at the gate this morning. Having his breakfast with me may have had something to do with it. His breakfast is quickly despatched and I am in the saddle by 6.45am. We clip clop up our lane, heading out to the near woods via the livery yard down Fielden Lane. Dog walkers are out in ones and twos. Some greet us, some do not, but I greet them all cheerily, which may have put their noses out of joint. It does not do to be too familiar so early of an English morning.

Callum was feeling good, doing a little two-step here and there at odd ghosts he saw or felt in the towering summer hedges. His neck gleamed gold and copper in the early morning sun, and as ever, my heart lifted to be abroad on such a fine horse.

As soon as we reached the Forest, there were spider-webs in the grass, hundreds of them, small parachutes that their owners used to reach the green from the sky, like regiments of parachute troops. And just then a huge, chocolate-brown buzzard curved lazily overhead, taking avoiding action round a giant oak, like a feather-clad Lancaster bomber which may well have dropped the spider troops.

Softly, and then louder, the Gatwick-bound aircraft were above us, coming in from their first early morning flights of the day from Morocco, the Balearic Islands and mainland Spain, Portugal, France and the islands of Cyprus and Sicily – bringing holidaymakers home to an England awash with its own beach weather on this perfect summer's day.

Callum feels well and sound, and happy to find the bracken at perfect mouth height. His gold head swings from side to side like a hungry best man at a wedding buffet. I tuck my legs close to his flanks to avoid getting my spur-clad feet caught up in all this vibrant green food. The early flies are easily whisked away with my three-foot length of beech branch, working as a second tail whisk for his head and shoulders with a flick down his side when he tries to quiver a horsefly away. The beech leaves are a dark green now, no longer the pulsing neon-yellow green of early spring.

I look for a small figure in red among the dappled dark beneath the trees, but there is no Little Red Riding Hood, just the odd deer crossing our path silently, like an image from the margin of an illustrated vellum gospel. There is a hush in the air, promising a hot day ahead.

And then disaster strikes. I let Callum graze for a minute while I type a note to myself. Suddenly he shakes his neck, and the reins slip down that long dinosaur curve all the way to the ground, and just then he takes a step forward. His leg is now tangled in the reins. Cursing myself I drop my phone in the grass and dismount fast. The big horse stands immobile, knowing he is caught up. I have him free in a long 30 seconds and breathe again. I hunt for my phone and pocket it.

Now I have to mount this monster and there is not a log in sight. I lengthen my left stirrup leather and put my foot in relatively easily. The horse stands stock still, bless him, as I bounce gently on my right leg with its brand-new knee. Everything works and once more I am back in the saddle. I shorten the stirrup leather, and we are off again among the burgeoning bracken. No damage done.

Into the Enchanted Forest with Callum

The rest of the ride is uneventful and two hours later we pull up at Callum's new home, the field in front of the cottage. It has been pure bliss from start to finish and my respect for the sense and discipline of this lovely horse is enhanced. What he thinks of me is perhaps best glossed over. At 10pm, with the heat of the day finally cooled, I go out to check on him and the final aerial display of the day greets me, a huge harvest moon rising over Callum's field, burnishing my golden boy silver in the moonlight.

Julian Roup

Into the Enchanted Forest with Callum

LAZY, HAZY, CRAZY DAYS OF SUMMER

Summer 2025

It's high summer in the Sussex Weald now and things have slowed down to a bucolic drawl. You can, if you listen hard, hear the grass growing and the lazy sound of horse tails swishing in the deep shade of oaks and beeches. Callum is living out 24/7 and is in horse heaven. If he has a complaint, it's that he can't get to the three broodmares in the next field, thanks to a stout five-bar metal gate.

The blackberries are ripening in the hedgerows alongside the cow parsley and the honeysuckle that scents the air with notes of ripe melon. And at dusk and dawn the sun burnishes everything in a honey treacle light as this neverending summer goes on and on and on, as if rain, autumn and winter have been banned for good. It would all be a bit nervous-making if one could summon up the energy to worry.

In reality, we have passed summer's highpoint, the Summer Solstice, back on 21 June , and so the longest day has passed, the Druids have done their thing at Stonehenge, but we are still meandering our way through July and holiday August is just around the corner. It is, as Nat King Cole sang, 'Those lazy, hazy, crazy days of summer'. But not all is perfect.

The horrors of Gaza, the rumbles from the Ukraine

and Russia, and the political turmoil in America fill the papers, a screeching descant to the choir of cicadas, swallows and wood pigeons here in southeast England, where desperate migrants continue to paddle hard across the Channel, seeking sanctuary.

But if you can shut out the clamouring horror, this ice-cream summer rolls on. Callum and my calendar are punctuated by his six-weekly visits from Toby the farrier, and by gentle rides in the woods. Yesterday, daydreaming in Hundred Acre Wood, we heard the sound of horses trotting. The couple I'd seen before, riding the bay and the grey, passed briskly by, not spotting us, a bare hundred foot to their left, deep in the gloom. I shortened my reins to control Callum's interest, but to my amazement he wasn't bothered, and we sauntered out of the wood and went to bathe his feet in the nearby dew pond. He does surprise me from time to time. Being out at grass 24x7 is working wonders upon his love of alarms and excursions!

My weekly visits to Windmill Feeds have slowed right down, now that my lad is feeding at an all-you-can-eat buffet in his field. I started a count of what was on offer but lost track after four different kinds of grasses and more plant varieties in the hedges than I had names for. A competitive show jumping friend has offered us free tickets for Hickstead, the international horse jumping venue 15 miles away. We might take up her kind offer. The lure of watching international show jumping at a venue we covered as junior reporters when we first arrived here in 1980 could be fun, with a bit of shopping thrown in for good measure.

Thirty miles away as the seagull flies, France is preparing to down tools for the whole month of August. How civilised. My morning and evening routine comprises of nothing much more than taking Callum his balancer mash and chopped alfalfa, laced with Bute, a painkiller for his arthritis, and all sorts of trace elements; putting on and taking off his fly mask; rubbing his head and tugging his fly-rug forward to stop it chafing his chest. And that's him sorted, if

Into the Enchanted Forest with Callum

I'm not riding.

Jan is kindly editing this new book, as she has done for each of my six books currently on Amazon. I may have ambitions to be another Steinbeck or Hemingway but to Jan – who has written and edited at the *FT,* the *Guardian,* the *Observer* and *The Spectator,* among others – I am just another writer who is mildly dyslexic. Her own three books and a book of poetry due out in January will soon be joined by another novel. This 260-year-old cottage might look like snoozeville, but in fact it is a humming hive of literary industry, nothing short of a word factory.

There is a shortage of cupboard space in the old house and so winter coats of every kind hang behind utility room doors and kitchen doors, a mute reminder that colder days will be coming. Even as I recline on my steamer chair at the top of the garden, tapping away at my computer under a sun umbrella, thoughts of managing Callum in the winter nibble away at the edge of my mind. I am reassured somewhat by the array of New Zealand rugs in our stables and tack room.

This has been a remarkably silent summer as the farm which surrounds our cottage is for sale, and the DIY livery yard next door with its fifty stables is closed. So the usual daily movement of cars and horses up and down the lane is gone for now, while a new owner is being sought. The silence will not last, that is for sure, but for now, the loudest noise is the cockerel next door with his harem of hens. In the woods behind the cottage, the tree fellers are hard at work cropping pines, something To which Callum pays little attention to on our rides, despite the massive size of the machinery involved.

In the garden I watch the swallows who've raised another brood in our stables, darting in and out, cutting parabolas above the cottage and the old oak tree, harvesting flies and midges, building up reserves that will power them back down the length of Europe and Africa come September. It is a bittersweet thought that they will be leaving us in September and I envy them their destination – my motherland,.

But I can't complain; this summer has been more Cape Town than Crowborough. I look up, hearing honking, and a V-formation of Canada Geese over-flies the garden, heading for fresh fields.

Into the Enchanted Forest with Callum

ASHDOWN FOREST – BIG CAT COUNTRY?

Summer 2025

I was out riding in Tilhill Forest when Callum and I had a big cat scare. I cannot absolutely swear to it, but I saw some kind of large lion coloured cat at the southern edge of Crowborough, around noon, on 5 August, near the Army Camp woods. We were on the last hill, heading home, when my horse gave a violent shy and as I looked into the woods to our left where something had spooked him, I spotted the rear quarters of a huge cat walking in that slinking mode they have when hunting. I shouted and pushed the horse to move briskly past this place to get home, making as much noise as I could. About a hundred yards later I stopped Callum, who was still quite lit up, and turned him to look back down the hill to see if I could spot the animal, but all was still.

Thinking about this as I unsaddled Callum at his field a few minutes later, I remembered something else that had happened on this ride about twenty minutes before our sighting of the cat. I was riding quietly at the walk when my horse suddenly shot forward so violently that I half came out of the saddle. I was annoyed with him, but thought he may have been stung by one of the wasps or hornets we'd passed through. Thinking back on this, it may be that the cat had crossed the road just behind us when we passed. Horses have 180-degree vision in each eye, so can see as clearly behind them as in front. He'd taken quite some stopping.

I have ridden these woods for 45 years and have on occasion spotted something odd, but almost invariably it turned out to be a muntjac deer that also moves in an odd creeping motion. Some people say they have spotted wild boar, which is possible, as some escaped from a breeding operation that ran here for several years.

I will be keeping a sharp lookout when I go out riding again. There are so many deer that live around here that we regularly see up to thirty at dusk and dawn coming out of the woods to feed in the grass pastures. My horse pays them no heed when we pass them in the woods, even when the stags are roaring in the autumn rut. A few evenings ago, I went to take Callum's fly mask off at 9pm and he was lying down with deer grazing around him, not bothered in the least. So I know for sure it wasn't a deer that startled us.

Intrigued, I did an Internet search for big cats in Sussex, and this is what I turned up in the *Evening Argus*, Brighton [2020]: 'The police stated that there had been three reports during 2020 which included someone in Arundel, who reported that they may have seen a lion cub. While another person in Crowborough said they saw a large wild cat at the scene of a road crash. And in Hartfield, a person reported seeing a lion in a field.'

In South Africa I have been close to large cats, lions, leopards and cheetahs in game parks, so I'm familiar with their size, colour and way of moving. But I never expected to come across anything like this morning's sighting here in England. Finding it hard to believe what Callum and I had seen, I reached out to the members of the Ashdown Forest Wildlife Facebook group who have a deep and intimate knowledge of the area, fully expecting them to rubbish my talk of a big cat sighting, but that was far from the case. It seems I am not alone or crazy. There were hundreds of responses reporting big cat sightings across southern England as well as deer and sheep carcasses cached high up in trees. The big cat sightings included lynx, pumas, servals in and around Ditchling, Cuckfield, Hartfield, Crowborough, and Brighton, all within a 25-mile radius.

A LIFE OF RIDING AND WRITING

I have loved horses for a lifetime; they have been a passion and a salvation. The only other activities that come close are reading, I love books, as does Jan, and one day our cottage is going to collapse under their weight. In my middle years, I discovered a late-blooming love of writing that went way beyond the journalism I did to earn a crust. I have been fortunate to be able to link these passions together – horses, writing and reading.

I grew up in Cape Town and lived there till I was 30. The city has left a deep mark on me, and I still think of it as home in many ways. I was a hopeless student, and I mean truly hopeless. This was aggravated by the fact that I attended the South African College School, SACS, as it is known, which, back in the 1950s and '60s, was largely focused on academic and sporting pursuits, neither of which appealed to me. I sloped off from school as fast as I could when the final bell rang to go horse-riding on the Cape Flats, the beaches, in Tokai Forest and the mountain above Groot and Klein Constantia. When my troubled schooling ended, I did my National Service and was possibly an even more hopeless soldier than I had been a student.

I worked for the family business, Enterprise Bakeries, for seven years, selling biscuits, which I think I was reasonably good at, though I found it a trial at times, but I had no idea about what to do with my life. It was only when

Into the Enchanted Forest with Callum

I was 26 that I finally got a sense of direction and took myself off to Rhodes University as a mature student (a laughable description, in my case).

There, I studied Journalism and Anthropology, and it felt like I had come home. I worked holiday jobs at the *Cape Times* and the *Cape Argus*, and this confirmed my love of writing. After university, Jan – another writer (*The Class of '79, The World Beneath*, among others) – and I emigrated to the UK in 1980 and worked on local papers in Sussex. She then moved to the BBC, the *FT* and *The Guardian*, and I changed direction and moved into public relations for a variety of clients, eventually going in-house as Director of Press and Marketing for Bonhams, the international fine art auction house, which sold Old Master paintings, wine, classic cars, antiquities, silver, jewellery, ceramics and furniture among its sixty specialist departments.

It was another education, and I loved working there. I played a small part in growing the company to its current presence in twenty-seven countries. At 65, I retired and opened my own media consultancy, which includes auction houses in the UK, the USA, France, South Africa and Australia. It provided a never-ending array of fascinating stories, from getting a dinosaur skeleton into the Eiffel Tower in Paris and into London's Heathrow Airport, to selling cars worth millions, a 1736 violin made in Cremona for £4 million, and a newly discovered Caravaggio found in the attic of a French farmhouse near Toulouse, which was valued at $100 million.

When Covid struck, I was 69, with a number of health issues, so was not sure that I would see my 70th birthday. This ignited a frenzy of writing, which found expression in three books in the two years in which effectively we lived in lockdown. The three titles are: *Life in a Time of Plague*; *Into the Secret Heart of Ashdown Forest – A Horseman's Country Diary*; and *First Catch Your Calamari – Travels with an Appetite*. I also added three new chapters to my first book, *A Fisherman in the Saddle*, first published by Jacana 20 years ago in South Africa before my British publisher, BLKDOG, brought out a new edition last year. It has been a very productive and creative time.

I kept a diary during the first year of Covid because I was not sure that I would survive, and I was also incandescent with rage at the ineptitude, corruption and general mismanagement of Boris Johnson and his government. I found writing the book cathartic and was delighted when Alec Hogg of BizNews, a South African business news portal, asked me to produce it as a series of podcasts, which I did, and then it was published as a book by BLKDOG.

Why do humans write? Well, I suppose we write for a variety of reasons, but in my case, I find it one of the most deeply pleasurable activities imaginable. When it is going well, you get a feeling that you are not so much writing as much as someone else is writing through you. It is very difficult to explain, but many writers have referred to this experience.

And then there is the pleasure of holding your book in your hands, the result of so many hours, days and weeks of thought. And finally, there is the truly profound pleasure of the feedback from readers, some of whom have really been touched by the writing, and this is hugely satisfying and humbling. I once had a call from a man of 78 who had survived life-threatening surgery to thank me for *Into the Secret Heart of Ashdown Forest*, an area he knows well and loves. He said that reading the book helped his recovery, and he vowed to walk the places described in the book once more when he can.

I suppose you could say that I write two kinds of books, personal memoir and political books. The latter is represented by *Boerejood*, (recently republished by BLKDOG) which was an attempt to understand the coming of democracy to South Africa without an all-out revolution.

I could not get my head around the Afrikaners settling for one man, one vote without a fight. It came as such a surprise to me. The book tries to unpack this conundrum.

And *Life in a Time of Plague* oscillates between the microcosm of our proscribed lives during lockdown and the catastrophic mismanagement by government in the UK and the USA in particular.

My other books of personal memoir hinge on my love of landscape, of being out under the sky fishing or horse-riding – being a figure in the landscape. The Japanese use the term forest bathing, and I suppose it is the love of this kind of activity that drives these books – *A Fisherman in the Saddle* and *Into the Secret Heart of Ashdown Forest*. It's all about the power of nature to cure so many of our ills, both physical and mental.

These days, I read non-fiction, travel, biography and history. My touchstones and mentors are Ernest Hemingway, John Steinbeck and John Fowles of *The French Lieutenant's Woman* fame. But it was his book *The Magus* that really got me writing. I read widely, and now and again a writer would allude to 'the Other' in some way or other – the experience of various tribal peoples (which led me to study Anthropology at university), a presence felt among the troops of the First World War, books about nature and the spirits of the woods, children's books with their magic doors into other worlds. Among my books were some now discredited writers: Lobsang Rampa (unmasked as Cyril Henry Hoskin), author of *The Third Eye*; Erich von Däniken, who wrote of the markings on the Andean desert in *Chariots of the Gods* ; Carlos Castaneda, whose book *The Teachings of Don Juan: A Yaqui Way of Knowledge* reveals truths that emerge in drug-induced states; and Laurens van der Post, whose books tell about his experience with the *Bushmen of the Kalahari* (the San people). These all seemed to touch on the issues that fascinated me – access to a world beyond my understanding.

The fact that these writers have turned out to be unreliable witnesses is of no account. Sometimes, the way to truth is shown by fools, by the illiterate, or by the innocence of children. These writers were, in their way, all seeking to articulate belief systems that spoke of ways and means that were not currently available or fashionable. They tapped into the great human hunger to understand why we are here, to make sense of this world, and in this they showed something true. Man cannot and does not entirely live by bread alone. We want more. We want to return to Eden, to innocence, to a life lived with meaning in harmony with the universe. And it is this that I seek.

I read, in later years, the book *The Songlines* by Bruce Chatwin, which reveals how the Australian Aborigines sang their known world into existence. Using song, they created word and melody maps of their world, which allowed them to walk securely down the songlines that offered safe passage in a harsh landscape they have inhabited for 70,000 years. They combined the sacred and the profane, and honoured their world with their culture. It was all of a piece. The land was their culture, and their culture was the land.

The Romans believed that to walk was to effect a cure. There is something in the act of going on a journey, however small, that offers us the opportunity to experience our world and the worlds it disguises.

To travel is to open up the potential for being opened up. The Muslim is required to make the journey to Mecca at least once in his or her life. It is a spiritual journey of enlightenment, and one wonders whether it is the journey or the experience in Mecca itself which offers the greatest lessons.

Silence is sacred. Quakers acknowledge this in their silent meeting houses. Out of silence and contemplation comes wisdom. There is a woman in Britain who has had media attention for her writing and her commitment to silence and her removal to the most remote places in the country, to seek out the most intense experience of silence available to her. In *A Book of Silence*, Sara Maitland has moved into the silence, the better to pray and to contemplate the richness of life. I believe she is on to something profoundly important. The Bible is full of men and women who sought out silence and prayer and contemplation as a means of revelation.

Where is all this taking me? I don't know. Maybe nowhere. But as I grow older, I am in search of something to help me understand my life's journey. I sense that I have missed much, that I am impoverished with the richness of the twentieth and twenty-first centuries. I would like to get a glimpse of God's face before I pass into the silence of death. I would like to be more than an unthinking ant.

So, I listen to the call of the wild, to the song of birds, the rush of water, the wind in the trees. I stop and look into the gloom of woods and note the new growth, the slow, silent turning of the world. I pick up stones and caress them. For in doing these things, I am honouring the world and healing myself, and giving a chance for 'the Other' to manifest itself. It may take a lifetime, it may never happen, but at least I would not have travelled unaware, blind to what lies about me, to beauty.

An interviewer once asked me: what, in my opinion, was the meaning of life? Good Lord! I'm working on finding answers to that, but thus far I haven't a clue; I just bumble along, making it up as I go along. I would say kindness is part of it, just being kind, something I fail at regularly, but I do try harder now I'm older. And I would say trying to realise your talents and make the most of them. And love – of life, of people. And having a passion. A life lived without a passion for something is a lukewarm kind of life. And trying not to worry so much. We are here and gone so quickly. Try to be happy. Just surviving is a victory.

Forest Bathing & Wild Desserts

Summer 2025

Sometimes nothing worth describing happens out there. You tack up and disappear into the woods and Callum behaves, is really chilled out, and just wombles about. We amble back and forth through our home range and stop at all our old markers, a bite of ivy on the old Victorian bridge at the base of the hill where it crosses a small, still stream now that it is August. In the Spring it will be a raging torrent, but for now all is peace and quiet on Ashdown Forest.

The Foresters with their ten-ton machines are gone and if you could hear it, the only sound other than birdsong would be the faint squeak of swelling among blackberries, acorns and chestnuts. Here Callum buries his head in the low hanging branches of a beech and munches to his heart's content. Now as we pass the lake, he trims the bracken with easeful swipes.

We pass through the mid-week emptiness of the camp where a few people have bought the right to pitch tents for some of their own forest bathing. The growing log piles left by the loggers scents the air with pine and spruce. It is a good place to breath deep. And then it's back home up the soft sandy canter track and Callum does his dolphin moves, gently, collectedly, almost as if he remembers he is carrying an old crock. And I am grateful to him and the woods. Then we are home, and nothing to report, nothing, and yet, so much. In fact, there is a lot going on. After our extraordinary six-month long summer this year of 2025, which started at the beginning of March, all the plants are fruiting and nutting weeks earlier than usual, in August instead of September.

The oak trees are carrying enough acorns to re-tree the Earth if every acorn sprouted, the blackberries have set a new record for freight of fruit, and the chestnuts are coming through now too, but whether they will find enough moisture to plump up is anybody's guess. Our two apple trees and a damson tree could supply the wholesale fruit trade, no problem. What a summer it's been!

Callum's four-acre field has six-foot-high hedgerows around three sides, which gives him about 250 yards of blackberries on the briars that intertwine with the beech hedge, making an almost impenetrable barrier. It is a sight to see this huge horse working his way delicately down the hedgerow snacking as he goes, blackberry picking, and only the sweetest. If someone asked me to describe Callum's character, nature and temperament, I would have to think hard, for it is complex, and multilayered as a Greek filo pastry baklava, full of honey, but with nuts in equal measure. If you could conjure up a human equivalent of my horse, then imagine a dignified British, senior civil servant, a Mandarin of the Court of Saint James, setting out by ship for the Imperial Court in Peking during the time of the opium wars. A handsome, courtly man, impeccably dressed, but with a well disguised history as a frontline soldier in India and Afghanistan, knowing things about killing people that his smooth exterior cloaks beautifully.

What is confusing is that 90 per cent of the time, Callum is lazier and slower moving than a sloth – except when he is not. In fact, he is like that beautifully balanced tool so beloved of barbers, the cut-throat razor. Used carefully, it delivers a very close shave, and one places oneself in the hands of the man wielding it with expectation. But as some Mafiosi's have found, once the hot towels go on, there is no knowing what the cut-throat will do. With Callum, it is much the same. One can never rely on the laziness to last.

Had I known this about Callum, I would never have bought him. But he takes the eye and has paces to die for. And the rest? Well, nobody wants to live forever. The deal I made with Callum was more insightful than I ever imagined possible when at 69 I bought him, six years ago. He was to be my 'Old Man's Horse'. A less likely candidate would be hard to find to fulfil this function. But then, as I explained to him, his role was, after some years, to plant me deep on Ashdown Forest to ensure that I never sat drooling in front of a TV set in some retirement home, wearing incontinent nappies, and totally gaga. And to give Callum his due, he has worked hard to fulfil his part of the bargain. But to his surprise and mine, we are still both alive, and the partnership carries on.

HOW NOT TO BUY A HORSE

There is something that goes horribly wrong when passionate horse lovers go in search of a new horse. Perhaps it's because it is such an emotional process that the potential for the wheels to come off are huge. Some of my own mistakes and some near misses over the years include the following, a far from exhaustive list, but exhausting all the same:

There was the grey Irish Sports Horse, 'Wish', whose video showed the dealer clambering under him from one side to the other and doing every kind of calisthenic exercise on his back. When shipped to us from Ireland he arrived a hand smaller than advertised (maybe he'd shrunk in the sea air). The vet showed us the X-rays, and he was gone in the knees. But this did not stop him rearing in his stable to chop at you with his front feet. He made the return trip to Ireland, hopefully not shrinking any further on the sea crossing. Then there was Liam, a very bad horse from a very bad, in fact notorious dealer.

What the hell were we thinking? At the viewing the dealer asked a passing groom to tell us just how bombproof the horse was. She smiled and kept walking. We ignored that red flag, got him home and within days it had bolted with me, back from the Forest into his stable, almost decapitating me in the process. He went back to the dealer, but we did not get our deposit back.

The first horse we bought in England was a thin dark bay gelding named George. We tried him out and liked him enough to say we were interested. But something about the seller and their story – the horse had been 'resting' over the winter, living out – made us change our mind. We said we were no longer interested. The dealer then went ballistic and blackmailed us with threats to have us expelled from England, shortly after we had arrived, unless we bought the horse. (Unlikely, as by then we had work permits!) But we were so green, so naïve and not wanting to rock the boat with the authorities, that we bought the horse. I then spent a year or two breaking it of its habit of whipping round 180 degrees when cantering. It had been over-jumped and was utterly sour. Gentle hacking for a year pretty much cured him.

Years later, we drove hundreds of miles looking for an Arab for Jan. One horse, whose owner had brought it to a show outside Blackpool refused to leave its trailer. We passed.

Then there was the bay gelding that lashed out at the owner with both hind legs as she walked into his box with the halter. Red faces all round and a quick departure by us. There was another George, a lovely horse in every way, who I galloped up the Berkshire Downs. The vet found that he had a heart defect and could have collapsed under me during that hill-topping gallop.

And poor Red, whom we had home on a week's trial. It turned out that his back was totally shot from a jumping fall. Our vet asked me on the day of the vetting: "You haven't ridden this fellow yet have you?" He went back – to what sort of future, God only knows.

There was a black mare who began to go mad a minute after I got on her back. The owners said she did not like men, suggesting I dismount promptly. We drove away wondering at the sanity of some people.

There is no guarantee for success, I know, I've learned this the hard way. But here are some 14 steps to map your way into and out of this horse-buying morass, which should be signposted: BUYER BEWARE – HERE BE DRAGONS.

1. Get a feel for the market. The Covid years, for example, sent horse prices here in the UK skyrocketing. They have since come down somewhat.
2. Decide what you want, how much you have to spend and stick to it if you can.
3. Remember, everybody lies, including that sweet old lady owner who served you a scrumptious cream tea, and was in tears at having to sell her 'heart horse'.
4. Ask why they are selling. And listen and watch them, ever so carefully, as they spin their yarn.
5. Spend time with the horse. As much time as you can. Ask for a trial period if at all possible.
6. Ride the horse in an indoor or outdoor school and ride it again on an accompanied outride and then on your own, if that is how the horse will be used.
7. Research the back story – find the breeder and previous owners if at all possible. All of them will potentially lie or be economical with the truth. Remember, they are beneficiaries of the horse being sold as stated – i.e. good in every way.
8. Find a trustworthy local vet and give it a five-star vetting, with X-rays and a blood test to check for unseen horrors and evidence of the horse having been drugged.
9. Don't fall in love, don't fall in love, don't fall in love.
10. Don't buy sight unseen or go via a proxy.
11. Avoid horses with evidence of external cancers.
12. Find a wing man or wing woman who is much more experienced and professional than you. View video up-front and eliminate anything that looks uneven or lame. Get them to ride the horse first to get a trusted second opinion.
13. Get the seller to write down the horse's current exercise and feed programme and any tips on managing its particular quirks. This will help to speed up the settling-in period.

14. Be aware that it will take you the best part of a year to truly know what you have bought.

Do keep looking, however dispirited you get, because there *are* good horses out there. We've owned some saints as well as horses who – after some retraining – turned into good, honest citizens.

A HORSEMAN'S TAPESTRY OF TIME

When you've had the privilege of riding the same piece of country for more than forty years, in some ways it takes on the patina of a much-loved children's book, sort of super-real, an ever-changing but unchanging place that one calls home. And the horse is the mechanism in which this idealised landscape is stitched together, until your own presence there becomes part of it too, a horseman in the woods, another illustration in this book of hours, days, months and years.

The horse, a gleaming golden needle, weaves his glinting thread through dappled leaf-lace shadows on the wood path, back and forth across the days, warping and woofing a memory garment, shuttlecocking a tapestry calendar of days.

It is a wood psalter of summer greens, autumn golds and winter greys, the sound descant to these colours, are the 'plock-plock-plock' of hoof on stones. the 'diff-duff-diff' on earth, the swishing through grass, and the sibilance of swept-past branches of beech, birch and sweet chestnut.

The tapestry edge is enlivened by birds, squirrels, deer peering from the woods, the viper and the badger too, the wild boar, the fox and the neighbour's peacock, the crow, the magpie, the robin and the buzzard. And once, just once, a milk-white stag in the mist. They stalk the edge of this memory-garment in a frieze of forget-me-nots.

Slowly, at his own pace, the horse criss-crosses these lines of thread pulled tight, of vegetation and sound and the green smell of leaf and the damp of the rain fresh ground. Now it hangs on my bedroom wall, this image, this calendar of days, though the horse is long gone, his bones beneath his favourite field. His steps echo in my head, his gleaming coat reflecting sunlight.

To see this book of days, this tapestry of time, this soup of vegetation and sun and wind, all I need do is close my eyes and it hangs once more before me in whatever place I find myself.

He did well, my golden needle, carrying me through streams and meadows, woods and hills, through the bracken, my hips rocking in the saddle with the same sweet motion that creates new life, but our rides birth children of another kind, memory sons and daughters, always with you, always bringing gifts.

I wonder if when I'm dust, I may give this tapestry to you who still inhabit the world of woods and horses? But I suspect this tapestry of my time spent here with horses is not transferable; each of us must make our own and hold it for a keepsake to remind us in the great beyond that once we lived in a paradise of sorts.

Julian Roup
East Sussex
August 2025

PRAISE FOR BOOKS BY JULIAN ROUP

INTO THE SECRET HEART OF ASHDOWN FOREST: A HORSEMAN'S COUNTRY DIARY

From Amazon

Paul McKinnell:
5.0 out of 5 stars
A love letter to our home
Reviewed in the United Kingdom on 16 June 2023

'I met Julian and Janice out riding this morning and our conversation prompted me to write a few words about this beautiful book.
It is a rare thing to find a book which speaks intimately of a place both you and the author know and love, but even if you aren't acquainted with Ashdown the appeal is just as strong. Julian brings this magical place to life on the page with a rare depth of feeling. Essential reading and highly recommended – a modern-day equivalent to Nan Shepherd's, The Living Mountain, set in Scotland, but with Julian's book, for the other end of the country!'

Mark Whyman:
Into the Secret Heart of Ashdown Forest
5.0 out of 5 stars Inner calm and peace

Reviewed in the United Kingdom on 1 December 2022
'I read this book during the worst of the lockdown and I'm sorry, I should've written this review a long time ago.
This amazing book took me to another place when the world was closing in around me. It transported me to the Ashdown Forest. I could almost hear the wind through the trees and feel the breeze on my face.
For anybody that knows this part of the world, it is an essential read and for anybody that would like to know this part of the world it is equally an essential read.
Well done Julian ,you helped keep me sane.'

Amazon Customer:
5.0 out of 5 stars The perfect antidote to the craziness and upheaval of 2020/21
Reviewed in the United Kingdom on 1 November 2021
'This highly readable new book by Julian Roup takes as it's central premise the author's visits to Ashdown Forest in the company of his horse, Callum. But in telling the story of these visits it covers so much more; the author's own childhood in South Africa and his carving out of an entirely new existence in a country thousands of miles away; his life-long relationship with horses and the enrichment – and mischief! – they have brought; the lore of this Forest itself and the way a regular visitor might experience its secrets in a way others might miss. Above all it is a hymn to the ways that getting into the heart of somewhere like Ashdown can be just what is needed to remind us of what it is to be human. As the Covid Pandemic starts to loosen its grip and we assess the damage wrought by 18 months of upheaval I found this book an uplifting alternative to the day's headlines, and a reminder that to journey into one of our green cathedrals is to find a kind of peace that flows with the rhythm of footsteps - or hoofbeats.'

Chalky
5.0 out of 5 stars Excellent read.

Reviewed in the United Kingdom on 28 November 2021
'Ashdown Forest is very close to my heart, I myself spend many hours there with my camera, so this book means a lot.'

Diane Rainbow-Towers
5.0 out of 5 stars A beautifully written book
Reviewed in the United Kingdom on 10 April 2021
'This book was a real tonic to read, especially on dull rainy days. I felt like I was actually riding out with the author through Ashdown Forest. His obvious love for his horse, his observation of nature and his humour shine through. Sorry when I came to the end of the book.'

JJB
5.0 out of 5 stars Lovely book, beautifully written
Reviewed in the United Kingdom on 2 April 2021
'I really enjoyed this book. It is beautifully written with heartfelt detail. It was a pleasure to learn more about the amazing Ashdown Forest that I have been lucky to have on my doorstep for many years.'

Lene Gurney
5.0 out of 5 stars Entertaining page turner
Reviewed in the United Kingdom on 19 March 2021
'This diary, with its detailed description of the countryside of the Ashdown Forest and great illustrations, is an entertaining page turner.'

Mr Paul Nott
5.0 out of 5 stars Magical ride through fascinating landscape
Reviewed in the United Kingdom on 1 February 2022
'Reading this book is like a ride in a great balloon which floats over the Ashdown Forest and drops down onto interesting and exciting places. No wonder it became home for some of our most famous writers such as Sir Arthur Conan Doyle, A.A. Milne, W.B. Yeats, and Ezra Pound. You also feel the great enthusiasm Julian Roup has for nature, the beautiful

landscape, and his magnificent horse, Callum, who takes him from one treasure in the Forest to the next. The book is well written and an uplifting way to recover from the restraints of the pandemic.'

Izzy P
5.0 out of 5 stars Immersive window into the wonders of hacking!
Reviewed in the United Kingdom on 7 September 2021

'As a window into the day-to-day enchantment of hacking, Into the Secret Heart of the Ashdown Forest resonates with riders and non-riders alike. This book is a wondrous ode to the Ashdown Forest and horsey worlds captured in all their magic, idiosyncrasies, beauty and ugliness.
Roup's stories will touch the heart of locals who are familiar with the Forest's histories whilst painting a vivid, immersive picture for those who have not have not. So beautifully written that you feel like you're out on a horse yourself!
Written in diary entries, this book is a cosy yet addictive read, which I thoroughly enjoyed & would 100% recommend.'

Simon H Taylor
5.0 out of 5 stars book review
Reviewed in the United Kingdom on 23 March 2021
'This is a wonderful book...a love story really...love for our stunning Ashdown Forest and for horses! Julian has the ability to take you with him as he explores the valleys and streams and hidden magical places. A must-read for horsemen/women and country lovers alike .'

'Author Julian Roup offers a lyrical love letter to Ashdown Forest after a 40-year affair. Wry and vivid, Julian's memoir chronicles the life of the author and the ten square miles of country he calls his Kingdom. He promises the book is as good as a brisk walk in the woods on an autumn day.'

Phil Hewitt, *Sussex Express*

REVIEWS OF *LIFE IN A TIME OF PLAGUE*

'It is a wonderful account of the time of coronavirus; I especially like the reverie at the end with its sense of time regained in that Proustian way. Julian Roup has a great gift for evocation and description.'
Bernard O'Donoghue, Whitbread Prize winning Irish poet, Oxford don, author of *Seamus Heaney and the Language of Poetry*.

'Witty, incisive, irreverent, iconoclastic.'
George Plumptre, CEO National Garden Scheme, author of *The English Country House Garden and Royal Gardens of Europe*.

'Julian Roup tells the story of his corner of rural Britain under the first 75 days of lockdown. His beautiful writing captures the way the world slowed down amid the strangeness of the new reality. The book is a snapshot of the details that make up the fabric of history – thinking back on memories of friends passed, observations on humanity and the natural world in his East Sussex valley, and of course his lovely horse Callum. Riders will appreciate how horses – in both reality and in our imagination – serve as an escape.'
Horse & Hound

REVIEWS OF *A FISHERMAN IN THE SADDLE*

'This is storytelling charged with raw emotion and always a deep appreciation for the sheer beauty and the enduring magic of nature which transcends politics, implosion of families, emigration. Horses, the author says, became 'my nation, my friends, my identity, my medicine. When I am in the saddle I'm home."
Robyn Cohen, *The Cape Times*

'Every now and then a gem of a new book lands on my desk: sometimes but rarely a diamond. This is one. I laughed. I cried. I was deeply moved. This is among the best books I have ever read about fishing, horses, growing up, the pain of maturity, leaving one's homeland and the things that make up the richness of life.'

Dave Bristow, *Getaway Magazine*

'The ability of horses to help and heal is boundless. In A Fisherman in the Saddle, Julian Roup explains how he feels about horses. 'The feeling of elation, of freedom, of excitement was indescribable. It was like being given wings and the gift of flight. I was hooked for life.' I know the feeling, and I hope many others discover it for themselves.'

Octavia Pollock, *Country Life*

REVIEWS OF *BOEREJOOD*

'Brilliant, just terrific, really very, very good. Engaged, intelligent, personal, fast moving and funny.'

Graham Watts, *Financial Times*, London

'A delicate exploration of a society 10 years after the end of apartheid and the onset of majority rule. Roup has no nostalgia for the old regime, but immense sadness for the embattlement of the Afrikaans language and culture.'

John Lloyd, Editor, *FT Weekend Magazine*

'Author Julian Roup offers a lyrical love letter to Ashdown Forest after a 40-year affair. Wry and vivid, Julian's memoir chronicles the life of the author and the ten square miles of country he calls his Kingdom. He promises the book is as good as a brisk walk in the woods on an autumn day.'

Phil Hewitt, *Sussex Express*

Other titles by BLKDOG Publishing for your consideration:

Britannia: The Wall
By Richard Denham & M. J. Trow

THE END OF ROMAN BRITAIN BEGINS.

The story opens in 367 AD. Four soldiers - Justinus, Paternus, Leocadius and Vitalis - are out hunting for food supplies at an outpost of Hadrian's Wall, when the Wall comes under attack.

The four find their fort destroyed, their comrades killed, and Paternus is unable to find his wife and son. As they run south to Eboracum, they realize that this is no ordinary border raid. Ranged against the Romans at the edge of the world are four different peoples, and they have banded together under a mysterious leader who wears a silver mask and uses the name Valentinus - man of Valentia, the turbulent area north of the Wall.

Faced with questions they are hard-pressed to answer, Leocadius blurts out a story that makes the men Heroes of the Wall. Their lives change not only when Valentinus begins his lethal sweep across Britannia but as soon as Leo's lie is out in the world, growing and changing as it goes.

**Goblin Market
By Maryanne Coleman**

Have you ever wondered what happened to the faeries you used to believe in? They lived at the bottom of the garden and left rings in the grass and sparkling glamour in the air to remind you where they were. But that was then - now you might find them in places you might not think to look. They might be stacking shelves, delivering milk or weighing babies at the clinic. Open your eyes and keep your wits about you and you might see them.

But no one is looking any more and that is hard for a Faerie Queen to bear and Titania has had enough. When Titania stamps her foot, everyone in Faerieland jumps; publicity is what they need. Television, magazines. But that sort of thing is much more the remit of the bad boys of the Unseelie Court, the ones who weave a new kind of magic; the World Wide Web. Here is Puck re-learning how to fly; Leanne the agent who really is a vampire; Oberon's Boys playing cards behind the wainscoting; Black Annis, the bag-lady from Hainault, all gathered in a Restoration comedy that is strictly twenty-first century.

Fade
By Bethan White

There is nothing extraordinary about Chris Rowan. Each day he wakes to the same faces, has the same breakfast, the same commute, the same sort of homes he tries to rent out to unsuspecting tenants.

There is nothing extraordinary about Chris Rowan. That is apart from the black dog that haunts his nightmares and an unexpected encounter with a long forgotten demon from his past. A nudge that will send Chris on his own downward spiral, from which there may be no escape.

There is nothing extraordinary about Chris Rowan...

www.blkdogpublishing.com

www.ingramcontent.com/pod-product-compliance
Lightning Source LLC
Chambersburg PA
CBHW032100090426
42743CB00007B/187